If Holden Caulfield Were in My Classroom

If
Holden
Caulfield
Were in My Classroom

Inspiring Love, Creativity, and
Intelligence in Middle School Kids

Bernie Schein

SENTIENT PUBLICATIONS

First Sentient Publications edition 2008
Copyright © 2008 by Bernard Schein

A paperback original

Cover design by Kim Johansen, Black Dog Design
Book design by Adam Schnitzmeier

Library of Congress Cataloging-in-Publication Data

Schein, Bernard, 1944-
If Holden Caulfield were in my classroom : inspiring love, creativity, and intelligence in middle school kids / by Bernard Schein.
  p. cm.
  ISBN 978-1-59181-076-6
  1. Middle school teaching. 2. School environment. 3. Middle school students--Psychology. I. Title.

LB1623.S33 2008
373.1102--dc22
 2007051932

Printed in the United States of America

10 9 8 7 6 5 4 3 2 1

SENTIENT PUBLICATIONS
A Limited Liability Company
1113 Spruce Street
Boulder, CO 80302
www.sentientpublications.com

Neither a lofty degree of intelligence or creativity nor both together go to the making of genius. Only love can do that. Love, love, love, that is the soul of genius.

—Mozart

Contents

Foreword

by Pat Conroy

Bᴇʀɴɪᴇ Sᴄʜᴇɪɴ ʜᴀs ʙᴇᴇɴ ᴀ ʟᴜᴍɪɴᴏᴜs ᴀɴᴅ ᴄᴏɴᴛᴇɴᴛɪᴏᴜs presence in my life ever since I heard his high pitched laughter echoing through the halls of Beaufort High School in 1961. His laugh remains indescribable today and sounds as though it is coming from a creature produced by the mating of a lunatic and a hyena. His laughter still serves as portent for his joyousness and irrepressible humor. Bernie is one of the funniest men I've ever met, one of the greatest teachers I've ever watched, and one of the best writing teachers I've ever met in my life. He has served as one of the first readers for all my books and novels, and has been a character in two of them. He reads my books with tenderness and devotion for the written word and an all-seeing critical eye that have proven invaluable to me over the course of a long career. He just read my newest novel, *South of Broad,* and his unreadable graffiti is all over a thousand pages of manuscript. His criticism is judicious and always to the point. But his true genius lies in his rare ability to praise. No one can praise you like Bernie Schein. No one.

It was our mutual passion for education and literature that sealed our friendship. When I returned to teach at Beaufort High School after my graduation from the Citadel, I found out on the first day of school in 1967 that I loved every single thing about teaching except the paperwork. We talked theories of education, ways to teach, the almighty importance of inspiration in a classroom, and the high crime of boring any child who walked into our classroom. He bought me a copy of A.S Neill's *Summerhill*, which became a seminal book in my life. When Bernie and I traveled to England the next summer, I hit the museums and the pubs, but Bernie left London on a train and spent the day at Summerhill schmoozing with the great A. S. Neill himself. Bernie was always a little more committed to education than I was. This book is simply glorious proof of that proposition.

In the seventies and eighties, I was a frequent visitor to the seventh and eighth grade classes that Bernie taught at the Paideia School in Atlanta. Bernie let me walk into his classroom at will, but I tried to time my visits so I could listen to Bernie teach his kids literature or writing. Sometimes Bernie would have me talk about my own writing, and the kids would ask me questions about the book I was writing at the time. Once I walked into a class when Bernie was leading a discussion about my own novel, *The Great Santini*, in which a character based on Bernie plays a major role in the book. No one can teach a book better than Bernie Schein. He was telling his kids things about my novel I had never dreamed of in my life. He would break it into incongruent parts, then make it soar into bright life again.

In his writing class, he was masterful and he would coax stories from his kids that were the finest things ever written by seventh graders in Atlanta or any other city. Bernie did it by complete immersion into the emotional and spiritual life of any child who walked into his classroom. He was charismatic and wide-eyed and controversial. The great men always are, and Bernie Schein is the best I've ever seen. The kids he taught were the luckiest kids in the state of Georgia.

I've been begging Bernie to write this book for years. He has come up with something astonishing and original. It does not tell you how to teach or to think, but it is a manual that tells you how to live, how to feel deeply, how to enrich your time on earth. It is a book that is part philosophy, part self-help guide, a text of revelation, and an ode to the beauty of law and the wisdom of justice. I know about every kid that Bernie writes about in this marvelous book. I read their stories. They were lucky to encounter as very young people a man on fire. Bernie Schein has been a life-changing force in my life. Now, with this book, he can be one in yours.

Letter from the Headmaster

A GOOD FRIEND OF MINE, AN EXPERIENCED ELEMENTARY school principal, once advised me that he thought that gifted teachers often skate on thin ice and, furthermore, that the really gifted teachers will be found on ice so thin, so far out, that the rest of us do not see how they keep from crashing through. I have remembered this advice as I have looked out my windows across the small patch of greenery which separates my office at Paideia from Bernie Schein's classroom. Bernie has been over there for twenty-seven of the years I have been head of Paideia School. I have watched him teach and talked with him far into the night about teaching, children, and human development. I have seen him skate places the rest of us fear to go, teach in ways not easily explained, and affect children more than anyone ever thought possible. He is the most personal teacher I have ever known, and also the most exciting. He is an ongoing pain in my administrative neck, and he has been the teacher of choice for each of my three children.

Experienced teachers understand that the more one knows about one child, the more one knows about all children. The same can be said of teachers: the better we know one, the better we understand what is possible for all of us. It would be a mistake to read this book as another how-to pedagogical manual, a compendium of what to say when, curriculum tricks, or different ways to set up a classroom. Instead of focusing on the details, a reader should take in the greater story, which is about the mystery of the inner lives of children and the intellectual and emotional growth that is possible when they are able to bring their entire selves to school. Bernie Schein's account of his classroom is not just a description of the ways of one talented teacher; it describes what is possible in teaching in general. Like accounts of explorers of old, it tells us of lands many of us may not have known existed nor fully appreciated.

William James is reported to have said that while method and organization means much in a school, there is no substitute for a cast of contagious characters. Bernie Schein's contagion is more than his personality, which alternates between being outrageously funny and unspeakably flamboyant. Underlying his personality are qualities we want for the teachers of every child. Bernie is passionate about teaching and confident of the difference it can make in the life of a child. What happens in school is important. Of course, one should expect such conviction among teachers, but some pay only lip service to the notion of the importance of their work, and too many others have learned, in the myriad of ways we discourage professionals, not to have such expectations. All sorts of research supports the proposition that teachers who have high expectations and who believe what they do is important inspire greater learning among their students.

Bernie not only expects great things from all his students, I have *never* seen him give up on anyone student. "Never" is such a categorical word that I always (another categorical word) cringe when I hear it. This is one of the few instances that it actually applies. To never give up sounds like terminal naiveté or a malady that will land one on *Oprah*. In teachers also blessed with discerning judgment, it is a godsend. All of us know schools that all too quickly give up. The teachers we remember, often the ones who made a difference in our lives, are those who had faith in our ability to do what we were not ourselves sure we could do. In the sense that parents should have unconditional love for their children, teachers should have unconditional faith in their students' ability to grow.

Bernie is no Pollyanna, certainly no sap. Over the years more than a few parents have asked me to intercede on their child's behalf in the hopes that Bernie would be less demanding. I do not accede to this request but instead insist that they talk directly to Bernie (which is where they should have gone in the first place). When they do, they hear something more important than the squeals of their temporarily overwhelmed adolescent. They hear the compliment and hopefulness inherent in great expectations and a reassurance that devastating failure is not an option.

There are many messages in this book, but for me the underlying optimism about growth and the insights into the lives of children are most important. It would be a mistake for those of us who teach children to rush to school and try to replicate an environment it has taken this gifted man years to evolve. Since we teach with our selves, it is not possible to copy someone else's style. The voice needs to be our own in the same way the children in this book are gaining their own voice. But it would also be a mistake to believe that the many struggles, passions, and lives of the children revealed in this book exist and can be heard only to a few rare teachers. We can all learn to listen and to respond in our own way. Our children, and the schools and families they grow up in, will be healthier when we do.

Paul Bianchi
Atlanta, Georgia

If Holden Caulfield Were in My Classroom

Introduction

MARVIN PAZOL, A STUDENT IN MY MIDDLE SCHOOL
classroom at Paideia, a rigorous, progressive private school
in Atlanta, somersaults wildly and uncontrollably in a dizzy-
ing neurosphere of the wrong friends, the wrong activities, the
wrong ambition, someone else's life. A refugee of Saigon, Norman Stewart, Americanized only by name, seeks his abandoned
soul in the belongings of his classmates. Dazzling with research
papers, footnotes and the accoutrements of academia, Lisa
Overton's stories, essays, arguments and speeches are lifeless
because she is loveless; her watchwords are safety and caution,
her forays into dramatic presentations abrupt dead-ends.

Betsy Robinson seeks her lost father through a Byzan-
tine maze of impossible relationships; her stories, attempts at
autobiographical fiction, do not make sense because her life
doesn't. Still shouldering the trauma of betrayal by her first
intimate friend back in third grade, Marie Zelgado parries her
classmates' attempts at social intimacy through what I term the

liberal's handgun, the put-down. Danny Field's learning disabilities are not nearly so problematic as his denial of them. Ian Gardiner's not lazy; he's anxious and afraid. Because Raquel Millsey, however irrationally, is so burdened with responsibility for her father's death, she's unable to assume responsibility for her behavior elsewhere, particularly when a social conflict arises; so she "blames."

A member of the class congress—a group of students elected by the class to make laws for the classroom—Jamila Cade is consistently vague about the laws she proposes and the arguments and speeches she makes on their behalf; she is particularly vague about those which concern racism among her classmates. A black kid in a predominantly white school, when she looks in the mirror she is vague as to whom she sees.

From what I have observed in my middle school classroom of seventh and eighth graders at Paideia for over thirty years, and before that as a school principal and educational consultant, contrary to traditional educational theory and practice the true liberators of love, creativity, and intelligence are emotion, not rationality, the heart and soul, not the brain, feelings rather than thought, personality and character rather than I.Q. tests and standardized test scores. Further, love, creativity, and intelligence are naturally inseparable, indivisible, and intertwined. Talent and intelligence are not traits to be absorbed, but rather inherent parts of the personality to be discovered, liberated, and cultivated. All kids are talented and smart beyond what most of us can even imagine, as I hope to show in this book, because all can feel and think, in that order.

I am not speaking here of a soft, sentimental, touchy-feely education; my students have been known to become hysterical, par for their ages, over the amount and rigor of the work I demand.

They read and reread, for example, great works. Of what

value, however, is *Lord of the Flies* if within Golding's characters my students fail to decipher their own character and those of their friends, families, and classmates? Is the American Revolution a vague, distant abstraction if they fail to recognize their own need for freedom, independence, power, and of course money? Of what use is a comma or a semicolon if kids have nothing important, insightful, or amusing to say?

The purpose of *If Holden Caulfield Were in My Classroom* is to show you that they do.

So again contrary to conventional educational theory and practice as well as the spate of best-sellers on the subject, my primary, fundamental question when a student enters my classroom is not What does he need to know?

It is Who is he?

Founded over thirty years ago by a group of faculty (many a nucleus from Harvard's Graduate School of Education) and parents, Paideia is private, obstinately small (750 kids), and fiercely individualistic and iconoclastic. Philosophically compatible, no two teachers, however, are exactly alike. We want to learn from the kids as we teach them. Befitting the Greek word Paideia (suggesting the total, overall development of the child), the one common interest was the student's social, moral, and artistic growth as well as that of his intellect.

My own education was a drab, dreary process, largely rote and mechanical. School had nothing to do with life; intellect had nothing to do with personality; art was basically dissociative. What was important then was to say nothing original, meaningful, or dangerous.

There was no emotion.

It was what was omitted from my own education that was the inspiration for the education I offer my own students. Having no real models or examples I give them what I did not get in school and then follow them where they take me.

I want passion, humor, and subtlety, and I want it to come from them.

The history of the world—the great, classical, universal themes of history and literature—is in the heart of each child. What is more tender and terrifying than first love? Is there one among us who has not betrayed (or been betrayed by) a friend for popularity? Death, illness, love, loss, greed, acquisitiveness, ambition, sibling rivalry, sexism, racism, identity, violence, romance, sex—these themes are not strangers to kids. To some degree they have suffered and enjoyed every emotion that an adult might feel. Who among us has not succumbed to peer pressure, whether from classmates or colleagues, and brought at least a smidgen of shame, self-consciousness, or guilt upon ourselves? Who among us has not sought love and attention through self-destructive means: alcohol, drugs, withdrawal, abrasiveness, acting like a jerk? The problem of identity begins as soon as the child becomes aware of other people, regardless of class, culture, or race. The death of a loved one—neighbor, friend, parent, or grandparent—can cause shock, grief, confusion, sadness, guilt, shame, or anxiety regardless of age. The dreams of kids, of power and achievement and respect in school, in athletics, in drama, in social areas, die as hard as they do in adults. Romance is exhilarating and terrifying, whether you're thirteen or thirty-three. Since Cain and Abel older siblings have wanted younger ones eliminated. Forays into sex, whether a first kiss or sexual intercourse, can result in joy and tenderness or shame and self-consciousness. Unrequited love—the issues are not only timeless but ageless.

Very early in my teaching career it surprised me that such emotions were so *present* in my students, perhaps because in my own education they were ignored or overlooked. What surprised me even more is the degree to which they inspire and enrich the structure, organization, and language of my students' stories, speeches, and essays.

Even grammar becomes more important to them because it is important for them to say not only what they want to say, but what they need to say—clearly as well as compellingly.

To be interesting one must be understood.

I require of my students a minimum of twenty pages per week on their stories. We talk about them in creative writing classes and story conferences—sometimes in groups, sometimes individually. Usually this results in their locating exactly *what* the story is. Once they do so, it largely tells itself. It takes five or six weeks to write a good story. The best are read to the class.

As with all aspects of my classroom, it is truth, always initially unknown to them and to me, that I am seeking. What is needed to find it—courage, honesty, depth, and often humor— is what liberates and makes them happier. It is what, I also hope to show, enables them to love.

Through their stories, as well as counseling sessions often involving my entire classroom, they begin to see what is not true in their worlds, what is not true in themselves. They can see, for example, that the put-down may be a subversive form of flattery, that the loneliest kid in the classroom may be a snob, that the victim can be a sycophant, the bully a coward, that blame is self-destructive and self-pity manipulative, that underneath the most harrowing abuse is dormant love in the back farthermost corner of the soul, waiting to be kissed and awakened.

Open to their own world, as you will see, they become more open to the world of literature, which I also teach. To *see*—in my mind that is the ultimate form of intelligence. To see, and to be able to express what you see.

In Salinger's *Catcher in the Rye,* Holden Caulfield epitomizes the self-destructive teen, the virtuoso of the put-down, finding fault, as you'll see my students point out, with everyone and everything but himself, lonely and alienated, reacting to the world with either cynicism or indifference. Blind to himself, he's blind to his world. So, however, are my students initially. Blind to themselves, they're blind to him. They see enough of themselves in him they at first slam the book shut and declare it "boring." The glare of their own reflection too strong, they turn away from it. As they do, they inevitably turn away from themselves, their true needs, desires, and aspirations, away too from those of their family, friends, and classmates, becoming more and more and more like Holden himself, the guy they least want to be.

Once they see themselves, their own fears and foibles and wariness, what innocence has been lost to make them so fearful, as it was with Holden, they can see, as you will, not only Holden himself, but who they truly are, their friends, family, and classmates. Reading the book with an open heart and open mind, they read themselves; reading themselves, they read, if you will, the room.

In short, they become perceptive.

More than book bannings by reactionary school boards, self-censorship, I've learned, presents the greatest threat to kids' freedom and happiness—in fact, to democracy in general. But I'll tell you this: even if I had to pry my students open with a crowbar, they were always grateful and appreciative because it always made them happier. Kids want the truth, for the simple reason that, as the old saying goes, it sets them free.

If Holden Caulfield were in my classroom, I think he'd have a blast.

Early in my first year at Paideia, I could see that my kids' thoughts and feelings in my American History class were largely reorganized and regurgitated from the texts and class discussions. Did they really understand such abstract issues as "justice," "balance of power," "law versus freedom," "conflict of interest," etc. without concretely and personally experiencing them?

Opportunity for enlightenment surfaced when someone unplugged the fish tank.

I had only been at Paideia a few months when I walked in my classroom one morning to find my students mourning three gaily-colored fish floating lifelessly in the class fish tank.

A kid held up the cord. "Somebody unplugged it," he screamed.

"Who did it?" shouted the kids. Why did they do it? they asked. What should the punishment be?

"Who decides?" I asked.

"You," they shouted.

"Not me," I said. "I'm too busy. Besides, why should I care about three dead fish?"

"Do you, really," I said, plunging ahead, "when it seems to me you don't even care about yourselves? Do you feel safe, fully alive, able to express yourselves in the classroom and at recess or do you tell yourself you do? I see subtle, but devastating put-downs, exclusion, bullying, sucking-up. Popular kids drop a pencil and suck-ups scramble to pick it up for them. I mean, it's disgusting. There are people who are afraid of speaking up in class because of what a classmate might say."

I saw a few curious, shame-faced grins so I went on. "Lunches are stolen, I've seen sandwiches taken outright. Nobody does anything. Is this the way you really want to live? How about people going in your lockers, reading personal notes? Am I right?

"Can you really do your work in study periods with all this horse crap going on? The pushing and shoving may satisfy those who are pushing and shoving, but what about the rest of you? Show some courage, tell me the truth—you won't regret it, I promise—what bothers you more: three dead fish or the people around you?"

"Three dead fish," volunteered Warren Bradley. Warren was the most popular, consequently the most feared member of the classroom at the time.

"And what might be Warren's motive," I asked the class, "for that particular answer?"

Teddy Simpson looked at Warren, then at me, his smile hesitant.

"Teddy?"

"He's one of the bullies," he said.

"Is that true?" I asked the class. "No, wait; you tell me first, Warren. What's the truth? I promise, whatever it is, you'll feel better afterwards. Okay?"

Of course, everyone *knew* the truth. They waited, curious, as Warren ticked off the pros and cons—fight or surrender—in his head.

"All I'm asking for is the truth, Warren. I'll believe you, whatever you tell me. You won't regret it…

"Yeah," he said, "I am a bully."

"How do you feel about it?" I asked.

He didn't know.

"Embarassed?"

He nodded.

"A bit ashamed?"

"A little. Yes. But…"

"Yes?"

He smiled, uncertainly.

"Go ahead, Warren, it'll be all right, whatever it is."

"I feel relieved."

"Good," I said. "Anything else?"

He didn't want to say anymore, but clearly something was on his mind.

"Say it, Warren, whatever it is. You're doing great."

"Okay. Well I'm mad at you, Teddy, and the rest of you. The whole class…Why didn't you tell me before? I thought you were my friends. Why didn't you stop me? I'm mad. I mean, I understand, but some of the things I didn't even know you minded. When I'd grab your cookie, Hermie, you'd laugh about it. Hell, you were just about offering it to me."

"I was scared," said Hermie.

"I didn't say anything," said Teddy, "because I didn't want you doing it to me."

"You were afraid?" I asked Teddy.

"Yes."

"So was I," said Warren. "That's why I did it. I didn't want anyone doing it to me."

"Wow," said the class.

"This is neat," said Hermie.

"Yeah," said Teddy.

"How do you feel about Warren now?" I asked the class. "The same? Different?"

"Much different," said Teddy. He looked at Warren. "I feel like I could talk to you now."

"The rest of you? Hermie?" Hermie gave a thumbs up sign.

The class applauded.

From the dilemma of the promptly forgotten goldfish emerged a greater sensitivity, on the part of my students, to their own needs for security and freedom within the classroom community. Further discussion fostered the consensus that they could protect themselves only if they had the force of law behind them. It became clear to me that not only did they want to understand themselves and their classmates, but that they had a basic desire to be good; in fact, heroically so.

Using the United States Constitution as a guide, but only as a guide, as well as law books and law dictionaries, the kids wrote and ultimately ratified the class constitution in which was established the rights, laws, and procedures of the class government and court system, the same one, almost twenty years later, in which Betsy Robinson would be tried for slander.

To safeguard against corruption, exploitation, and favoritism, which already they had suffered *without* a *government*, a separation of powers, intentionally balanced, was established. Congress, composed of six members and a chairperson, made laws and proposed them to the class; the class could approve them only with a two thirds majority vote. Court, over which a judge presided, interpreted and enforced the laws; trial was by jury. All public officials campaigned for election; all were subject to impeachment.

Formidably abstract ideas such as balance of power, justice, or invasion of privacy were at once more complex and more easily understood because they were personal. Regarding, for example, invasion of privacy, they wanted the thief caught, they said, but they didn't want some nosy district attorney reading personal notes stuffed away in their cubbies; thus search warrants must be approved by a judge, there must be reason for suspicion, and the owner of the cubby must be present during the search. Because of their stage of development, that age where many sway back and forth with the current from the concrete to the abstract, they would often dissect issues with such a fine and discriminating enthusiasm that I would have to guide them in their return to their original principles.

The issues, like the number of crimes to which most of them most of the time readily confessed, seemed infinitesimal, as they do to this day.

I devised a semester-long preparatory course, much of which involves expository writing, speech making, debating, and the cultivation of such skills as research and recall. It prepares kids not only for academic and adult life, it enables them to participate in the government and court system of the classroom itself. The text for the course eventually became the class constitution, an intricately detailed, richly complex document which after thirty years is still being revised and amended.

All the students do in the class government and court system is constantly subjected to criticism and evaluation, both by the class and by me. A lawyer whose opening statement (an oral essay) lacks sufficient research and evidence may be charged with obstruction of justice, reprimanded or punished by the Class Bar Association, and last and probably least, receive a poor evaluation from me.

Sloth is intolerable to me because it's dumb, to the class because they're affected.

When a kid does great everyone learns and prospers. That, I think, is community.

So though I do so in my own fashion, I teach what is conventionally termed English (literature, writing, and grammar), social studies (the class government and court system, U.S. history) and I conduct counseling sessions, which often include the entire class, since all can learn from and even help each other.

My classroom consists of thirty seventh and eighth graders—middle school, the most neglected, forgotten age in American education. Seen generally either as an extension of the elementary years or as a lower appendage of the high school, little is known about these years: little has been written about them. Few adults, in fact, are willing to have anything to do with them. Teachers make a beeline for the lower or upper grades. Parents throw up their hands in frustration and fantasize about furloughs and leaves of absences.

But if you ignore them, they won't go away.

Students enter my classroom from Paideia's lower school, from private schools around the area, and from public schools. They will seem unusually bright to you because they are speaking from their hearts. Were all kids to do so, they would all be smart. Many of my kids do score impressively on standardized tests; a surprising number also suffer from learning disabilities or attention deficit disorder.

They visit other teachers for science, math, art, music, physical education, and a foreign language. The remainder of their time is mine to schedule as I wish, which I adjust accordingly

Paideia is in the verdant, established, Emory University neighborhood of northeast Atlanta. The Center for Disease Control is several blocks over, as well as the Carter Center. The school is in a residential neighborhood. Two blocks long, the architecture is an eclectic mix of English Tudor, Georgian mansions, and modern condo-style classrooms. It begins with preschool and graduates high school seniors.

My classroom is on the first floor of a two-story Georgian house. I have three rooms: a study area, a conference room which also serves as my office, and a large classroom with tables and chairs which readily converts into a courtroom every Friday afternoon.

I came to Paideia to teach, not to administer. I had been a teaching principal, a full principal, and an educational consultant. The more supervisory sessions I held, conferences I conducted, and speeches I made, the more full of shit I began to realize I was.

There were no kids to teach me, and I wanted to learn. So through mutual friends I was invited to join the Paideia faculty.

If Holden Caulfield Were in My Classroom is not about the school; it is about the students in my classroom, from which over the past thirty years I have rarely emerged. One must write, I teach my kids, about what one knows most intimately and about what most matters. So my classroom is the centerpiece of this book.

But my work and the results I've gotten do not depend upon one personality or one group of kids. Teachers I've supervised and mentored or otherwise worked with over the years have gotten pretty much the same results I have. *If Holden Caulfield Were in My Classroom* is itself thirty years teaching experience distilled into one. I have worked also with high school kids in workshops and classes; evenings I counsel and teach adults creative writing. Though space precludes this work being included here, the results are the same.

My students generally do very well in high school, in college, and in life. Many tell me that they miss what they had in their middle school classroom; that they wish that real life, in fact, was more real, less contrived, less false and untrue. They leave my classroom, as a rule, knowing who they are and consequently what they want. They want to learn, to grow and to be successful—as do all kids, once liberated.

Through the trial of Betsy Robinson, as well as the side stories of the participants, I hope that teachers will see how to probe their students' hearts and open up their souls to find those timeless, fundamentally human themes and issues that inspire them to break the surface of the water, shake the hair out of their eyes, and emerge fully into the sunlight. I have included a section for teachers at the end of the book to further explain the way my classroom works.

If you are a parent reading this, it's my intention that by knowing and understanding my students you will more easily and readily know and recognize your own children. Recognition is what brings them out.

For purposes of disguise as much as effect, kids are composites and events and incidents have been compressed into the year 1990, sixteen years before I would leave Paideia and Atlanta and return to the Lowcountry, where I began my teaching career. The kids' written stories, of course, are untouched by anybody but them.

If my kids seem unusually bright and talented, it is because, inspired, they speak truly from their hearts and souls. If they seem to have suffered abnormally, that's not the case. Statistically, the rates of divorce, abuse, and neglect in my classroom conform to the national average. Neurosis, I have found, *is* normal, as normal among children as among adults. Tragedy is universal. What distinguishes my classroom from most is that it is the recognition of such tragedy that inspires, enriches, and ennobles my students.

The heart is the key.

The Principals

Betsy Robinson

Betsy Robinson's story is not yet over, even though she has finished it and it is tidily packaged and presented.

The story, which she wrote for class, begins with a tribute to family life. However, following her parents' divorce, the reader sees her wandering alone among Danish furniture, touching glass here, contemplating an abstract painting there, as if her father's new condominium were a new planet onto which she had somehow wandered. The furniture was selected by a woman, and she knew the woman, this secretary and mistress who had stolen her father, in whose outer office Betsy had drawn pictures while waiting for her father. As she wanders about this strange planet, the reader senses she is contemplating the devastation of her own family life.

She seems a lost thirteen-year-old looking for a father. Yet one senses from her detached presentation that for her the separation is too painful to speak about in an intimate manner.

Betsy left Ben Keller, her boyfriend, as she has often left friends in her life, using an assortment of avoidance techniques and put-downs. After all, her parents had taught her, if you can't say anything nice, don't say anything at all. So suddenly Ben's jokes were no longer funny, his conversation boring. What do you say, after all, when you can no longer say anything nice?

Life is terrible, says Betsy's mother. She is talking to me outside the door of Betsy's hospital room, where Betsy has had her stomach pumped after an overdose of her mother's sleeping pills. I have learned a lesson from this, says her mother: illusion is sickness. The truth catches up with you. Betsy's hurt, she's angry. Help her to get it out, Bernie, she said, or she'll try to kill herself again. I know it. She's going to get him for this.

Upon her return to school Betsy told me in a counseling session with the class that she had attempted suicide because her father had left her.

"I hate him," she said, "I really hate him. I need him, Bernie. He's gone. It's…"

"Painful?"

She nodded, looking away.

"You love him."

She nodded, holding back tears.

"Why don't you tell him that," I said, "instead of killing yourself?"

I will never forget her answer.

"It's harder," she said. "Much harder."

She'd just continue making a fool of herself, she said.

It was more fun.

And she did. When a girl fails to get love from her father, she will seek relief in all the wrong places: suicide, as in Betsy's case; drugs; alcohol; failure in school; extreme and unusual disobedience at home; extreme and unusual inattention to chores; the silent treatment; running away; anorexia; precocious sex.

"Does your father show you affection, Betsy?" I asked. "Any at all? I mean, does he try?"

"Why, yes," she said.

"How?"

"You know, he'll put his arm around me or say something nice, you know, things like that."

"And your reaction?"

She growled.

"Your father doesn't love you," I asked, "or you don't love him?"

She smiled.

"You're leaving him, you know."

She smiled again.

"To get, Betsy, you've got to give."

"Like I said, I'd rather make a fool of myself."

So she flirted, she teased; she'd periodically check to be sure that the top button of her blouse remained unbuttoned. She leaned over at the most inappropriate times. In midclass boys trailed off in midcomment. Some shamelessly ogled; others were more cool. She left suggestive notes in less-than-discreet places. One advised Joseph, the boy she went with after Dwight, whom she went with after Dennis, whom she went with after Lewis, whom she went with after Ben, on the advantages of Trojans.

One boy, however, she could not successfully charm: Maury Michaels' boyfriend, Charlie Webb. He shamelessly stared at Betsy's breasts, usually with a pleasant smile on his face, and she shamelessly flirted, but his Kroger ring was on Maury's finger, and his necklace hung around Maury's neck.

Betsy was insanely jealous, absolutely obsessed. Through no fault of her own Maury had now assumed the role of The

Other Woman, Betsy's father's secretary and mistress. Maury's mere presence seemed to Betsy a rebuke and a rejection, superficially at least an unpleasant reminder of the paramour whom Betsy wanted nothing so much as to marinate in poison. Maury was naturally aggressive in class discussions. Now if she so much as raised her hand in class to answer a teacher's question, it earned her a martyr's sigh or an impatient tapping of the pencil from Betsy. A comment, an insight, or a reaction from Maury in any class discussion invited a smirk, a grimace, or a subtle glare from Betsy.

Maury handled it with characteristic simplicity and assertiveness.

"Fuck you, Betsy."

At which point Betsy would retreat, only to return to her own internal headquarters to plot an even more subtle attack.

"Bernie," said Maury, furious, frustrated, and incredibly embarrassed, "everybody in this classroom thinks I stuff my bra. That bitch. I can't believe she told people that."

"Betsy?"

"Duh...who else, the wicked witch of the west?"

"Charge her. Bust her ass. Maul her. Talk to Norman. He's the DA."

"Do you know what *that* son of a bitch asked me? He asked me if it was *true!*"

"To find out if he'd have a slander case, Maury, I'm sure. Norman's much too shy and reticent to have really wondered."

"Slander? Hey, that's a great idea."

"Norman," I said, passing him on his way to class, "it was Betsy, right?"

"Of course"

"How do you know?"

"Everybody knows, even if they don't *know*, you know what I mean? Well, everybody except maybe you."

"Can you prove it?"

"I've already started," he said. "First I had to be certain it wasn't true. I'm waiting for Maury to file charges."

"She will," I said. "Oh God, here she comes now."

"Norman," she said, interrupting. "I want to press charges against Betsy for slander. She started the rumor. She told Anna."

"And she told Frannie," said Norman. "I've already begun interviewing."

"Can you *believe* Betsy?" asked Maury.

"I hope so," said Norman.

"What do you mean?" asked Maury.

"If nobody believes her," said Norman, "we don't have a case."

BETSY MAKES A FOOL OF HERSELF

Shortly after Norman notified Betsy that she had been charged with slander for instigating and spreading the rumor that Maury wore a padded bra, Betsy herself came to school braless, wearing a provocative tank top. We were in literature class, discussing Chaim Potok's *My Name is Asher Lev*. Betsy dropped a pencil, leaning over seductively to pick it up. After a few minutes she bent over to tie her shoe. Finally, to make sure she captured everyone's attention, she placed her elbows on the table, the tank top falling dangerously low, and she remained that way, as if it were nothing unusual to be sitting in class, discussing Asher Lev's motivation for terminating his artistic endeavors, with one's breasts spilling all over the table.

"Betsy," I said, "your tits are sticking out."

"I'm not certain that has anything to do with the book we're discussing," she said.

"Oh," I said, "but it does. Always. Who can tell me how?"

"We can't understand Asher's motivation for whatever he might do," said Frannie McGee, "if we can't understand our own?"

"Right. If Asher's motivation for quitting drawing is guilt, if he sees it as frivolous in the face of his father's work, who has caused him to feel this way?"

"His father," yelled out about half the class.

"And who has made you feel the way you do, Betsy? Who is causing you, as you've admitted, to continue making 'a fool' of yourself? What, Betsy, is your motivation for suddenly sharing your breasts with the entire world? Very simply, if Asher Lev's motive for terminating his art is guilt, what is yours for exposing your breasts?"

"Asher Lev's father is running his life," said Anna Rossini.

"Mine's not even in my life," said Betsy.

"Ah, okay, Asher Lev wants his dad off his back?" I offered.

"He wants to *please* his father," said Frannie. "He wants…"

"Acceptance?" I asked.

"Yeah," She said.

"And Betsy," I asked, "what does Betsy want?"

"Oh," said Frannie, "the same thing."

"You think you're so smart, Bernie," Betsy said.

"I am. I am. Now, Betsy, you'll call Dad crying, and you'll say Bernie doesn't let you wear what you want to school, and out of guilt—as Asher Lev's father supports his ancestors—your father will support you and you'll holler about children's rights since he's a lawyer."

"Well, it is my right to wear what I want."

"Not in this class. Dress like that again, and *I'm* calling your father and telling him to come pick you up. Then you'll still get what you want. Asher Lev wants his dad out of his life, according to Anna, and you want yours in. Or according to Frannie, you *both* want your fathers, probably a deeper interpretation. Hey, it'll all work out. Look, Betsy, you *are* making a fool of yourself."

"By wearing what I want?"

"Just for the sake of curiosity," I asked the boys in the class, "how do you feel about it?"

They felt uncomfortable, they said. They didn't know where to "put" their eyes. It "kind of" made them feel like perverts, they said. All, that is, but Rick Broderick and Adam Wade. They liked it. They were popular.

More importantly, asked the boys and the girls, why did she need to do it, to call attention to herself in this manner?

"Good question," I said, even though they had actually already answered it, because now they had discovered it for themselves.

She would no more get what she truly needed and wanted from her father by exposing her breasts to her classmates than Asher Lev would get from his father by hiding his art.

Paul Bianchi, headmaster, approached me the next afternoon as I was leaving school. He's one of my best friends.

"Bernie, if I ask you if you told Betsy Robinson in front of an entire literature class that her tits were sticking out, in exactly those words, is the answer going to be what I expect? No, no, wait. Don't answer that, please." He stuffed his fingers in his ears. "Are you answering?"

"No, I'm saying 'Paul Bianchi is a fool.' Can you hear that?"

"No, I can't, since generally I'm regarded as presidential material."

"Willy called?" Willy was Betsy's father.

"Willy doesn't worry me. He knows you, he trusts you, *he's* a fool."

We both laughed. "He mentioned it—he knows he's got a problem with Betsy, you know that—he was calling about a board matter. What concerns me, Bernie, as always, is whoever *didn't* call. Someone outside your class who might not know you. Look, friend to friend, colleague to colleague—"

"Fool to fool?"

"Fool to fool. Did you have to say it like that? I mean, 'Your *tits* are sticking out'?

"Absolutely."

"Do you mind if I ask why?"

"Well, they *were*, Paul."

"I understand, I understand. No, I'm *trying* Bernie, I'm trying. *In that way*, Bernie. Did you have to say it *in that way*?"

"Yep."

"Why? Again, if you don't mind me asking. Far be it from me to interfere with Michelangelo while he's on the scaffold."

"Given the nature of what she was doing, and why she was doing it—parading her tits before the classroom, most of whom were uncomfortable as hell with it—it wouldn't have been honest to say it any other way. Her tits were sticking out. Simple as that. She wasn't making a fashion statement, Paul, this wasn't naiveté, it was tits and ass. What I said was real. It was also absolutely necessary. Because it was funny. It was certainly what she wanted. When the tension was released everybody got to express themselves about it, including her. She got to hear them, and believe me, at least superficially, that is what she wanted. The kids got to go a bit deeper into themselves, as well as the character of Asher Lev, as well as Betsy herself. What was she doing, why was she doing it? If children do not have their fathers' acceptance, what effect does it have on them? Would exposing her breasts to her classmates—or going from boy to boy, for that matter—ultimately get her what she wanted, what she needed? What need was being expressed, in other words, underneath that show? Would it be met, in that particular way, or would she merely be ogled or disdained? Paul, listen closely: she got to hear that they like her and respect her truly for who she is. For them she doesn't need to parade her tits in front of their eyes. That must be a very nice thing to hear."

"The lesson here, Paul, is 'What is love?' and 'How do I get it?'"

"From Willy," Paul said. "From Willy."

"Right," I said, "from Willy."

NORMAN STEWART, THE DISTRICT ATTORNEY

The district attorney for the class, Norman Stewart, is the prosecutor in the trial of Betsy Robinson. He is a short, muscular gymnast, a Vietnamese refugee who is the only kid in the class with a perceptible mustache—in a year he will begin shaving. The adopted son of a Unitarian couple, he has no memory of his natural parents; he was part of the evacuation of Saigon.

Naturally distrustful, Norman perceived any social slight, intended or no, as a rejection: "Mom says I've got to get off the phone so she can use it, Norman"; a greeting that looked as if it might have been aimed elsewhere; a refused invitation—"Sorry, I'm invited to Robert's this weekend, how about the next one?"

All were sources of anxiety, resentment, jealousy, rage, and confusion, hardening his heart. Any kid I might suggest as a prospective friend, or who might offer himself, Norman ridiculed as too "insecure" or "boring" or, his latest phrase, "incompatible due to different interests."

He was really fucked up.

He was so lonely and so angry that one night he rode his bike over to the school, sneaked into the classroom through an unlocked window, turned over all the cubbies, and stole all his classmates' money.

"Somebody better make friends with him quick," I told the class, "or we're all going to be broke."

Every time I'd walk by him I'd grab my wallet.

"Norman," I'd say, grabbing him by the shoulders, "I love you. I love you. Is my money safe?"

I drove him crazy until he admitted one day in class why he'd done it.

"I'm angry," he said.

"At whom?"

"At this class, everyone."

"Why?"

"I don't have any friends."

"Who do you want to be friends with? Everybody I mention you say is boring."

"I don't know—Joseph, Checker maybe, Rick."

"Why them? You want to be friends with *them*."

"They're popular. Through them I can make other friends. Then I'll be popular."

"You want to be friends with them, or to *use* them?"

"I want to use them for popularity, for respect, to be top dog, you know?" He smiled at himself. "But I didn't know that."

"Until now."

"Right." He looked at them, all three of whom seemed to waver between relief and resentment. "Sorry, guys."

They shrugged.

"So who do you really want to be friends with?"

"I don't know."

Meanwhile, Danny Fields and Jonathan Paul, both of whom shared the same temperament and interests as Norman, looked furious.

"Spill the beans, Norman."

"Can I think about it?"

"No, you'll think yourself out of it. Why can't you tell me?"

"I don't know who they are yet. I have to think."

"But in the blink of an eye you told us who you *didn't* want to be friends with. Why?"

"It was easy."

"Because you really didn't prefer them?"

"Yeah."

"Because it was safe?"

"Yes."

"Because you *knew* you'd be rejected?"

"Yes."

"So you're only trying to be friends with those who you *know* are going to reject you? Why?"

"It won't hurt."

"Do you really want to be friends with those guys?"

"Not especially. No offense, guys."

They shrugged again, palms open.

"What makes you so afraid, Norman? Help me, Bubba."

"I don't know, Bubba."

"If I ask you who you most wanted to be close with in here, could you tell me?"

"Maybe. No."

"But *you* know."

He nodded.

"Okay, let's see where this fear comes from."

"Other friends left me."

"They left you, or you left them?"

"Oh. Maybe I left them."

"How?"

"By being annoying, avoiding them, putting them down."

"Why?"

"I thought they'd leave me."

"Why?"

"Because they did."

"Norman, that doesn't make sense."

"I know."

"Come over here beside me. That's it, walk on over here. Now lie down on the floor where you can relax. What takes years for adults can take minutes for kids. You'll be more comfortable afterwards. Lie down. I'm going to hold your hand just so you'll be safe. Try not to molest me."

He giggled. So did the class.

"Okay, I'm going to count to five slowly."

"This is stupid. Bernie, do I have to?"

"Yes. Just shut up. Okay? That's it. Relax. Move your hands, relax your arms. I want you to go back all the way through childhood and let's see where that feeling comes from. Okay. Good, that's it, one…two…three…four…five…."

The class was quiet. I had done this periodically with all of them, as a group, to get to the essence of their feelings not only to enhance their relationships, but also to enable them to discover the source of their conflicts in their stories and debates and court cases. Tension has to clear before the heart can open.

After about ten minutes his body jolted and jumped as if it had been electrically charged. I heard: "They didn't want me." Then: "Why wasn't I good enough?"

He was referring, of course, to his birth parents.

Later he would return to an even earlier time where he would see himself playing with his mother, feel the warmth and tenderness of a baby swathed in blankets, of being held and cuddled, but for now, all I said was, "You know that's not true, don't you?"

He nodded Yes and No.

"In your head you know it?"

"You just told me," he said, suddenly feisty.

"But not in your heart?"

"I want to be friends with Danny and Jonathan," he said dusting off his trousers.

Danny and Jonathan understood. They had wanted to be friends with him too. That's why they'd been angry with him. Norman had actually been a snob, seeking power, i.e. popularity and social status, as a substitute for intimacy. Fear made him that way.

They understood, because Norman understood, and he had shown them.

The class applauded his courage and insight, his willingness to dare, to show his humanity, to illuminate, at least in part, their own souls as he bared his own.

Distrust, however, would resurface again and again over the course of his middle school years. At the point at which he turned away from his birth mother, thrust amid a desperate, screaming throng through the gates of the American embassy in Saigon toward a pale, uniformed nurse on the other side, he turned away, he would eventually remember, from himself, from love, security, and warmth, from his mother's bosom. Toward the close of his eighth-grade year that child, glimpsed through a fog of memory, arms outstretched in his mother's, would cry out to him. Norman was afraid that if he returned to him and claimed him as his own, he would disappear forever into that seemingly vast eternal fog that separated them. He was terrified beyond measure, as are all abandoned children, that he would be lost forever to memory, grief, loneliness, and insanity, forever out of control. Let memory claim you, I urged. Allow yourself to disappear. Let yourself go crazy. Your feelings will take you through the fog, and when you return, I promise you, it will have lifted. Completely let yourself go. Become that small child. Let him in. And as the child came out, Norman would.

Still, a beginning—an initial connection to that child—had been made, and an auspicious beginning it was.

When he ran for district attorney, he won.

"I know the criminal mind," he announced in his campaign speech. "I have one."

Now *he* was poking fun at himself. Much healthier.

FAYE BROWN, DEFENSE ATTORNEY

Betsy's lawyer, Faye Brown, was a brilliant attorney. She was a superstitious, aggressive, likable obsessive-compulsive kid who publicly fell apart before each trial. She would fly into a manic hysteria, complaining that her client should fire her, that both of them would be publicly humiliated, that she simply had no case. She would throw up her arms, papers flying all over the room, until sympathy, in the form of evidence, information, potential witnesses, ideas rushed in from every corner.

If she didn't get what she needed, and witnesses heretofore unheard of did not come rushing in from the most unlikely places, she'd wait until the next day and try again.

She was a great actress.

"Boy," she said to me one afternoon after a particularly rambunctious bout of hysteria, "being a lawyer is exhausting."

Obsessive people often get what they want because they are so single-minded they will stop at nothing to achieve resolution. Insecurity and uncertainty are unhinging, and consequently become the source of their drive. Faye's insecurity and hysteria were sympathetic because they were real.

Uncannily shrewd, Faye would do anything, as a lawyer, to get to her particular truth. When I caught Alec lying about having read his literature assignment, she argued for and won an outright acquittal: according to *Webster's*, she explained, to cheat is to deceive and mislead; the teacher Bernie, she said, was neither deceived nor misled; therefore Alec did not cheat.

"Alec attempted to cheat," she argued, "but he failed at it. You cannot find me guilty of theft if I do not take your money, no matter how hard I try. You may, however, find me guilty of attempted theft, attempted robbery. What Alec did was attempt to cheat. Unfortunately he was not charged with that crime. I urge congress to bring it up as a law—attempted cheating—and to bring that law before the class and pass it so Alec can never again get away with this.

"If, however, you find him guilty of a crime he did not commit—cheating—then you are saying that the actual law itself, all these laws on which we have worked so diligently, do not matter. So if you find him guilty of a crime he did not commit—cheating—we are all in danger.

"The matter before the court is to find him not guilty of cheating."

Her advice to Betsy: Keep your mouth shut. Talk to no one. If they place you under subpoena, plead the fifth. It may look peculiar, but your testimony can only hurt you. They have to prove that your comments were false, malicious, and hurt Maury's reputation. That is a big job. Let's not help them. Besides, everybody knows the comments were malicious, that your motive was jealousy, that you hate Maury because you love her boyfriend.

Faye!

Faye's not the point. Motive is. If witnesses testify to it, it's hearsay; if you say it, it's direct testimony. The burden of proof is on the prosecution; they have to prove you were malicious beyond a reasonable doubt. That's hard, without direct testimony, and the only person capable of providing it is you. That's the weak spot in their case.

It wasn't really malicious, said Betsy. I mean, I didn't really want to hurt her.

Yeah, Betsy, said Faye, studying her papers. Right. Right.

Norman Stewart

"Bernie," Norman said, "are you busy?"

"No."

"Oh, can I come in then?"

He was already in. I put down the essay I was evaluating. It was Amy Levenson's. She was arguing for a law against social conspiracies, usually, according to her evidence, a group of friends plotting to scapegoat one of their own.

"I've got a problem, the slander case against Betsy. Frannie and Anna are avoiding me. I can't get them to testify."

"Have you subpoenaed them?"

"Yeah. But when I approach them or even phone them at night they're always busy. And when they do talk they're so vague I can't even tell what they're saying. Everybody knows Betsy told them Maury stuffed her bra. I can't get them to tell me."

"What does the constitution say?"

"Here, I've got it right here. Dwight can give them contempt, I can charge them with obstruction of justice."

"Wait, they're not protecting themselves. You've told them they won't be charged for spreading the rumor?"

He nodded. "They're protecting Betsy. They're close friends."

"Right. Are we thinking the same thing?"

"Well, if they testify, what's the word…"

"Reluctantly?"

"Reluctantly. Yeah. If they have to be forced to testify against their closest friend, that shows their loyalty."

"Yes."

"The jury'll believe them if they know that. And I don't think Frannie, at least, and maybe Anna would have told other people if they hadn't believed Betsy…"

"Great, keep going, and if they believed her…"

"They'd have to have thought less of Maury."

"Give me the definition of slander."

Norman pulled out his law dictionary. "It has to be false, malicious, and harmful to her reputation."

"It was false…"

"Everybody knows Betsy's jealous."

"And Maury's reputation?"

"Well, if they believed Betsy, like I said, then they had to have thought less of Maury…"

"Maybe. Also, if they believed Betsy, it's more likely people they told believed *them*."

"That's what I was getting at."

"Check. Be sure."

"I will. I don't like surprises."

"How do they make you feel?"

"Scared."

"You know why…"

"Yes, Bernie. We've been over that."

"Right. Oh, Norman," I said as he was leaving. "Good thinking, Bubba."

"Thanks, Bubba."

"Right."

DWIGHT ALLGOOD, JUDGE

When Dwight Allgood stole into his father's bathroom late one night and slashed his wrists, he hoped his father, who had physically abused him, would find him. See, see what you've done, he wanted to say. Now I've finished the job. Fortunately, he admitted, for the sake of himself and his mother, whom he could not bear to hurt, he botched the job. He was terribly ashamed of his inability to love his father; all he could feel was hatred and fear. At the age of thirteen he was terrified of his anger, so frightened that already he was afraid to have children of his own.

What Dwight does is to withhold tenderness and affection; he is too frightened to show it. I feel certain that this feeds his father's resentment and anger and violence.

Dwight told me that he dreamed of a big, Irish cop kicking his father's ass in their living room. Again and again and again. After which Dwight would stand over his helpless father and point at him and say: "See, you bastard. See how it feels?"

And then he burst into tears: he had punched his little brother for failing to give back his baseball glove.

Who cares about the glove? he said. He's my brother. I love him.

And when he realizes that his grandfather beat up his father, he sees himself caught up in a spiral, a vortex, a legacy of violence and anger and injustice.

What, he says, does one do with it?

One expresses it, one reports it, and one discovers his own consequential self-destructive neuroses. For example, Dwight, a very bright, capable student, sabotages himself at every opportunity to avoid an excellent evaluation overall in his schoolwork; this is to avoid becoming in any way possible his father, a Harvard graduate and famed botanist, and to deprive him of the satisfaction of a child who is an excellent student; you can't hit a kid for making B's.

After he learns that what has happened is not in any way his fault, that in no way might a six-year-old be responsible for his thirty-year-old father slugging him, then it may occur to him that what self-destructive things he might be doing now are meant to deepen the deterioration of his and his father's relationship.

Remember, what Dwight wants, for his own sake, is to be

able to love him.

To tame the beast raging in his own soul he must embrace him. He wasn't bad; his father was.

Then what one does—at least this is what Dwight did—is to run for judge.

Dwight is tall, easily blushes, and generally walks, as you might imagine, as if he is in perpetual fear of ambush. But on the afternoon of his campaign speech all I could see was his height.

"I know what it means," he said, "to be treated unfairly; I know what it feels like to be assaulted, harassed, and bullied. My father, as most of you know, has managed to make me his punching bag since I was six. Six." He paused, and took in his audience with the confidence of a heavyweight; it was as if he'd been dreaming this speech for years. "I understand, I swear to you, the feeling of anger, of helplessness, and of shame that comes from powerlessness and unfairness. I promise you justice. My passion will not be crazy. I ask you, I beg you, to allow me to use it to help you—to help myself. I will not become those judges and public officials who served this class years ago and who became, in a small way, my dad. They too were the powerful, and they too were unfair."

His opponent, Helen Wright, he charged, lived a *"Leave It to Beaver"* existence; that was the picture, he said, that she had chosen to present. If she had never been treated unfairly, where then was her passion for justice? From where did it come?

When the election results were announced—Dwight won— Helen, his opponent, was devastated. She'd never lost anything before, and though her father was hospitalized for depression, her younger brother was suicidal, and her mother so frightened as to be neutralized—Helen was, as she presented herself behind the lectern and in day-to-day life, excellent academically. She was perfect, as many of her friends and teachers felt, and as her classmates were now telling her as she wept loudly and inconsolably in front of them.

"You're great, Helen."

"Not a hair," said Dwight, with great affection, "is ever out of place!"

She looked at him and smiled.

He smiled back, again not with triumph—in fact, as elated as he was, he felt a bit guilty—but with affection.

"That's the problem," she said ruefully. "It's hard to be truthful when you're perfect."

Dwight proposed what he called a System of Administering Penalties that would necessarily be applied to every student in the class, regardless of personality, position, or power. It was a specific formula, a scale in which the guilty party's sentence would be systematically increased in accordance with the frequency and severity of the crime. Perjury would require a harsh sentence regardless of how often the defendant committed it. Failure to Return Class Property to its Proper Place, however, would suggest a sentence that would increase in length each time the person was found guilty of either that particular crime or one similar in significance—perhaps three days clean-up of the study area room the first time; six the second; nine the third, and so forth.

Still, what if the judge chose to ignore his system?

He suggested that congress and the class amend the constitution and that his System for Administering Penalties be placed under the heading Duties and Responsibilities of Judges, since already a judge could be impeached for "Failing to do his job adequately."

Failing impeachment, he reasoned, the judge could be suspended or disbarred by the Class Bar Association.

So Dwight, both passionate and intelligent, an abused child compelled and determined to have justice in his own life, would preside over the trial of Betsy Robinson.

Several years before Dwight Allgood entered my class-room, social influence, more than any other factor, became po-litical power.

Until, following the naturally sluggish, circuitous, mean-dering stream of the history of the world, the masses, under the leadership of Rodney Shelton, revolted.

Rodney was an established member of the elite, those ma-cho boys and personality-parading girls obsessed with the art of one-upmanship, scholars in the science of exclusion and degra-dation. They knew what clothes to wear—and were terrified not to, and what jokes to laugh at—whether or not they caught on, and their mutual camaraderie was based chiefly on their fear of each other and their contempt for the masses.

The boys were macho, the girls pretty and loud.

They were, as they are in all classrooms, the Popular Group.

The masses were the Unpopular Group.

I knew that the Popular Group's habits of sneaking out of their bedroom windows at night to smoke, drink, and experi-ment with pot and sex were largely out of fear, as was their cloned posture, their way of lounging in a chair, their walk, their uniformed laughter, their contempt of their classmates.

Rodney, however, seemed somehow *better*. *Special*. His face seemed more alive, he seemed more sensitive and helpful to his classmates, the masses.

His athleticism and his machismo, identification badges of the popular boys, seemed all pretense to me.

I wondered, if one day the Popular Group stayed home, would Rodney Shelton have the time of his life at school?

What neither Rodney nor I knew at the time was that he was gay.

The popular kids ruled the classroom, and of course the masses hated their guts. But as much as they were despised, they were feared. Their personalities were strong, and they were charming. They knew when to fight, when to charm, and when to woo and placate and sympathize.

They were great politicians.

Few kids would have ever dreamed of not voting for them.

If Freddie Cox, the most popular one of them all, told a joke, his cohorts were a veritable laugh track. If an unpopular kid laughed, the Popular Group stopped abruptly, turned, and stared until he disappeared into the woodwork. If an unpopular kid actually spoke in the presence of the Group, they turned as if he were a fly unworthy of swatting, a rebellion too minor to quash. They rendered him invisible. The fear of ridicule had ground class discussion to a halt. Unpopular kids were intimidated into allowing popular kids to copy answers off their test papers. A story by an unpopular kid read aloud to the class was dismissed with sneers and nitpicking.

At recess one day I heard Freddie say, "Davey Markham is so stupid. Watch this. When I say, 'When the sun sets, the chicken sleeps,' everybody laugh real loud. Okay. Here goes. 'When the sun sets, the chicken sleeps.' Isn't that hilarious!" His cohorts doubled over, overcome with laughter that appeared genuine.

Davey was sitting alone over in the corner, working on his homework, and when he heard the laughter he looked up.

"Tell Davey the joke," Freddie said to Rodney. "Go ahead. You can tell he wants to hear it. He feels left out. Don't you, Davey. Tell him, Rodney. Be a friend."

"Yeah," chorused the group, pushing Rodney over there.

Wavering between good and evil, right and wrong, courage and cowardice, Rodney chose the latter, pretending perhaps even to himself that he was more than ready and eager.

"This is really funny," he said walking over to Davey. He placed his hands on the table, palms down, looking into Davey's eyes.

A bit unnerved, Davey nevertheless smiled in anticipation. He couldn't afford to miss this. The ridicule would be too great. Also he was flattered. Rodney Shelton, of the Popular Group, was including him!

"When the sun sets, Davey, the chicken sleeps."

The Popular Group laughed like crazy. Rodney doubled over, apparently unable to contain himself. "Isn't that a riot?" said Ginger Collins. "Ohmigod."

Puzzled only for a second, Davey joined in, as if it was the funniest thing he'd ever heard.

"You get it?" said Rodney, apparently almost choking.

"Yes," said Davey, still rollicking along. "Oh my God, man. That's really funny."

"Isn't it?" said Rodney.

Davey nodded, chuckling, still unable to shake it off. "That's funny, man. That's really funny."

"What's funny, Davey?" asked Rodney, looking directly at him, his palms still flat on the table.

"The joke, man. The joke's funny."

"There is no joke, Davey. There's nothing to get," he said, walking off. "Jesus, you're stupid."

"What a fuckin' dork," said Freddie, his arm around Rodney. "What a piece of shit."

"Can you believe that dork?" said Ginger.

Until Davey was left sitting there alone.

I hate pious teachers. A good teacher has to be willing to dirty his hands, to fight for his kids sometimes by fighting them. Inaction in a case like this would have been a terrible action. To the degree that Davey knew he was pretending, Rodney knew he himself was pretending.

That was my opening. Second semester was approaching, and elections were coming up. Something had to be done. Favoritism toward the elite reigned over the class government and court system. Popular kids didn't just steal lunches, for example, they openly took them. The unpopular kids appeared to happily give them up. When they stuffed Drew Little in the trash can, he acted like he was having the time of his life. Freddie Cox, who happened to be the class judge at the time, let any popular kid off the hook, if the class district attorney, also a popular kid, ever filed charges against them in the first place, which he rarely did. Extortion, put-downs, discrimination, assault and battery, invasion of privacy, slander, and gossip were rampant, all of which kept the masses intimidated. The only way they got off the hook was if they bribed Freddie or the DA. The elite controlled congress, so impeachment was impossible. In fact, if an unpopular kid even tried to charge a popular kid, he himself was brought before the court on fabricated charges of framing or vengeful prosecution.

They were bad, but you have to remember, they couldn't have been happy—the popular kids, whether they knew it or not, were themselves scared of each other. They were bad in order to discover—even if by force—what it took in order to be good.

Had they needed to have their butts kicked for every kid to feel safe and secure, I would have done so.

The problem is they wouldn't have learned.

My job is to teach.

The immediate dilemma was that with elections coming up, no one had the courage to run against the popular kids.

The offices were listed on the blackboard: DA, congress, judge, etc. Candidates had to sign their names underneath the office for which they were running by the closing of school,

January 1st. Only the incumbents, all popular kids, had signed up to run, one per office.

When I asked why there was no opposition, the incumbents replied that they'd done a great job; consequently, no platform or issues presented themselves on which opposing candidates might run.

"Wow," I said. "That's pretty neat. Everybody give them a big hand." The class applauded with great enthusiasm. I thought to myself: this is not merely nuts, it's so thoughtless as to be pathetic. Only Rodney seemed elsewhere, as if by dissociating from the discussion he could avoid his shame and guilt.

"Rodney?" I asked.

He shook his head, placed it in his arms, and glanced about the room. "Nothing. Really it's nothing."

Silence.

"It's nothing," he insisted. Again, total silence.

"Bernie! Stop, I swear. I don't have anything. How many times do I have to say it. God."

"Yes you do, Rodney. You do have something. 'When the sun sets, Rodney, the chicken sleeps.' Favoritism. Favoritism's the issue. That was a put-down. You weren't charged. The bribery, the pushing, the shoving, the extortion, the thefts and harassment. Hey, when I think about it, Rodney, when I think about you and your buddies, there seem to be *lots* of issues, all revolving around the theme of favoritism."

Rodney was clearly embarrassed, as well as curious.

However, Freddie Cox said, "Why do we need the court system anyway? We don't need rules."

I leapt across the table, wrestled Freddie to the floor (nearly jerking out my back in the process), and pinned him, my fist cocked and poised over his face, ready to be launched.

He was stricken with terror.

"How do you feel about rules now?" I asked. "There's no

court system, Freddie, no headmaster, no parents, no Board of Education, only me, Freddie, and I enjoy beating the shit out of people weaker than me. Do you? Here," I said, helping him up. "Sit down."

A curious energy was stirring among the masses, in fact, among everyone perhaps but Freddie. And even *his* soul was bubbling and fermenting. For the first time, he was vulnerable.

"Every day when I come home," said Rodney, "my mom asks, 'Did you have a nice day, Rodney?' and I always, every day, say 'Yes,' you know, with all this fake enthusiasm."

"And every day you're lying."

"Yes."

"How do you feel about that?"

"Guilty. I'm sorry, y'all, I'm ashamed. I feel like a traitor somehow, to my mom, yes, but more to myself. I mean, throwing the football every afternoon, laughing at jokes I don't get. Sorry, Davey, I know just how I made you feel, I don't blame you for hating me, but I hope you don't…"

Davey said nothing.

"…reading the sports section, which I hate, so I'll have something to talk about, so I won't be ridiculed. The way I walk, talk, sit in my chair—it's like I'm a copy of you, Freddie, and that's not your fault, it's just not me. I don't blame all of you," he said looking at the masses, "for hating me. I hate myself. I've been cruel. I've been an ass-kisser. I'm sorry. Run for office. You've got my vote. I'm sorry, Davey. I hope after a while, at least, you won't hate me. I want a new life, new friends."

"Are you for real?" I asked him.

"Yes," he said.

"Do you guys believe him?"

"I believe him," said Davey.

The masses murmured their agreement.

No one argued to the contrary. Only Freddie had a sneer

on his face, and that was not enough to withstand the excitement forming among the masses. "There are more of you than them," I said. "There always are."

Rodney called a meeting of the masses, and within minutes candidates' names were supplied for offices. Later in their speeches they cited instance after instance of favoritism practiced by the incumbents against whom they were running. Their message was that they had taken it long enough, they were organized, and they were ready to fight. They had been afraid and they had learned, they claimed, what fear could do to them, so never again would they suffer such humiliation. Where he was afraid before, said Davey, now he was mad. He ended his campaign speech for district attorney with, "Watch out."

The incumbents' speeches were equally interesting. Running against Rodney for judge, Freddie began his speech, in all sincerity, with "I am, and have always been, an asshole." He felt guilty, he said, and he had enjoyed it at the same time. He attacked his opponent, Rodney Shelton, for not having been honest with him in the first place, for pretending to be his friend, for going along when he *knew* it was wrong. Freddie hadn't stopped to think about what he'd been doing, he hadn't known. Why? Because Rodney had been too weak and cowardly to tell him. He held up twenty-seven court sheets as proof of his sincerity. "I have pressed and filed charges against myself for put-downs, assault and battery, extortion, slander, and failing to uphold the class constitution. I plead guilty and welcome the punishment for every charge. Because I am guilty, and I am sorry. Rodney is good, but is he strong? If you were *me* would you trust him? I'm here to *prove* to you that I'm good, that I'm not the asshole I was, I'm running to earn your trust. And unlike Rodney, I will be strong."

Only in this race did the block voting disintegrate. Freddie won by one vote. But power was restored to the people, of whom most certainly Freddie was now one.

In the lore and tradition of my classroom, the stories of Rodney and Freddie and the corruption in their classroom assumed the status of legend, cited years later, for example, when Norman Stewart ran for district attorney and Dwight Allgood ran for judge.

Faye Brown

"Bernie," said Faye Brown, "Norman won't give me his evidence. According to the class constitution, the defense attorney gets to see the prosecution's evidence."

"Come on in, Faye. Make yourself at home."

"Thanks," she said, making herself at home. "I'm exhausted. How ya doin'?"

"You want something."

"Yep."

"You want me to make Norman give you his evidence. He obviously doesn't have to yet or you would have gone to Dwight. What does the constitution say?"

"Bernie—"

"What does the constitution say?"

"He's got a week."

"What can I do?"

"Overrule it. You're the teacher. The constitution says you can overrule it. The board can overrule you, the headmaster can overrule you, and you can overrule the constitution. Bernie, he's making me wait on purpose, he's going to hang on till the last minute, giving me as little time as he can get away with."

"Faye, you can anticipate most of it. What's he got to prove? False, malicious, and harmful to reputation."

"I know all that. I've got to come up with something that'll surprise him. I can't have Betsy testify, she'll have to tell the truth. That certainly won't help her."

I smiled. That was funny.

"Hmm…Damn!"

"Where you going?"

"See ya," she said. "Thanks."

"What'd I do?"

She was already out the door.

MAURY MICHAELS, THE PLAINTIFF

Maury Michaels is a spunky, aggressive kid, busily freckled, with enormous brown eyes that registered epiphanies in classes and storywriting conferences like they were birthday presents. She loved to learn.

We were in a pre-story writing conference, the purpose of which was to come up with a story idea, in my office.

"You know, Maury, not many girls your age are as serious about their boyfriends as you. I mean, you guys actually date. You make out and stuff."

"I hate Betsy Robinson. She's such a jealous bitch."

"Okay, she spread a rumor. What's the big deal? It's middle school. Gossip and rumor are the nutrients of your social lives. Without them, let's face it, you have to deal with reality. Right? Isn't that much too threatening? Anyway, why such intensity, I mean, at thirteen?"

"There's no story there."

"Are you sure, Maury? Are you close with your dad, or distant…?"

"Look, I know my story, Bernie. Can we get off this other stuff?"

"Yeah, if it's a good one."

"It is."

But it wasn't. The safe and easy, even for a student as feisty and aggressive as Maury, beckon like sirens. Decoys are everywhere, and hers, of which at the time we were both unaware, was the semifinals of the Atlanta Lawn Tennis Association in which she had to play her best friend. Unable to face the prospect of defeating her in public, she said, Maury discovered herself sitting at midcourt in midmatch, crying.

I admit I was puzzled. Normally whom would you rather beat than your best friend? Besides, Maury was one of the most competitive kids in the class.

"And then I have to go home and listen to my father lecture me on Playing to Win and Doing My Best and Handling Pressure and he's never even home. Why, he didn't even come with us on vacation.

"He's never home, Bernie. He's never there. Then he has the gall to pry into my social life. I hate him."

"What do you mean?"

"He asked about the necklace Charlie Webb gave me." She fingered the necklace, sadly. "He hadn't noticed it for weeks, then he's all over me about it. I know he cares but he's not showing it. As far as I'm concerned, it was none of his business."

She stopped. Then: "Oh my God, Bernie," she said, her eyes registering the epiphany. "I *have* missed the story. It's my father."

"Would you have beaten her?"

She shook her head. "No. I was afraid."

"So you get back at your father by withholding information from him."

"Yes, I ignore him. It drives him crazy. He's dying to know about Charlie, and I won't tell him anything. Also, the salad plates."

"The salad plates?"

"My job, after the table is set for dinner, is to set out the salad plates. I don't do it. He's been working all day, he comes home for a relaxed meal, he wants to start with his salad. The plate's never there. Every evening it's the same thing: 'Where are the salad plates, Maury?'

'Why, in the cabinets, I imagine, where they belong.'

'Get them, Maury,' he says, seething.

"I do, but I amble as slowly as possible to the kitchen, then slam the cabinet doors as loud as I can."

"You've got to talk to him," I said.

She was stunned. "Why?"

"It's a wonderful, marvelous conflict—universal, neurotic. It's terrific. But in order for it to be a story, the conflict must be resolved. For resolution, you need confrontation. You know that. You can't write a story that's still continuing. How will you end it?"

"I don't think I can."

But two weeks later she received an ovation from her teacher and classmates for her story, "The Salad Plates."

According to her story, she waited an entire afternoon on the sun porch—so anxious she couldn't even read—for her father to come home for dinner.

She heard his Volvo pulling up in the driveway.

The car door slammed.

She met him in the kitchen. He was reading his mail. "I miss you, Daddy," she said.

And that was it. All defenses broke. It was the first time, she wrote, that she'd ever seen a grown man weep; it frightened her.

He listened, explaining why he had to work such late hours, why he'd had to miss the family vacation. The thing he wanted more than anything, he told her, was a close, intimate family; yet he also had to work to make the money to send her to the private school she loved. Sometimes he felt other family members—Maury included—weren't doing their parts. It made him angry to have to get on her about her room. He felt lonely sometimes, like he was the only one serious about doing his part. Yet she was right, he said, and he would have to do something about it. He handled it. He took responsibility. "We'll get through this," he promised her. "It's tough, but we'll get through it."

Later that evening after everyone else had gone to bed, they walked upstairs, their arms about each other, pausing awkwardly, tentatively, on the landing before going to their bedrooms. She placed her arm around her father's waist, and he placed his around hers.

"I love you, Daddy," she said, looking up at him.

"I love you too, Maury."

If only all of us could be so unaware as Maury.

The Witnesses

WITNESS LIST

PROSECUTION		DEFENSE
Frannie McGee	Riley Andrews	None
Anna Rossini	Laura Daye	
R.L. Peabody	Tessa Monroe	
Lanny Butler	Lisa Overton***	
Betsy Robinson*	Albert Herman	
Ian Gardiner	Marie Zelgado	
Checker Blumenthal	Raquel Millsey	
Jamila Cade	Joseph Cohen	
Sunaina Shah	Carrie Enright	
Faye Brown**	Amy Levenson	
Rick Broderick		
Tommi Albright		

*Though not offering direct testimony, Betsy's attorney concedes that her client made the statement, "Maury wears a padded bra."

**Class constitution allows lawyers to serve as witnesses. Under subpoena Faye will testify that she did hear the rumor.

***Also court officer

Each witness, apart from the trial itself, lives his own life and consequently has his own story. The conflicts—the trials, if you will—in his own life are those of any kid in my classroom.

FRANNIE MCGEE

The chairperson of the class congress, Frannie McGee, tall and blonde, attractive and intelligent, is tense, angry, and frustrated. Despite her ready humor, a mild tension always seems to radiate from her; she is a perfectionist yet an anomaly; a terrible speller, for example, with an unerring ear for language. Now, however, she suffers a significantly greater, more profound personal dichotomy: she is in love with the boy most responsible for her misery.

In a world traditionally made more beautiful by the splendor of the male athlete, Frannie's legs are the swiftest and the most articulate—as well as the loveliest, according to the boys—in the middle school. Her athletic instincts are quick and aggressive, as are those of Rick Broderick, her prospective boyfriend. Her vision of the playing field and basketball court is a universe from which entire worlds are created.

Her prospective boyfriend is her nemesis. She is the best female athlete for her age I have ever seen (she will attend college on an athletic scholarship), and it is he who is largely responsible for her exclusion from the games and events that matter so much to her. Her exclusion is the source of her immense anger, frustration, and vulnerability.

Rick is himself an interesting concoction—clever, attractive, and good-looking, there is a sweetness in his blue eyes that belies his daily attire: fatigues, camouflage jacket, and combat boots. Where in his eyes adults see the traces of angels, kids see what he shows: the superior, arrogant heart of a swashbuckling pirate. Yet they are attracted to him. Naturally he is the most feared, popular boy in the classroom.

I once said to him: "Rick, you're like everyone else I know—you're both bad and good; it's a question of which you prefer to express."

He smiled and thanked me, a polite, deferential statement of gratitude that did nothing so much as reassure me of my ineffectiveness.

It would take the hurt and angry Frannie to bring out his best.

She was not feared, but she was immensely well-liked and eminently respected. As chairperson of the class congress, she presided over a group of five elected representatives who met weekly with the class to discuss and debate issues and to introduce legislation that the class had the power to ultimately approve or reject.

The issues raised and discussed, often heatedly and formally, are generally unlike those raised by conventional class or student governments in conventional classrooms or schools. I am not talking about raising money for the middle school dance or organizing gifts for UNESCO or serving as a surrogate mouthpiece for the faculty, but rather such issues as violence and harassment in the classroom, social insensitivity, bribery and corruption in the class court, plagiarism, verbal assault.

Is it just and fair for the strong to bully the weak? If not, what can and should be done about it? Is ridicule fair? Why is it that at most only token "black" music is played at the middle school dance? Is it plagiarism if one student overhears another's idea and uses it as a story? I can't work, argues one student, with Johnny horsing around. Cheating. Favoritism. Perjury. Obstruction of justice.

Who, in particular, is doing what to whom?

The point that Frannie McGee was arguing in her weekly congress meeting with the class is that there is sexual discrimination taking place on campus during school hours; she cited twenty-three instances. Politically astute, she omitted the names of the offenders in favor of currying their potential votes for her bill. The subject has been pending for two years. Paideia is a liberal institution; no one wants to be embarrassed, and she was attempting to use that to her advantage. She was also, however, tired and frustrated.

She concluded her argument: "Girls have been excluded, and the proving ground is the playing field and the basketball court at recess. I have cited twenty-three instances. If I ask to join a boys' pickup game, it is full, or they argue that my joining the game would make the sides uneven; five minutes later, however, when a boy asks to join, suddenly there is room, or uneven sides seem to no longer matter. No girl has ever played quarterback at recess, and the fastest girls in the class with hands as reliable as any boy's are rarely thrown or passed the ball. In softball we bat seventh, eighth, and ninth; girls never pitch, catch, or play first base."

Rick Broderick raised his hand. As chairperson of congress, Frannie McGee's duty was to call on all persons with relevant comments, failing which, she herself could be charged with favoritism and abuse of authority. Frannie called on Rick with visible reluctance: according to rumors, she'd kissed him at the middle school dance; also, according to the classroom gossip, if she ever mustered up the courage, which was doubtful, she was going to ask him, in the vernacular of the kids, to go with her.

"Why do we need a law for this?" he asked. "I never realized it was happening. Just ask, I'll be happy to have you join my team."

"Then why haven't you?" she shot back

His face reddened; he was angry. "I didn't know," he said. His tone was pleading, as if he were trying his best for fairness and justice, and then the truth came out: "Why do you care so much? If we've got a game going, why don't you just form your own?"

She looked directly at him, the most feared, popular boy in the classroom. "The reason I care," she said, "is because I'm better than you."

"That's true, Rick," said Joseph Cohen, who can be funny and self-deprecating. "She *is* better than you. She's better than all of us."

"Which is why," said Kathleen Rabinowitz, "you don't want her to play."

"Maybe that's why a bill's never been passed," said Betsy Robinson.

"Damn right," said Anna Rossini, who normally tired quickly of discourse but loved a passionate cause and who would never have let anything or anyone interfere with *her* freedom.

Marvin Pazol, notoriously unathletic, raised his hand. "You girls may be right, because they let me play," he said. Everyone laughed.

And Lester Hardwicke added, "Girls aren't the only people in this classroom who've been excluded. I have, and so have others I can name."

"Then let's change the wording," Frannie offered, "from sexual discrimination to social discrimination."

"That's ridiculous," said Joseph Cohen. "A law against all social discrimination in the classroom means that I may have no best friend, that I must give everyone in the class equal time, and that whatever private, confidential, and intimate information I might confess to one classmate I must confess to all."

"He's right," said Kathleen. "I mean, what if he doesn't know whether they're interested? Will he then have to seek them out and ask? I mean, it's ridiculous. Can you imagine it? I can see it now: 'Hi, are you interested in who I have a crush on. My name's Joseph, incidentally. I'll be happy to tell you.' I mean, it's ridiculous."

Eventually the social discrimination bill was passed, in a modified form that at the time seemed to appease everyone: No one may be excluded from any school game, exercise, or activity. What Frannie soon realized, however, was that it did nothing to solve her original problem of sexism on the playground. The boys really didn't accept her. She practically had to scream for the ball. After several weeks once again the sides were "too full." Rick Broderick said: "It's not because you're a girl, Frannie."

But it was.

She charged Rick Broderick and his friends, all boys, with social discrimination for excluding her and her friends, all girls, from school games.

Acting as his own attorney, Rick argued that it was not social discrimination but discrimination based on ability. "There is no law," he said, "against it. This is not social discrimination. No boy, for example, has been excluded. Girls have been excluded because generally, well, they are not as good as the boys. It would bring down our game. It would not be fair. That is not social discrimination."

For Frannie to argue that she alone was as good as the boys, which was true, would mean that, at most, *she* would get to play. Her case was built on the fact that she and her friends were excluded. And she couldn't make a case that they were excluded for social reasons. Besides, she told the jury, she didn't want to be "just one of the boys."

She couldn't help but point out, however, that Lester Hardwicke, who had lured her into the social discrimination bill over the sexual one, was now a defendant in the case.

"Truly," she said turning from the jury, looking directly at him, "you're now one of them. Congratulations, Lester," she said, smiling at him, before she sat down to close her case.

The girls were depressed. And despite her dramatic finish, she knew she had lost the case.

"You presented a good case," Rick told her afterward. He looked uneasy. "Really."

"I fell right into their trap," she told me later. "I hate Lester. I hate all of them."

"Rick?" I asked her.

She shrugged.

"What do I do now?" she asked.

"Write a great story. Go back to when it all started. Make them quake in their shoes. Tell the truth. This isn't the first time this has happened."

"It's happened all my life."

"When was the very first time? Go back…"

She relaxed, and after a few minutes she ran out.

She had it.

She read the class her story on a Friday morning in December. She hoped, she said, looking at Rick, that the class might be interested.

She could remember, she read, the day she discovered she was a girl. It was a time of innocence, of after-school play, of no homework. Her best friend's name was Randy, a neighbor in first grade whom she had not once thought of as a boy, and every afternoon they made faces, which they'd practiced in the bathroom mirror, at old Mr. Turner's vegetable garden, for the simple reason that he periodically presented his vegetables as gifts to their parents, and they, the kids themselves, hated them.

As she had not once contemplated Randy as a boy, so had she neglected to think of herself as a girl. She was aware only that she could outwrestle and outrun him, and he was smarter than she was. One Saturday morning she ran over to his house to play just as she had done every Saturday morning for as long as she could remember. The front door was open, so she peered through the screen door into the living room.

"Hey, Randy," she yelled, "let's play."

There was no answer. An ironing board, at which Randy's mother was working, was set up, and the television was on. Off to the right, almost in the hallway, she could make out Randy and another boy about his age and height wearing a baseball glove, a baseball cap, and a jersey with the number thirteen on it.

"Hey," she repeated, "wanna play?"

"We're going to play baseball," Randy said.

She and Randy had played baseball a thousand times; if either had had another friend over, it had never mattered the slightest; they all played. It was simply an unspoken tradition.

"Oh, great," she said, excited. "Can I play?"

She doesn't know why she asked. She must have sensed something awry, without wanting to face it, or else she would have assumed she could play, as both always had.

"No," he said.

She was so taken aback that her voice came in almost a whisper.

"Why not, Randy?" she asked, frightened that her small, lovely world of milk and cookies, of tadpoles down by the creek, of Mr. Turner's vegetable garden was about to end.

He did not articulate his answer with courage and eloquence; he couldn't; he was a boy who was ashamed. His mother, who was working very intently at the ironing board, told Frannie it was all a part of growing up, which confused Frannie, as she simply did not know what that meant.

He told her the truth.

"You're a girl," he said.

She looked up at the class.

"A girl," she repeated.

"What does it mean," she asked the class, tears unashamedly

streaming down her face, "to be a girl in this classroom, at this school—not back then but now, right here—in this goddamn shithole of a classroom."

Rick Broderick raised his hand: "I move that there may be no discrimination by any one person or group of people who are members of this class on the basis of sex."

"I second it."

"I third it."

Every hand rose.

Frannie had enriched a classroom community with the gift of herself, and in accepting it Rick Broderick had discovered within himself the gift of humility and grace.

All of the tension disappeared from her face.

"Thank you," she said to them. "Thank you."

In a small way, a lifelong struggle had been won.

Anna Rossini, R.L. Peabody, and Lanny Butler

We are all ignorant; consequently we can all learn. We're all gifted—most of us damned good at at least something—and all defective. Were we to be perceived as we truly are, most of us would be bright, and most of us would be dumb.

The truest measure of intelligence, of the genuine and capable learner, in my opinion, is his humility. One's genuine and hearty welcome of one's own ignorance and stupidity, one's slowness and sluggishness at catching on or figuring out, and one's awe at the mystery of creation—particularly one's own—is to learning what foreplay is to orgasm and what the knowledge of one's own evil is to a life of goodness and decency.

Arrogance, for the student no less than anyone else, is a fraudulent representation of oneself. Straight-A students with perfect standardized test scores, on their way to Yale, Harvard, and professional success also can be classically dull, earnest, and exceptionally submissive. Yet if the man obsessed with facts and footnotes shrinks in horror from his own poem, the poet or artist can find himself anesthetized into a stupor over the prospects of writing a research paper.

Look at Anna Rossini, probably the most gifted, prolific writer in the classroom. Not only is she the weakest math student, but also her vocabulary—not her manipulation and use of the words she knows but the extent of her vocabulary—is only average, according to standardized tests, and according to her stories; her reading is only average, better on fiction and literary passages than academic texts; her spelling is actually weak, her grammar fair, her ear for and use of language superior. Her academic essays and research papers are mediocre, her stories and poems sublime. She might lack the capacity of a scholar, but for how long? Besides, who cares whether Anna's a scholar when she's a brilliant poet and storywriter? Were Fitzgerald and Hemingway critiqued for the studies they compiled at Yale and Princeton? She can date Reality all through high school, but she doesn't need to spend her life with him.

Fitzgerald couldn't spell. And no one's perusing his trunks for old math tests.

Let's get more specific: the expert in grammar may in fact hobble through the English language like a literary cripple. Critics can't necessarily write. Vice versa. Teachers can't necessarily write. Vice versa. Analyzing the English language, to some degree, is different from using it: acing a grammar test is a passive, receptive act involving the skill of locating, analyzing, and correcting errors, perhaps memorizing, understanding, and applying rules, following and using someone else's directions. *Writing* grammatically is active, generative, and utilitarian.

Let's look at reading: the Atlanta novelist Pat Conroy has always been an exceptionally wise, profound, and expansive—not to say inspiring—reader of great literary works; his vocabulary is so diverse and expansive he could devise his own S.A.T.

in ten minutes. Yet Conroy, my favorite novelist, refuses to divulge an S.A.T. score taken more than thirty years ago.

Neither will I.

Do you know why? They're low.

You would expect the math score to be relatively unimpressive, but our verbal scores?

Stupidity bonded us for life.

Until we discovered *why* they were low.

"I was bored," Pat says.

I was bored also, reading middle school place descriptions and character sketches. They were uninspired. "They're clear," I told the class, "but clarity isn't enough."

"What would you have us do?" asked R.L Peabody. "Levitate?"

R.L. was as severely learning disabled as any student I've ever taught. She was enormously quick-witted and possessed a startling vocabulary; she was in fact a prodigious, voracious reader. Unfortunately, all she could do, schoolwise, was read. She couldn't write—even at age fourteen she reversed letters—and her math skills were centuries below grade level. She had been kept back a year in fourth grade.

"I'm not required to write," she announced, "I have learning disabilities."

"And I don't have to pass you," I told R.L., "I have authority."

"My life's miserable," she told me. "I would probably characterize it as lethargic."

"Describe it. Give me one day in the life of R.L. Peabody. You're at your best when you're miserable."

"You really think so?"

"Absolutely, R.L., that's when I like you best."

She hugged herself. "Thank you. That's when I like

myself best. I can't spell, Bernie. I'm a horrible writer. I get disorganized."

"Believe me, R.L., your misery will organize itself, unless you consciously organize and shape it in real life."

"You mean I don't have any excuses left? My spelling and grammar?" She asked hopefully.

"Use a computer, R.L., one with a grammar and spellcheck. It's amazing, as you already know, what they can do."

"Yeah," she said, "too bad. Technology is making me write."

"You got it."

The Hard Life and Good Times of R.L. Peabody
R.L. Peabody

My father, I think, is on every committee there ever was. My parents are neat dressers. I'd get a purple mohawk just to be different from them. Recently, I heard my mother saying that she had spent all this money on me. I had a computer, and a tutor, and an allowance, and all she came out with was your average teenager. WWWWWEEEEEELLLL, EXCUSE ME.

It was Sunday and I had to go to youth group. My mother walked in and said, "Take off that tee-shirt and put on one with a collar."

Well! I was insulted. That was my favorite tee-shirt.

Several seconds later my father walked in and said, "Have you done your homework?"

"No, I just have a little bit of math to do." I sat there for a minute.

"Well, do it!"

I sat down to do my math when my mother rushed in and said, "Why don't you put on your shirt?"

"Well, Dad said…"

"I don't care what your father said!"

I started to put on my shirt when—wouldn't you know it—my father rushed in and said, "Why aren't you doing your homework?"

"Well, Mom said…"

"So what! Do your homework."

Now you know why teenage suicides are up.

My parents put a lot of pressure on me because they want me to be the best I can. This in turn is driving me crazy.

I think that insanity runs in the family. First my aunt (who was at Westminster) got so sick of study hall that she threw her books out the window. Second, it is a tradition to fight with your mother. I fight with my mother. My mother fought with hers. I think I'll commit myself to an institution where all I will have is peace and quiet, and there won't be people running in saying, "Have you done your homework yet?" Maybe this is a good idea. I don't know.

I called my father to tell him that I got a note this week for not finishing my work. He nearly plastered me to the wall with threats.

I will describe a normal day in my life.

There isn't one.

Anyway, here is my life after three o'clock. I get out of school and go to the carpool. Dennis (eight years old) whines, "You're not my mother so you can't tell me to put on my seat belt!" Then he proceeds to show off his toy robot that is plastic and costs nineteen dollars. Howie screams, "By the power of Greyskull, I have the power!" Louise cries because Dennis has told her to shut up. Michelle, my younger sister, hits me for no good reason. Hugo picks on Dennis and makes him cry and then he doesn't stop. Mrs. Parker (a.k.a. Goody-Two-Shoes Harper) panics and yells, "Are we all here?" about a thousand times, and off we go. We almost get into a wreck and Mrs. Harper screams, "YOU BASTARD!!! Oh! Excuse me, children."

Finally we get to my house. "Thank you," I say politely. I think, "Thank you for getting me home in one piece." I should start taking the bus.

I'm walking up the stairs to our door. Our door is about two inches thick and looks like the entrance to Dracula's castle. Slam, I'm inside.

"Hi Honey, how was your day?"

"O.K.," I say drably.

"Want a snack?" Mom says with a smile on her face.

"Sure," I say, thinking that it sure had taken her a long time to ask. We walk into our ultra-funky kitchen. It is ultra-funky because just about everything is shades of white and shining. But the six burners and two ovens make the room instantly hot when my mother cooks. She holds out some grapes. They look about a thousand years old. They are brown and greasy and just plain gross-looking.

"Thanks," I lie.

I'm walking up the stairs to my poster-filled room. My dog wanders in. He's black and white and looks like he's been hit by a steam roller. He's about a thousand years old.

I go and sit on my bed. Michelle comes dancing in in her new pink toe shoes. Michelle is really nice, but she has a mad dog temper. Making her mad is like putting a cat into a bathtub.

"Look at my new shoes!" she says happily.

"Nice." I act really suave.

I really am more impressed than I act. She is better than me in a lot of ways, especially dancing.

It is five o'clock and I start to do my homework. I finish that as quickly as I can, because it is so boring. I go and get the basketball and start to play one on one. It is really, really hard because:

A. There is only one person playing, and

B. I am losing.

7:00 p.m.: I go inside because I hear Mother calling.

"R.L., dinner time."

I go to dinner and see on my plate that I have green peas, carrots, mashed potatoes and gravy. I think, "What can I do with this?"

I start assembling my peas into a line, and I appoint the leader. He starts the attack and rolls into the mashed potatoes, and the gravy pours on top of him. "I'm drowning!!!" He yells with pain in his voice. So I decide to put him out of his misery, and I eat him. "Attack," I hear the second in command yell. All the peas roll into the mashed potatoes and gravy. The giant carrot is about to attack the mashed potatoes when my illusion is broken by a scream.

"R.L., your food is for eating and not for playing in," Mom says.

"But Mom, I am in the middle of an important battle."

"EAT!"

8:00 p.m.: It's time to take a bath. I do that without drowning. Now it's prime time on T.V. I fight it by playing computer games. I am playing Castle Wolfenstine. The guard tells me to stop and I don't. He shoots me.

8:30 p.m.: I finish what homework I didn't do at 5:00. Then I turn on prime time and watch an exciting rendition of "The A-Team." "Mr. T." looks uglier than ever. Then I turn to Channel 36 and finish watching a dumb horror movie. If I had named it I would have named it Godzilla Meets Funny-Looking Spider-Thing.

9:30: I go and kiss my mom and dad goodnight. From then on, I usually am free to do what I want, but sometimes Dad tells me to go to sleep. Tonight he doesn't.

11:30 p.m.: I turn to see Johnny Carson telling dumb jokes. I get sleepy and get up and walk the ever-seeming a thousand miles to my T.V. and back.

"O.K., get comfortable."

I'm still not comfortable, I think.

Finally, I get to sleep only to wake up and find the lights in my room on. I get up and secretly wonder if the bogeyman is in my closet. I cuddle down in my bed and fall asleep.

Here ends an average day in R.L. Peabody's life.

After the story, which the class seemed to like—particularly the one-on-one basketball game—everyone applauded and commented, everyone, that is, but Ian Gardiner.

"Are you jealous?" asked Lanny Butler. "I am. It was great."

"It was really funny," said Anna Rossini.

R.L. couldn't help but smile; she respected Anna. "Thanks," she said.

Then R.L. looked at Ian. "I don't understand. What was it

you didn't like?" Her smile had disappeared now and she looked almost pale. Self-doubt, sometimes overwhelming anyway because of her history with learning disabilities, was knocking at her door, threatening re-entrance.

He shrugged. "I just didn't think it was very funny."

"Come on, Ian," said Lanny.

Maury Michaels rolled her eyes. "He's jealous. Come out with it, Ian, it's not fair to R.L."

"To R.L.?" I asked.

"I don't want him doing it to me when *my* story's read," said Maury.

"Me neither," said Anna.

"Out with it, Ian," I said. "Even if you didn't like it you could have applauded unless you wanted her to feel bad, to notice. What's *your* story?"

"She's insulting—little subversive comments in math class. She does it all the time. Little comments every time I raise my hand or go to the chalkboard."

"He's right," said R.L. "I do. I hadn't realized. I'm really sorry, Ian, no excuses, I really am. Oh my God this is so embarrassing. Will you let me explain why? Please? I'm really embarrassed and really sorry. I've done it to others too. I see by your faces. I'm sorry to everyone. Okay, listen, it's because I'm stupid in math, because I have absolutely no idea what is going on in there and never have, I mean, I've been like this all my life, stupid, I'm not making excuses I'm just trying to tell you why."

"Yes," he said. Now he surrendered. "Your story was really funny. I loved that one-on-one basketball game, and Mrs. Harper, she really is like that, I know her! And dinner at the Peabodys was really great, R.L."

She beamed: "Thank you, Ian."

"'Passions beat about Simon on the mountaintop with

awful wings,'" quoted Lanny. We were in literature class, discussing *Lord of the Flies*, and the same kid who first perceived Ian's motive for silently condemning R.L.'s story pointed out to the class the agonizing responsibility of sensitivity and goodness. "'Awful' wings," said Lanny. "Simon sees things that disturb him, that he doesn't want to see. He sees, 'mankind's essential illness.'"

"How do you know?"

"'Maybe the beast,' Simon said, 'is us.'"

The sadistic Roger, immediately before murdering with lust and exhilaration the decent, wise, asthmatic Piggy, looks down below, where he will push a boulder upon him, and sees him as a "bag of fat," a reference at which Riley Andrews laughed.

The entire class stared at Riley, though uneasily, because Riley's laugh was reflexive and involuntary. The meanest, most sadistic kid in the middle school, generally protected by a formidable system of sanctimony and denial, Riley, in a fashion, had been caught. No one else in the class even contemplated laughter at such an evil thought; they were staring, in fact, in horror. Riley turned to see his entire neighborhood gathered about, scrutinizing him, as if for the first time.

"'Maybe the beast is us'?" I offered.

Riley blushed, a bit sheepishly, and we all laughed.

"Why am I subjecting Riley to such embarrassment?" I asked.

No one knew.

Finally Lanny said, "Simon was an angel."

"What made him an angel, distinguishing him from the others?"

"He knew about the beast. He recognized 'mankind's essential illness—'"

"Which is?"

"Well..."

"Anyone?"

Silence.

"You can recognize it but not say it? It's that frightening?"

"Evil," said Lanny.

"Knowledge, that particular knowledge, made him good? How did it make *him* good?"

"He could see it," said Lanny, "in himself. 'Maybe,' he said, 'the beast is us.'"

"Is it?" I asked.

"Yes," said R.L. "Had I understood I was putting down Ian, I wouldn't have been doing it, since really I was putting down myself. It was myself I hated. Does that make sense?"

"Same here," said Ian. "Had I known really what I was doing I wouldn't have done it."

"And how did you feel when you found out?"

"Embarrassed," they both said at the same time, and laughed.

"Is embarrassment in this situation bad or good?"

"Good," said Ian. "It lets you know what you're doing. It makes you feel better."

"It stops you," said R.L.

"And are you embarrassed, Riley, about your put-downs, etc.?" I was purposely vague, lenient, so he would be less defensive.

"I think you should be embarrassed by this discussion," he said.

"I'm a 'beast' for bringing it up?"

"Yes, I think it's cruel."

"And Simon," asked Lanny, looking innocently at Riley Andrews, "was he cruel?"

Like Simon, Lanny sees subtlety, nuance, and suggestion long before anyone else, both in the story and in real life. He is a brilliant reader, and he is a brilliant student of his immediate society. Roger is not a major character in *Lord of the Flies*, yet later as Piggy's executioner, he becomes evil incarnate; around him is the terror of the hangman; hardly the Mafia don, he is nevertheless a hit man who thoroughly enjoys his work. Yet in Part I only one sentence is devoted to Roger, a description, however lethally suggestive, that in all my literature classes only Lanny perceived. Roger is described as "sly, furtive…possessed of an inner intensity of avoidance and secrecy."

"My God," asked Lanny, "what's Roger got to hide? Listen to this: 'Sly, furtive…possessed of an inner intensity of avoidance and secrecy.' An 'inner intensity…'"

"What does he have to hide?" I asked him.

"The beast inside him."

"And if it were to be brought out where he could see and recognize it for what it was…?"

I looked at Riley, hoping for a response, hoping that he could see.

"He would be Simon," said Lanny. "An angel."

"A good person."

"Yeah, a good person."

"And will that happen?"

I again looked toward Riley, who offered only a curiously unrevealing smile.

"He has too much to hide," said Lanny. "An *intensity* of avoidance and secrecy…God he's scary."

And so, like Simon, Lanny becomes a prophet. Sensitive, he sees.

Severely learning disabled, Lanny learned to read in fifth grade. His spelling and grammar were atrocious, his research papers and academic essays chaotic. His math was years below grade level. He suffered from attention deficit disorder. Inspiration, however, organized his stories. He was, as you have seen, extraordinarily intuitive and perceptive; a computer corrected his spelling and grammar errors; and like many ADD kids, the passionate and artistic compelled him. With people, whether in stories or real life, he was acutely attentive. Like most of us, he is smart and slow, only extraordinarily so. The discrepancies in his strengths and weaknesses as well as his erratic rate of development qualify him as learning disabled. To ignore these differences and to view him through a narrow conventional paradigm would be to snub his gifts, not the least of which you see here, in "The Party List," his short story that takes place in first grade.

The Party List

Lanny Butler

"Pause..." Miss Hester said. My pencil hovered over my paper. I was leaning over my desk. I didn't have to lift my head, I could see through the corners of my eyes, and the class's pencils moved across their papers. I looked back to mine. I closed my eyes, searching: "P-A-W-U-S? P-U-A-W-S-E?" I decided against both. I glanced up. Miss Hester was glaring at me, drumming her fingers on the spelling book. I sat back in my chair. Everyone else, I noticed with a quick sweep of my eyes, had long since finished the work and was waiting patiently.

"Have you finished yet?" Miss Hester said.

"Yes, ma'am," I replied as flatly as possible.

"Have you got it?" Her eyes were taunting but her face was blank. I bared my teeth. She would never just go on.

She would probe you.

"NO," I flung at her trying to conceal the anger that was rising. Her forehead wrinkled and her face flashed anger. She was preparing to say something. I corrected myself: "No, ma'am," in a forced sweetness. I braced myself for what was next.

"Why not?" A smile of satisfaction crossed her face for an instant when I flinched. I could have broken the wood desk I was sitting at with my fist at that moment. Instead, I put my arm over my chair and said with just the right sting, "Because I don't want to."

My body was warm and I could almost see the rays of hatred that I shot at Miss Hester.

"Out in the hall, that'll be the last time you'll ever disobey me on purpose."

I jumped to my feet and my desk tilted on two feet. I set it down and started for the door. I was almost out when she stopped me. "Wait."

She walked to the board brightly designed with balloons and bears some girls were chosen to make. In cutout construction paper "party" was stated. She moved her finger down the list of names and stopped at "Lanny B." and pulled the cap off a pen. I didn't see the rest, I was out in the hall.

I sat on the cold floor and pulled my legs together to sit cross-legged. I slipped my pencil out of my pocket and brushed the dust away from a space beside my legs. I leaned over and tried "POWSE." I moved my pencil away, looked at my work, and scratched it out.

Miss Hester's back was to us. She reached to the top of the chalkboard, and chalk squeaked out a math problem.

Moving away she put her finger to certain parts of the problem. She wrote next to them divisor, quotient, and dividend. Hands shot up. I looked to the board and back to Miss Hester.

My mind searched. A girl's hand went up beside me. Miss Hester nodded to her.

"Six," the girl answered.

I glanced to the chalkboard but could not comprehend. When my head returned to Miss Hester, she was waiting.

"Lanny, what is the answer to number eight?"

I gripped the corner of my desk. I searched my head for an answer. Nothing would come. I thought of the rest of the boys and girls rattling off the answers.

I gave it a shot. "Seven?"

"You weren't paying attention." Her voice was loud in my ears. "Stay in four days for lunch," she said. "Don't tell me you were paying attention."

She asked, "How many of you knew the answer?" I slid down in my seat.

Hands sprung up around me; I wanted to hide my face, and my mouth was dry.

"If you were listening you would have known the answer."

Miss Hester walked back to the board and resumed. She began to write a sequence of numbers. We were to raise our hand if we knew the answer of the problem she called out. She started: "6 minus 3?"

A girl beside me raised her hand and got it.

"7 plus 3?"

Miss Hester pointed to a black girl.

I tilted my head trying to follow. They got it so quickly. I bit my lip, and my mind started to get tangled, and I wished Miss Hester would slow down.

"10 plus 5?"

My mind began to shut off. I noticed a crack that crossed my desk. I placed my pencil into it and darkened the line. Someone's foot bumped mine, and I kicked it with my heel.

The line started to look like lightning so I drew a branch breaking where the line finished at the corner of my desk. It was her fault I didn't understand. I began to put Miss Hester under the falling limb.

I was interrupted.

"Lanny!" The shout sent my spine against the hard back of my chair. "Out!"

I didn't look at her. "Where? The hall?"

I bet her face was red.

"Don't be smart with me," she said and closed the door behind me.

I guessed I was getting used to getting yelled at because the second time it didn't hurt as much. But I knew why it wasn't as painful the second time: I really was not paying attention.

The next morning I got off the bus and met Welch Suggs. He was waiting for me inside the doors. We walked in the middle of a blob of children. They all talked noisily so Welch and I put our heads close together. Welch had coarse hair, he was small and a nerd. The kids called him Welch Sluggs. He was in Discovery class and went up to second grade for reading. We had a plan to scare the music teacher, a tall scarecrow woman with a bright orange wig. Welch had a plan to buy a smoke grenade that was advertised in a *Boys Life* mag, bring it to school, and wave it in her face.

The halls echoed with stomping tennis shoes and

children's voices. I wondered if any of them knew the lonely halls during class time like I did.

"Lanny, Lanny," Welch was saying. "I'll see you later."

I jerked out of my trance.

"Bye, I'll see you at break. I'll be in at lunch."

I went into the room marked Miss Hester's Class, First Grade. I went directly to my desk and shoved my lunch box into my desk and sat. I looked straight ahead avoiding the board which Miss Hester had marked on yesterday afternoon. It was the party chart; it had the names of all the kids in the class and two boxes by each name. There was a month between each party; if you got two marks before the party you were not included.

I was surprised to see Winfred walking in the classroom, barely lifting his feet from the floor. He looked at me from dark puffy eyes like he had had little sleep lately. He was black and thin.

"Hi," he said. I knew not to ask him where he'd been the last few days. He was often gone for sometimes weeks. He would become uneasy and worried, when you asked him where he'd been. He'd look at his shoes and would walk away if that was the only way to avoid answering you.

I saw Welch at break. We sat on top of the hill overlooking the gravel field playground and hardtop. My butt was in a tire. My hand shielded my eyes from the bright sun that reflected off the field.

Byron walked closer, kicking clouds of dust into the air. He stopped in front of me. I took my hand away for his shadow crossed me.

"What are-are-are-are you you bringing to the-the-the party?" he said. Byron had a stuttering problem.

I shrugged, "What are you bringing?" He seemed

happy I asked.

"Mom said I-I-I could make some p-pop-pop-pop," I opened my mouth to help but, "Popcorn!" he finished, breathing like he had pushed a heavy load.

Welch, who had been quiet, asked, "What did you say you were bringing?"

"Well, I haven't asked my mom yet," I said.

It was true I hadn't but I wondered if I should. I had missed all the other parties but I only had one "X" for this month.

Reading was next. We all got around a half circle table. Miss Hester was facing us on the other side. We finished a paragraph on "The First Basketball Game." It was something about a man putting a fruit basket on the wall. Miss Hester laid her book on the table.

"Why did Dr. Atkinson put a hole in the basket? Windell?"

"Cause he didn't wanna climb the ladder and get the ball," he said.

"Why did he get his students to play basketball?"

She scanned the group. "Amanda."

"Because they had nothing else to play," said Panda. We called her Amanda the Panda because of her love of the animal.

"Very good, Amanda."

"Lanny, how was this game developed by Dr. Atkinson?"

I could almost catch distaste in the way she spoke.

"I'm not sure," I said.

"What."

"I'm not real sure," I repeated, speaking a little louder.

"You mean, you don't know. Correct?"

"Uh huh," I looked into my lap.

"Amanda."

"Well, because...."

"Very good."

Even worse than staying in at lunch was being out. Miss Hester was a playground supervisor the next week and I had to stay out with her to sit out my lunch punishment.

The pole my back was to was beginning to get warm and the specks of granite came through my jeans. I was cross-legged with my coat on my lap. I insisted on bringing my coat out with me. Miss Hester was sitting on a long structure under the only two trees on the playground. The platform had been tacitly designated for teachers on playground patrol as soon as the warm season started. Often Miss Hester would end playground duty drenched with sweat. Because of her fat body she had it worse than anyone.

Miss Hester's large back was to me, so I slipped my hand into the pocket of my jacket and brought out a dark sleek Trans-Am. When I repainted the car one of the car doors was permanently shut with paint but one door and hood was still functional. I brushed my hand across the ground; a small cloud of dust rose and swirled a bit as it moved across the playground. I scanned the area for a tool to dig a garage. I stretched my arm and my hand went around a pine stick. I maneuvered my car avoiding the larger stones and crevices by putting on the turbo blasters and rearing onto the back tires. I made a low rumble when the Trans-Am inched along. I made a louder noise in the higher gear—it raced along through the particles of gravel—and of course the occasional "yee haw" imitating my idols, the Duke Boys. I was too busy keeping my car from skidding into the rut in the road that was slowly being formed to hear her heavy foot-steps. It wasn't until her shadow crossed my race track that I knew Miss Hester was standing over me. I knew I had done something terribly wrong. When I looked at her face, sweat beads were on top of her lip, her mouth was twisting in a frown and her eyes were menacing.

I guess I knew I wasn't supposed to play when I was be-ing punished. Miss Hester put an "X" on the board. I didn't know at the time I was getting in trouble on purpose; it was part of my defense. I really didn't care; I was angry, it was her fault. I wasn't paying attention, fine, as long as it was not my stupidity. First you try to understand and she says you weren't listening—anyone listening would have gotten it, she says, so next time when you begin to not understand you shut it out so that you don't get it because you really weren't paying attention, not because you didn't know the answer. Anything beats stupidity.

There was only a week before the party. I came into school Monday and Winfred was kind of leaning forward in his seat; his eyes were extra red and swollen. I heard about the yelling Winfred got when his book report wasn't in that morning. I looked up at the board and we both had two "X's."

Miss Hester passed out brownies on napkins and pop-corn in cups. I sat at my desk with my head down. Out-side the darkness of my folded arms kids were talking. I peeked through my arms and Winfred's back was moving like he was crying. I came out better than Winfred, I had a defense.

Miss Hester disproves the axiom that what we don't know won't hurt us. When Lanny was in first grade, access to knowledge about learning disabilities was less available than it is now.

His mother, herself a psychologist, transferred him to Paideia at the beginning of his third-grade year. Barbara Dunbar, our school psychologist, immediately had him tested for learning disabilities and attention deficit disorder, both of which the tests showed he had.

"I must be stupid," he told Barbara when informed of the results.

"On the contrary," she said. "If you weren't bright you wouldn't have the disabilities."

"Oh," he said, and was suddenly very attentive.

BETSY ROBINSON, KATHLEEN RABINOWITZ, AND JOSEPH COHEN

Repressing pain, conventional society and consequently conventional schools repress joy and love. The truth, on the other hand, enriches not only the lives of my students, but also their prose.

Before her parents' divorce, Betsy Robinson was uncreative and untalented. Both on paper and, for that matter, on stage she was emotionally parsimonious, unrevealing, and flat. Academically strong, she was flighty when confronted with her feelings. Trauma, however, changes one; it is a great motivator.

Betsy is remembering her wealthy, prominent family—both parents went, in their words, "up North" to Ivy League colleges, but nevertheless have always remained rooted and secure in Deep South, small-town values, the most dominant of which is the priority placed on appearances and manners. How one holds her fork, Betsy told me, meant everything in her family. Remember, all her life she was taught that if you can't say anything nice about someone, don't say anything at all, which is why, of course, Betsy couldn't write.

But now let me show you in a very brief excerpt at the beginning of Betsy's story—the remainder can only come later when her conflict with her father is resolved—the sudden irony, the maturity of perspective, the tenderness and affection, and the self-deprecation and wit that can materialize from loss and separation.

She is remembering her family before the divorce, when she was very young and they all were very happy.

I was very little then, and my family was very happy, and because I was the oldest, I was known as "the Big Girl." I loved that. When friends of my parents visited, my father and mother would pat me on the head and say, "This is Betsy. She's the Big Girl in the family." And because I was the Big Girl, on Sunday mornings, when my parents slept late, I'd get to go into their bedroom and chat with them while they had coffee in bed and read the newspaper. I got to do that because I was the Big Girl, the oldest of my brothers and sisters.

Well, one Sunday morning I walked into my parents' bedroom. It was funny. They were laughing and screaming and giggling. It looked like they were wrestling or tickling, like they'd do to me when we were playing, but when I opened the door and they saw me standing there they suddenly looked shocked and their faces were red as tomatoes and covers and sheets went flying everywhere as they pulled them up—they looked so frantic! And my father kept reaching uncomfortably under the covers for something.

And then they just lay there, they just lay there, their heads propped against the pillows, with these silly smiles on their faces, looking at me.

Just grinning.

What were they smiling about? I knew, of course. They were happy to see me!

By contrast, here is Kathleen Rabinowitz, finally accepting the fact of her parents' divorce. It took her a long time, as it will take Betsy. Until recently, if a man touched Kathleen, she'd flinch and scowl. Kathleen is an interesting mixture: She is overweight and glum, but she is also impressively athletic and is very, very funny. If I pretend to tousle her hair or give her a hug she laughs and giggles and points her finger and calls me a pervert.

At the end of her story she is beginning to accept and understand the divorce of her parents. She wrote that before the divorce she would tell her friends that her parents made her dust the entire living room, for free, or that they gave her only fifty cents allowance; after the divorce, however, she told them that her mom made her eat at least one piece of lettuce at dinner, and that her dad made her say "Excuse me" before leaving the table.

She was beginning to see, she wrote, "Mom as Mom and Dad as Dad"; they were slowly becoming "two separate people" instead of one set of "parents."

The symbol of her former family life had been the lush, vivid vegetable garden, from which on Sundays they picked fresh vegetables and made giant pots of spaghetti.

One day I was walking up the walkway, trying to avoid the cracks, when I saw a bright green weed twisting its way around a tomato plant. I almost started to cry on that sun-filled day, but I didn't. Instead I walked quietly over to the garden and yanked the weed out of the ground, blaming it for the divorce and remembering how the garden used to be weed-free. Days went by and every time I looked at the garden, there were more and more weeds. Finally the whole garden was only a mass of retired tomato plants and sad cucumbers. It was then when I actually realized that mom and dad were never going to be together, that our family was never going to be the way it used to be. Years passed and the weeds took over our yard. Mom hired a few guys to fix the yard up. Just a few days ago they planted grass over the old vegetable garden, over my mom and dad.

Then there is Joseph Cohen, on his relationship with his sister. He teases her unmercifully. He takes out his anger on her. He is thirteen, she is seven; once he told her she stunk. Joseph, however, also has a larger, more prominent side to him: he is funny, self-deprecating, and honest. "It feels good," he wrote in his story, "to have someone smaller than me to push around."

At first, he said, all he did was tease her; only later, when she began to subtly retaliate, did it escalate. Slowly, he said, she began to drive him crazy.

Her tactics were subtle. She would cry when informed he was to baby-sit her, which hurt his feelings. At every opportunity, she would disagree with him: On family nights out, if he wanted Chinese food, she'd want Mexican. She chose to play the piano, loud, only when he turned on the television.

"But worst of all," Joseph wrote, "was Susie lacing up her shoes…"

You see, every morning I have math first period. Which means I have to be at school at 8:30, or else I get a late mark. And this is perfect for Susie to get me back. She will get all ready for school by 8:15, except for her shoes and socks. You may think that putting on shoes and socks takes two or three minutes. But this is not any ordinary person putting on her shoes and socks; this is Susie. She can make the simple task of slipping on a pair of Nikes into a saga. First there is finding the shoes. I sometimes think Susie deliberately hides her shoes, just to prolong the whole ordeal. Once they are found she often realizes that her socks do not match her shoes, and she must change socks. By the time the socks are changed, it's about 8:25. By now I'm becoming annoyed. Only because I know her being slow is done deliberately to get me mad. But I try to show no emotion. In fact, I often drop hints like "Thank God I don't have math this morning, it doesn't matter if I'm late for school." Or I might say, "I love getting to school late, I love it." Even if it is totally untrue, I hope maybe if she thinks I don't care about getting to school late and what she is doing doesn't affect me in the least, then maybe she'll get ready quicker. But it never works. Sometimes I just relax on the sofa and watch t.v. and make it look like I could care less. But it gets hard to control my anger.

Next Susie will completely unlace her shoes, take out the shoe laces and flatten them. Press them to perfection. Then slowly, in a snail-like fashion, relace the shoes. Neatly and precisely. By this time I'm getting angry, real angry.

Susie finally places her left shoe on her left foot, tightens all of the laces, then ties her laces in one knot, then another, then another, and then another. She now has a quadruple knot. And her laces don't look like a bow; they look like some intricate macramé. Susie slowly repeats the same procedure for her right foot, yet slows down her steps a little bit more.

By now, I'm mad, and my anger is beginning to show through.

I begin dropping hints about there being a vegetable in the room. And how I'd love to get to school for grammar class, sixth period. I ask my mom if she'll write a note to my teacher, explaining why I missed a day of school.

"Dear Bernie," I'd say out loud, "I'm sorry Joseph missed school on Tuesday, but his sister had to put on her shoes. Love, Nancy."

Finally Susie will get both of her shoes on. Then she rolls down her socks, rolls them back up, rolls them back down, and folds them over twice. Then Susie checks for errors. She sees none and we're off to school at exactly 8:31.

Joseph was a bully, but Susie was a fighter. She continued to refuse to allow him to baby-sit her or even to be in the same room with him.

He attempted to make amends. They both enjoyed playing basketball; once when they were small they had played together after dark, using the goal over the driveway.

"Let's play basketball," he offered.

She refused, and the smile that played across her face was infuriating.

"You're cross-eyed," he screamed, which to a slight degree she was. "Why don't you get glasses? Why don't you look pretty? Everybody thinks you're ugly."

Would this never end?

Every time he struck out at her, he wrote, he seemed to suffer for it.

It could only get worse.

Finally he concluded his story.

One afternoon, he wrote, she came home from school and went to her room and did not come downstairs for dinner. Her mother was telling Joseph why.

"She's real upset because some boys at school called her fatso and cross-eyed. She said that she would've told us when she came in but she was scared you'd tease her about it."

It made me mad at first. Why would Susie think that I'd tease her about that? But as I walked upstairs towards my room and passed by Susie's open door, I saw her sitting on the bed hunched over crying. Her head was bobbing up and down with each sob. As I saw this, I grew angry, angry at those boys who did this to her. What right did they have to upset and hurt Susie so much? I wished I could've killed them. I hated to see Susie so hurt. But how could I have the right to get so mad at these boys when I did it myself. Why did I have a right to pick on Susie and make her upset if they didn't? I didn't. I couldn't tell how much I actually cared about Susie until someone else put her down, and I saw her hurt. I didn't realize until then what an asshole I had been. It took me all that time to realize how much I cared for her, and loved her.

I turned into Susie's room and went and sat down on the bed next to her. At first she shrugged me away, but this time I wasn't just going to leave and go off and get mad. I sat next to her for a few minutes quietly, then we started talking. I told her that she shouldn't worry about what those stupid boys said. They didn't know anything. I told her that they probably just said it because they were jealous of her and it was their only way of expressing it. I never came right out and apologized for teasing and picking on her so much. I wasn't sure if she'd understand, or believe it. But I think she understood, and began to forgive me. Because I stayed next to her in her room until her tears dried up, and then me and Susie went outside and played basketball all evening under the moonlight.

Betsy, Kathleen, and Joseph are not exceptional children. They are bright, however, as most are, and they have heart and soul, as children do. They do have an advantage: their parents are supportive, or at least respectful, of their education, as are the parents of most of the students I teach.

All kids, however, think and feel, and all have problems. All are human, and all suffer, at one level or another.

That is why, at bottom, they are all talented. Inspiration, as in Kathleen's story, perceptiveness and maturity, as in Joseph's, and irony, as in Betsy's, are all unscientific, immeasurable qualities far beyond what the best colleges in America might look for; yet all of us possess them.

Is that not odd?

Ian Gardiner

Repression, learning disabilities, emotional problems, weakness, sloth, apathy, distractibility, stress, pressure, and anxiety all intrude upon one's capacity for love, creativity, and intellectual achievement. The repressed student is too unrevealing to either make a true friend or to fashion from her life a work of art. She will shrink from the demands of her heart in the fashion of the student, weak and sluggish in mathematics, who shuns the chalkboard, to say nothing of her teacher's explanations and her homework.

Impenetrable fortresses, these students defend themselves against self-attack: the fear of rejection creating lovelessness, the fear of exposure camouflaging one's talent, the fear of stupidity leaving one dumb.

Whenever possible, and more often than not it is, my answer to every one of these problems is *do it anyway*.

In my own middle school classroom there is also pressure, though of a different nature. Success and failure are both more celebrated and more dramatic. Time spent on after-school work is enormous, not only because the artistic, political, and academic competition is intense, but also because of what makes it intense: most of what the kids do in my class is personal. The left brain is developed along with the right, the artistic and creative along with the academic and intellectual—the story, for example, as well as the essay. More work—more learning—usually takes more time. It often takes a kid fifty pages just to find his story. Originally, if you remember, Maury Michaels' story was about a tennis match between her and her best friend; Betsy Robinson's was about a wicked girlfriend—her father's secretary—who had "stolen" her father from her.

A story is ultimately a celebration of oneself, an offering of oneself to the classroom community. Everyone wants to be accepted, everyone wants to be celebrated; therein lies the motivation to write a story that is both true and beautiful. Above all, one must be interesting.

As they are all capable of goodness, so are they capable of writing wonderful stories. My students have taught me that talent and creativity are as commonplace and widespread as intelligence. They are simply infinitely more frightening.

The popular wisdom suggests that Americans would rather amuse themselves over shallow sit-coms, Reality TV, and the foibles of Paris and Brittany. Were that truly the case, however, Maury Michael's story would have been read as a tennis match between her and her best friend.

No genuine beast, no genuine beauty.

The greatest motivator in the world is the truth.

The particular intelligence neglected and repressed in American schools is perception, an eye and ear for the truth, an internal Geiger counter that vibrates at the first sign of fraud, pomposity, convention, and decorum. It is not enough for Lanny Butler to accurately perceive the evil Roger in *Lord of the Flies* or the melodrama—the idealization—of Atticus Finch in *To Kill a Mockingbird* or the hypocrisy of Holden Caulfield. Does he see it in his classroom, in his home, on the playground, in his social milieu; most importantly, does he see it in himself? When he points out that R.L. Peabody, whose evaluation in literature class made him runner-up, was favored with softer, easier questions, which incidentally was untrue, is he aware of his jealousy?

It takes courage to see it, it takes courage to point it out.

Not doing so creates neurosis and self-doubt.

The beast is stupidity and cowardice.

But it would be unfair to R.L. to stop here.

"She brags," said Anna Rossini. "After every test she asks Lanny what his grade was."

"Why?" I asked R.L.

It had never entered her mind. "I wanted him to know mine," she said.

Lanny smiled.

Anna was applauded.

More often than not, blame reverts back to oneself. The victims of Freddie Cox years ago in my classroom are as guilty as he was. Like him, they failed to speak. "I'm worried about you" or better still, "I care about you" usually means "I'm worried about myself" or "I care about myself." Piety gets you nowhere. When two close friends claim to have just "drifted apart," look for signs of betrayal. "I suffered, I feel guilty" more often than not means "I had the time of my life."

Like a good story, the truth is inevitably more interesting, more dramatic, and more effective than blame, self-pity, or piety.

It is also necessary for good work.

As Lanny rationalizes R.L.'s success, he rationalizes his own need to improve himself.

Giving less, he gets less.

Yet, remember, had Lanny not openly demeaned R.L., he would never have assumed responsibility for improving himself and his work.

Tragedy, failure, and ignorance are basic, inherent motivators.

All of us want to learn, to grow, to somehow better ourselves.

That is what makes us work.

Then, anxiety or no, they can Do It Anyway.

One kid, proficient in all things purely academic, continuously stumbled and faltered over grammar and punctuation rules. In a blatant act of sabotage, she told me in grammar class that she'd forgotten her book and her homework, which later that day I discovered, purely by accident, stuffed behind a bookshelf. Having been sexually abused, naturally she was fearful about exposing herself emotionally. If I learn where a comma goes, she reasoned, will I then have to write?

Stories?

Like those of my classmates?

Certainly.

And the reaction to her story warmed and gratified her.

Her courage and her humanity were applauded.

Because the deeper the fossil, the more valuable the find.

Like R.L. Peabody and Lanny Butler, both of whom have learning disabilities, Danny Fields learns in his own unique way. He hears only his own voice. However, he can see everything and everyone. He learns visually. "The subject usually appears before the verb, Danny. What is the subject of this sentence: 'Danny kissed Roberta Feelgood on her big toe, which was gross.'"

The more I explained, the more confused he became.

I wrote it on the board: 'Danny kissed Roberta Feelgood on her big toe, which was gross.'

"Danny!" he exclaimed.

"The verb?" I asked.

"Kissed!" he yelled.

Danny understands almost nothing I say. On the board, on

posters, he understands immediately.

I know what to do.

It's more tiring and more time-consuming to create visual lessons, but I must Do It Anyway.

Ian Gardiner, like many of us, had no substantive cognitive weaknesses. He understood the fear and anxiety and awful work habits underpinning his procrastination, and like many of us, he still couldn't Do It Anyway.

He was recalcitrant and lazy, the guy with a thousand excuses, all spawned from insecurity, anxiety, obstinacy, and sloth. His mind was enormous and expansive, his passion grand and inspired; at thirteen he was already over six feet tall, classically handsome, and beautifully proportioned. He was a cyclist, and I envisioned him with his great stature and grand passion straddling mountains and plying valleys. His descriptions and sketches were beautiful, as grand and expansive as Ian himself, but he lacked the rigor and stamina and complexity required of the story form. He lived in terror that he was stupid and would be discovered, so he did mostly half-assed work with a kind of arrogant insouciance.

He had entered my classroom from a conventional school, and I couldn't help notice that whenever possible every piece of writing he handed me in was done on a computer.

Ian had avoided schoolwork—written work, that is—since primary grades. His teachers had referred to penmanship as writing, and since there was little else offered in the way of writing he naturally assumed that indeed it *was* writing. That penmanship itself was a mechanical rather than an expressive act never occurred to him. Since his penmanship was awful—and it was—naturally he felt his writing was. No matter how much I tried to convince him otherwise, I could not expunge his shame. He could not get beyond it. He was like a person who wants to build a great house but he never does so because he's afraid he won't be able to clean it up.

On written tests Ian obsessively covered his writing with his forearm, glancing about, clearly inhibited, struggling mercilessly and obsessively over every letter. (Had he worked so assiduously on the rest of his work he'd have been an honor student.)

"No writer," I told him, "ever received a poor review for a bad hand."

"My grammar sucks too."

"Not in your writing."

"What do you mean?"

"The decision, Ian, to place a subject complement in a sentence instead of a direct object will never make an otherwise fertile and inspiring sentence barren."

He smiled. "I like *that* sentence."

Nothing, however, did any good. He had been hurt early. For six years penmanship had been writing, and his penmanship was almost indecipherable. The edifice of his self-esteem had crumbled to the foundation.

"You're out, Ian. You're gone. I'm not going to work if you don't. It's too frustrating. I spend an hour on every draft you give me, and you don't even give lip service to my criticism."

"But I turn it in. I'm not failing. I'm doing fairly well."

"Without question. 'Fairly well,' however, is not your best."

"You're expelling me from school for not doing my *best?*"

"Yep."

"Bernie, please. I'll do anything."

"No you won't."

"I will, please! This is my only chance."

"You've muffed it. You've pissed me off. I've worked my nuts off, and you haven't. So screw you."

He phoned my house every night for two weeks crying. His parents phoned. "We trust you, Bernie."

Well...

The kids asked what had happened. "Ya'll, he'd have to make up every assignment he missed and every assignment he did half-assed, which was most of them, for a semester. Why, he'd have to write four superb stories...he'd have to..." I went on and on...and on... "That'd be literally impossible," I told them.

That was all Ian needed.

His parents phoned: "We slip him his food under the door. He put his television out in the hall."

Six weeks later he returned triumphantly to school, an entourage of classmates carrying his work in. Piled on my desk, it seemed taller than Ian. He circled it like a skyscraper, admiring it from every angle.

"The quantity is there," I told him. "Now I'll have to judge the quality."

He stared at the skyscraper, admiring it. "It's good," he said. "Damn good.

"You know," he said, "I began to enjoy it. At times it became play."

He recently graduated with the highest honors in his class from Northwestern.

Ian Gardiner no longer has to Do It Anyway. He can just do it.

CHECKER BLUMENTHAL

In my middle school classroom, like everywhere else, it is evident that feelings can be wrong. I hate you, as often as not, means I love you.

Checker Blumenthal, for example, showed Rebecca Langly, the prettiest girl in the class, how much he loved her by turning up his nose, grimacing, sticking his finger down his throat (pretending to throw up), and calling her a scumbag. If she raised her hand in class he rolled his eyes. If she sat near him he sulked and moved away.

His stories about her were about her failures—long, tedious, scathing denunciations of her personality, looks, intellect, and social skills. He handed in draft after miserable draft.

"Why write about her," I asked finally, "if you hate her?"

"You told us to be honest," he blurted.

I smiled.

Finally she confronted him in front of the class in a group-counseling session. She was in tears. "Why?" she asked. "What have I ever done to you? If anything I've tried to be friendly."

Progress was being made: Checker was at a loss for words.

He squirmed. Drained of all pretense, he stared at the floor. He mumbled something but I couldn't make out what he said.

"*What?*" she said.

"I like you," he said.

Now *she* was at a loss for words.

He shrugged, sheepishly.

"Well," she said, "you sure have a hell of a way of showing it."

I could tell he was relieved. So was she.

So was I, to tell you the truth: I wouldn't have to read Checker's crap anymore.

Jamila Cade

The black child's (or the Indian or Asian child's) experience at Paideia is probably more akin to mine growing up Jewish in the small-town South than that of his predecessors in my hometown or the inner-city black kid. First, at Paideia his background is most often middle class. Second, his problem is more one of identity than overt racism. My home, to paraphrase Yeats, was full of passionate intensity—argument, hysteria, outrageous humor, excitement, music—whereas in the community itself argument was considered impolite, if not downright disagreeable, passion was for women who weren't brought up right, and music was, well, for girls. Athletics was the route to social success, and I learned quickly to play ball. As long as you played ball, you were liked, often popular, and as the son of respectable merchants and professionals—to say nothing of being one of God's chosen people—you were respected. You could even get away with being smart as long as it appeared effortless and casual. Gentiles loved our humor and our sense of family. We were nice folks, always polite, though we did like to watch our money.

Away from home every summer, I attended Camp Blue Star, which brimmed with urban Jews, all of whom talked like Yankees. Really fast. I was the only one with a Southern accent. Yiddish slang I had never heard. A Jew with a Southern accent was as alien to them as a Jewish hillbilly or a Jewish cowboy.

The black child at Paideia is similarly betwixt and between. (With middle-class values, however, she would be equally alien in an inner-city school.) If the mark of maturity is knowing and assuming responsibility for oneself, then for the minority kid the process is even more intense, perhaps more interesting, and certainly more confusing. Jamila Cade, a beautiful, passionate black girl who was a wonderful actress, was saddened and disappointed to discover, halfway through *Catcher in the Rye*, that Holden and his family weren't black. Black herself, she naturally assumed they were, since nowhere is it pointed out explicitly that they're white. Knowing that she had touched my heart, she later used it as an excuse for failing to complete her reading of the novel.

"You're a good actress," I told her, "but you ain't *that* good."

However, she was aware of her lie. She was just a kid trying to get out of her homework.

Jamila knows who she is, she is comfortable as an African-American female at Paideia, because she is comfortable as an African-American. She talks black, dresses black, and lobbies for black music at middle school dances. Because she is who she is, Jamila Cade is one of the most attractive, personable, well-liked, and well-respected kids in the class.

Her work is generally clear, involving, and exciting.

You can see and hear her. She is actually present and visible. When she makes a speech she can bring the house down.

About her little fib, she said, "My mama's gonna burn my backside."

It was not always this way, however. When she first entered my classroom she dressed very prim and proper, i.e. white, talked white, befriended only white kids, and thought black kids, like their music, were generally loud and obnoxious. On the other hand, she imagined racial slurs when they were not there and jumped quickly on whatever innocent party had sparked her imagination. In her stories she accused former white teachers of racial prejudice without any evidence to support her. (In fact, she would discover later she had *unwittingly* used racism as an excuse for her own laziness regarding her sloppy work and bad grades.) Dissatisfied with the overall ban on put-downs, Jamila insisted on a law specifically against racial put-downs. Yet she could find no evidence of any, and everyone told her the overall ban covered them anyway. Asked by her classmates why she wouldn't attend middle school dances, she looked down her nose at them and said, "What dance, honey?"

I couldn't find her, either in her work or in her personality. She didn't know who she was, so I didn't.

It was becoming increasingly clear that she wasn't making sense. The teachers and classmates to whom she referred weren't prejudiced; *she* was. The only kid in the class snubbing and "putting down blacks" was Jamila herself. And when she had said, "What dance, honey?"—a put-down of the white kids who were trying to include her—she was herself "putting down whites."

At every opportunity I exposed these contradictions to her.

She was working on her speech to the class trying to garner support for her racial put-down law and she could find no real evidence it was needed. Lester Hardwicke raised his hand. "It's you, Jamila, not us."

Confused, however, Jamila left her classmates in confusion.

"Your need for this law comes from somewhere, Jamila. Or else it doesn't. Your confusion, at least, comes from somewhere. Let's go back to when you first felt it. Come here and relax. Everybody be quiet," I told the class.

She lay on the floor, I held her hand, and relaxed her. "One...two...three..." I counted slowly, as she returned to her early childhood.

After about ten minutes she felt shame.

"I wanted to be white," she said.

In kindergarten at Paideia a white kid named Nathan had stared at a pile of dog feces on the playground, looked at Jamila, and said, "You're the color of dog crap, Jamila, so you *are* dog crap."

She looked at her classmates and teachers and saw truly for the first time that they all were white.

She was brown.

Am I dog crap? She wondered.

"I was terrified," she continued. "I didn't want to be ridiculed and left out. I wanted to be like they were. They were all I had, all I knew. Bernie, tell everybody not to tell the black kids in the other classes about this. They'll hate me. Please."

"They'll love you," I told her. "It's honest, and most of them have the same problem."

"Really?"

"You'll see. Put it all in your speech. They'll hear about it."

"I'm ashamed."

"Do you feel better?"

"I feel like I know who I am, an African-American. I'm Jamila. You know, all those black kids, the ones that wear those tee shirts that say 'I'm black' and put down whites all the time—I just realized, they're like me. They don't know what the hell they're doin' either. They ain't walkin' the walk, they ain't talkin' the talk. I'm screwed up, ain't I. Hey, you know why I put down those white kids about the middle school dance, you know why I don't go?"

I shook my head.

"'Cause I don't know how to dance black and I'm afraid they'll find out. Ain't that somethin'?"

"You're talkin' it now."

"Ain't I though? Ain't I. I sure am. I *like* it."

"Me too."

"How about you guys?" I asked the class.

"Cool," they said, smiling.

They were really behind her. They liked *her*.

"God, I'm sorry, y'all. But I'm mostly sorry to myself. *I'm* the one who's been prejudiced. I just didn't know who I was. Later, after kindergarten, I had this friend, she was black, Jessie, her name was Jessie, we were seven. She wouldn't play with any of my white dolls, she destroyed them all, she scared me almost as much as Nathan. She made me feel like there was something wrong with me. She'd only let me play with black dolls, she talked *bad* about white people, and if I didn't I felt like there was something wrong with me, like I was bad if I liked them, you know?"

"The racial put-down law? You know now what to do for your speech?"

She looked puzzled. "Well, *I've* been putting *everybody* down, black and white, but what bothers me is I've been putting myself down, real down."

"Still..."

"There's somethin' there. I just don't know what it is. I mean, the law would have helped *me*, but, I don't know, I don't know what it is..."

"Are you afraid Nathan will come back?"

"Yes," she said, searching my eyes to be certain he wouldn't.

"It takes a lot of courage to be who you are, Jamila. Would a law specifically against racial put-downs make it safer for you to do that, to have friends over at your house to see all that blackness, to eat black food, to hear black music, would it make it more inviting in the classroom if you knew as an African-American you were welcome? Would it be reassuring for you?"

Now, now there was relief. "Yes," she said.

"Tell them," I suggested. "Tell them that. Invite them, rather than attack them."

"Yeah," she said. "Yeah. That's good, Bernie. That's damn good. You know," she said, grinning, "you pretty smart."

"You want a law," I offered, "against the Nathans, the Jessies..."

"And *me*," she said.

The law passed.

A few weeks later, when I had them do character sketches of family members, she wrote about her great grandmother, a sharecropper's wife in rural Alabama whom she called Mama: "...a big, fat woman who wore the same night-gown all day with the same stray thread hanging alone beneath the armpit.

She was always perspiring, her sweat mixing with the smell of bacon grease and fatback on the stove. Chickens pecked at the dirt yard, which was swept by the broom leaning against the wooden steps to the front door. Pictures of Jesus were in every room. In the living room Grandpa snored in front of *Family Feud*...Mama greeted you, smothering you warmly in great folds of tits... ."

Her classmates loved it. It was novel and different, as was, finally, Jamila.

"Now how would you feel," I asked her, "taking your friends from Paideia down there with you when you visit?"

"Oh my Lord!" she said, and covered her face giggling.

That weekend, at the middle school dance, you should have seen her.

That chile, as they say, was movin'.

SUNAINA SHAH

Sunaina Shah was a raven-haired Indian beauty; her eyes were like almonds and her skin burnished to a golden brown. Her parents, one a psychologist and the other a podiatrist, were studiously religious immigrants, holding fast, for example, to the idea of an arranged marriage, as theirs was, for Sunaina. I recognized my own upbringing in hers.

"Marry a Gentile? What are you going to do when one day she gets mad at you and calls you a dirty Jew?"

That was ludicrous, I thought, and paid absolutely no attention to it.

And yet, in retrospect, what my parents were afraid of was what I was afraid of: *the unknown*. In my teenage years the route to popularity was smoking, drinking, and fornication. "Fitting in" meant popularity, much as it does now, and as superficial and snobby as I was, and as much as I bucked and shouted at them for being the "strictest parents in town, all of my friends say so," I was secretly and actually terrified that they might remove their tenderhooks from my Beaufort High School Band Jacket and release me into the clutches of debauchery.

Sunaina, whose parents, unlike mine, were immigrants and whose rein was so tight she came to school in a metaphorical harness, apparently had no such worry. She shucked them like two ears of corn. They made her life, she once told me, humiliating. No jeans, no R-rated movies, no rock concerts. Religion for breakfast, lunch, and dinner, Buddha for snacks. If she failed to clean her room, she would die and return to earth as a wharf rat. Sex, drugs, and alcohol were the lepers of America; touching them resulted in contagion. "If you ever took drugs or drank alcohol, or engaged in you-know-what, it would kill me, I would die, and you know you would then, after your death, return as a cockroach for having murdered me," her mother said. "Always remember your Indian values. Do you hear me, Sunaina?" "Yes, Mom," she'd sigh, as her boyfriend, Adam Wade, about whom her parents were oblivious, grazed like a superstud, befitting his reputation, in the pasture of her imagination.

"Then what did I say?" her mom asked.

"Mom, I don't know," she'd say, tired.

"You're not leaving the house until…"

"Our values are superior, Mom. Buddha was the greatest of all prophets. If I'm bad I'll become a cockroach."

Her retreat from her family and heritage was becoming a compulsion.

At school she didn't want to have to work "twice as hard as everybody else"—by her calculations that would mean studying six hours nightly—and her grades were low. She and Adam Wade draped themselves publicly all over each other at recess, but to her surprise and consternation instead of sharing his sexual "experience" he preferred talking about it.

She figured it was because she lacked it. By her calculations, he must have felt she wasn't ready for him. There was a drug dealer in the neighborhood, a high school kid, a true bona fide sleaze bag, the obvious choice. She invited him into her bedroom and late one night, after her parents had long been asleep, she unlatched her screen, let him in through her bedroom window, and proceeded to get stoned, sloshed, and screwed.

She didn't like the cigarettes, she said later. They made her cough.

Anyway, to her complete satisfaction, it seemed to me, her parents placed her on restriction.

Also to her complete satisfaction, she became, in the vernacular of the classroom gossip, a "woman" of experience.

But something else happened. Adam Wade, the class superstud, seemed terrified of her. He refused to even speak to her, except in a distant mumble when it couldn't be avoided. He avoided her as if she were a leper. A mere brush of her shoulder as she walked by him in the corridor would cause him to jump back, tainted, in horror.

It was time for a counseling session, a conference. The whole class was there, of course. Nothing was juicier than sex, gossip, scandal, romance, drugs, and liquor.

She had even smoked cigarettes.

Any time there is conflict there is a lesson to be learned.

"Why are you ignoring me?" she asked him. There was plea and entreaty in her voice, but he couldn't even look at her. He stared at the floor, vulnerable for the first time in his life.

"I don't respect you anymore. I'm sorry. How could you do that...God...How could you? I don't even know you..."

That was true. Neither did she know herself.

"What? What do you mean? You don't *know* me. You don't *know* me. But I thought that's what you wanted, it's all you talked about, experience, experience, experience, that's all you ever talked about. I did it for you, I thought you'd like me more..."

"I'm a virgin!" he screamed.

FAYE BROWN AND LANNY BUTLER

Faye Brown had the hots for Lanny Butler. She'd write him love letters, which she'd never send. Instead, she'd answer them herself; that way, she wrote in her story, she'd always get the answer she wanted. When her story was read to the class, however, Lanny loved it, and she got the answer she wanted. They lived in the same neighborhood, and once Lanny realized she liked him, he'd jog by her house, she'd wave from her upstairs bedroom window, run down, and they'd stand on the sidewalk saying things to each other like "Cool," "Awesome," "Man!" and "Ohmigod." They even went to the movie matinee together with Frannie and Rick and Joseph and Betsy, who kissed. Lanny and Faye kissed once, but it was a Truth or Dare game, and though each was rewarded for their calculations, it wasn't quite the same thing as kissing at a movie or at the middle school dance, which was Saturday night.

Big plans were in the making.

Now that Lanny was jogging by her house and sending her love notes and had taken her to the movies and had kissed her, even if it was Truth or Dare, all that was left was the Big Kiss at the dance, after which she would leak the news and all of her friends would come running up to her, oohing and aahing, wanting to know everything. She would, of course, tell them, as she was certain Lanny would. Then they would truly be a couple. He would present her his ring. In school, at recess, it would catch the sunlight.

The strategy for landing him, however, proved to be remarkably indirect and uncannily stupid. Now that she had him in her sights, she reversed herself. She spoke to him in a language incomprehensible to so authentic and sensitive a young man: the language of neurosis—when I was a teenager it was called playing "hard to get."

Ignore him, and he will grovel at your feet.

Faye's family was of Italian-American extraction, high-powered, fast-talking, pressure-packed; she thrived on it. Anxiety and hysteria were the charms she displayed on the necklace of her personality.

Her hysteria made her the most successful lawyer in the classroom. But to expose such a zealous heart in a relationship?

She *liked* him too much.

So, of course, she didn't.

You understand, don't you? She loved Lanny so she didn't want to show it so he would love her.

You can see how this might have caused Lanny to do a bit of head-scratching.

She performed magnificently. Her "work," as always, was exquisite. She followed her script mercilessly, right down to the last detail.

In fact, Faye Brown was so convincing an actress that playing Hard To Get made her downright inaccessible.

At the dance, draping herself all over Joseph Cohen, whom she knew secretly liked her, she began to wonder why Lanny wasn't fighting for her, his eyes aflame with revenge and desire. Why wasn't he tearing her away from the charming, self-deprecating Joseph and, as she had planned, whisking her off into Loveland?

Because he believed her! He watched them for a while; then he grew fidgety and apprehensive. Joseph was one of his best friends. He was confused. He was sure she'd liked him. Of course, it was a Truth or Dare game in which they'd kissed— maybe it had been only his fantasy and imagination that that kiss was also the consequence of her calculations. He stared at them. Boy, she really liked Joseph. Well, just goes to show... Besides, there was always Frannie, whom he'd also liked, in fact for as long as he could remember, and she had broken off with Rick. He knew she liked him a lot as a friend, and they talked easier than he and Faye anyway.

The best man won, he said to Joseph in the boys' bathroom, offering his hand—that's the way Lanny was, he was truly a nice guy—and by the end of the evening Frannie was flashing Lanny's ring in the girls' bathroom.

Understandably, Faye was aghast. He humiliated me, she told her friends, he used me. "Did he lead me on or what, I mean, this is total humiliation...Ohmigod..."

They pressed forward sympathetically, excited by the action.

"What if I'd gone after him. I mean, that would have been totally humiliating. Totally. Ohmigod."

"He used you, Faye," said Anna Rossini.

Anna patted Faye's shoulder as Faye cried, admitting to herself that yes, much as she hated admitting it, that was exactly what had happened.

The next morning, however, Faye was awakened by a phone call from Joseph.

Of course! Having draped herself all over him at the dance, having practically thrown herself at him, naturally he was calling to ask her to go with him.

"I love you," he said.

"Oh God," she said to herself.

Placing her hand over the mouthpiece, she screamed at the top of her lungs.

FRANNIE MCGEE AND RICK BRODERICK

Here's the reason Frannie started going with Lanny: Rick hardly ever "talked" with her, and he certainly seemed to have little, if any, interest in what she had to say.

At first she'd doubted herself. Was she somehow a bore?

Her conversations with him assumed a desperate, frantic tone, as if always she were seeing him in passing.

Was it like this before they had fondled each other so intimately?

Yes, she had to admit it.

That had been thrilling, the thought of it remained thrilling, but the fact is Rick was an insensitive bore. She had been seduced by his good looks, his athletic prowess, and though she disliked admitting it, his social status, his popularity.

She had also been seduced then by her own superficiality. Let's face it, she told me, he's not all that smart, and he's going to grow up to be one of those locker room guys who plays poker with the boys every Wednesday evening and wakes up to the sports section.

Then suddenly, talking to Lanny, it dawned on her that she was interesting.

That's why she broke up with Rick. Did it bother him?

Of course not, she told me, that had been the problem. Nothing did.

TOMMI ALBRIGHT AND RILEY ANDREWS

Rarely are there fist fights at Paideia; intelligent, civilized people usually resort to more subtle, effective ways of destroying each other. In my class, as in most liberal environments, the most commonly preferred handgun is the put-down, the ban on which is still hotly debated and discussed.

The meanest kid, not just in my classroom but in the entire middle school school, is Riley Andrews. He is a compulsive put-down artist always drawing and firing from the holster of piety and sanctimony. Only a weak athlete is criticized for throwing an errant pass. Why, Riley? I believe in a person doing his best, he responds. A beautiful story written by a classmate can be read and he'll pick out some insignificant detail and discuss it for five minutes. Why, Riley? Are you jealous? Of course not. The author was a good writer, and he simply wanted to make her better. He assumed that's why we were here, to learn and improve. Well, Riley, I certainly hope you don't grow up and view women the way you look at stories. He smiled and nodded. What could he say? I was his teacher, I was bigger than he was, and would have loved to whip his little ass. With a roll of his eyes or a conspiratorial whisper to a friend, he could keep an entire class from approaching the chalkboard in math or participating in class discussion in literature.

His primary victim was the weakest, most vulnerable kid in the middle school, Tommi Albright.

But she was also the biggest.

Her voice was throaty and husky—Winstons protruded from her pocketbook—and she could pass for twenty-five in any bar in Atlanta. Emotionally, physically, intellectually she was more mature than the middle school kids. Rather, she acted like she was. She alienated them with her Tough Broad act, her references to high school escapades, which rarely happened, over the weekends. The middle school kids frightened her. She wasn't interested in Truth or Dare and Who Likes Who and girls' basketball. She wanted to Talk Philosophy and Have a Good Laugh and every once in a while, Have a Good Screw.

All this was an act. She *was* different, and her difference—her truly incredible physical maturity—was what frightened her. On those few occasions when she left her act at home and behaved spontaneously, she was a delight. But she was scared to reveal herself. Too vulnerable. Asking her who she most wanted to be friends with in the classroom, she chose Faye, Frannie, Rick, and Joseph, the four most popular, socially attractive, sought-after people. All but Rick, that is. He was popular because he was feared. People were scared not to like him.

And vulnerability, she would tell me later, was what Riley

Andrews loved to spot.

He's good in literature class, I told her. He's sensitive.

His sensitivity, she told me, is what makes him dangerous.

She felt he could see right through her.

His cynical smile and conspiratorial whispers made her nights sleepless. Every day he would wait in the corridor with his friend, Adrian Priestly, and he would smile in her direction and whisper in Adrian's ear. She became so flustered she dropped her books.

One day in literature class I saw the kid—the real Tommi Albright—stand up for herself.

I read them a passage from *Catcher in the Rye*. There's a Princeton guy with one of those "tired, snobby voices" in the typical "tattersall vest" holding forth on this play that was supposed to be popular, trying to impress the girls standing around. He was the kind of guy who when he talked, Holden said, "You had to step back and give him room…"

Tommi was delighted.

"Classic," she said, a wonderful smile on her face. "Absolutely classic. God, am I thinking of a few people I know."

I saw Riley whisper in Adrian Priestly's ear, and I thought I heard the word "classic."

Tommi rose from her chair, pointed her finger at him, and said, "What'd you say?"

He pretended she wasn't talking to him.

"I said," she shouted, "What'd you say?"

"It was private and personal to Adrian."

"Well, share it, asshole."

He looked to me for help. I shrugged. "She's just trying to be helpful," I told him. "Constructive criticism."

"Why?" she said. "Why do you pick me to be cruel to?"

She was towering over the table, screaming.

He was scared. After all, she was the biggest kid in the school.

The class was ecstatic.

"Why?" she said. "Why me? Tell me now, you slimy little son of a bitch, or I'm coming over there, and I'm going to break your goddamn neck. DO YOU UNDERSTAND ME YOU FUCKING ASSHOLE."

The whole class laughed and applauded.

She had taken on the world, only to discover that the entire time the world was on her side.

He was cowed, shrunken in his chair, his eyes like a puppy's, pleading.

Riley had no choice. He told the truth. "You were vulnerable," he said.

She looked down at the shrunken, pathetic figure in his chair, and she said: "Well, let me ask you a question, you little son of a bitch."

He looked up.

"Who's vulnerable now?"

Riley's a good student, and basically he's a good kid, I think. He certainly can be kind and considerate: he brought me a load of firewood for Christmas, chopping it himself. He is sensitive. He comes by his meanness honestly: his father's the same way. However, unlike his father, he is now without either weapons or respect. Disarmed, he now is the one who is vulnerable.

Afraid, he has no choice now but to be nice. His sensitivity may deepen and broaden him. Poor himself, he has a vested interest in helping kindred spirits.

He became a leading advocate for the ban on verbal putdowns. Inadvertently I was right: she did help him.

LAURA DAYE AND TESSA MONROE

Laura Daye and Tessa Monroe were by all appearances best friends; they were not, however, close. While Laura was admired and respected by her friends and classmates, Tessa was not only respected, she was liked. Despite appearances, Tessa was more intimate and revealing with her friends other than Laura.

Tessa generally faced the world with her doors flung open. She was dramatic, competitive, accommodating, and honest. Talented, creative, and unusually perceptive unless she herself was rankled—academically she was flawed and inconsistent. A perspicacious reader of literature, she was weak decoding academic textbooks. Her ear for language was perfectly pitched, but she was weak in spelling and grammar. One of the best poets and most interesting story writers in the class, she shrunk in horror at the prospect of research papers. Original, tender and passionate, by nature an artist, she was as impatient with academia as she was with practicalities and logistics.

She was terribly conscientious, but you were never certain from day to day what color her hair was going to be.

Laura Daye, on the other hand, was a conventional teacher's dream. Poised, pretty, intellectual, and confident, she was a straight-A student, impeccably dressed, her achievement test scores in the statistical stratosphere. Her handwriting was neat, her hair always the color of rich fertile soil, carefully turned. Her sixth-grade teachers in the private school from which she transferred had characterized her as academically gifted, unfailingly polite and cheerful, and never a problem.

I appreciated her skills and thoughtfulness, but that she was never a problem, in my class, *was* the problem.

If there was no problem, what was there to truly discover? In her stories, her poems, her essays, her arguments, her debates, her literature classes? To what use might her skills be put, other than that of relaying or transmitting information to others like a conduit? Why acquire knowledge and information only to be unaffected by it? Why engage in a class government and court system if life is non-problematical? Why campaign for congress, propose a law, press charges against a classmate if never is there a need?

Imprisoned in her paradigm of rationality, she saw perfection; I saw fear.

To the degree Tessa was cognitively learning-disabled, which was mild, Laura was emotionally (and consequently) artistically disabled.

Where in academic classes like science, math, and history she was a vigorous participant in class discussions, in counseling sessions she was quiet except to comment on her classmates' issues. She offered none of her own.

Her creative writing was flat, her acting giddy, if not operatic and mildly hysteric.

She was unwittingly competitive, attempting to win friends by triumphing academically. She would often ask her classmates their test scores, shivering with manufactured anxiety, so that she might reveal hers.

In creative writing class where she was weak, and only the best stories were read aloud to the entire class, she would rarely applaud afterward, and usually ignored the thrust of the story, selecting instead a fairly inconsequential detail to point out and criticize.

Classmates retreated from her, guiltily.

After all, it had to be their problem. She didn't have any.

Tessa confessed to me she often acted irritably toward Laura without knowing why.

Then Laura began going a bit too far.

She courted Dwight Allgood, the judge in the class court system, also Tessa's boyfriend, by competing with him academically. When that failed to produce anything other than friendly academic rivalry, she began dropping comments here and there to her classmates about Tessa's questionable behavior, sexually, toward Dwight. On a day when Tessa was absent from school, Laura brought a claque of girls into my office, all of whom, as is the rule in middle school, were seething with melodrama and hype. However, very much in control, not "wanting to make too much of it," Laura expressed concern for Tessa's "rather slutty" behavior toward Dwight. Tessa, she said, "flirted shamelessly" with him and danced "awfully close" with him at the middle school dance.

The girls in my office—all but Laura, that is—couldn't wait to call Tessa that evening and tell her what Laura had said.

Tessa's response: "Bullshit." And she pressed charges against Laura for committing the crime of put-down, which (as you know) remains against the law in our classroom.

Testifying on her own behalf, from the witness chair toward the front of the classroom, Laura professed earnestly that she spoke not out of malice but out of "concern" for her best friend. "If I am guilty of anything," she swore passionately, "It is of caring. Is it wrong"—she appeared earnestly puzzled—"to care? I *care* about you," she said, her arms outstretched toward the plaintiff's table. "I care about your reputation."

When she said she just couldn't stand the thought of people talking badly about Tessa, one of the jurors raised his hand and asked for a hearing aid.

"Cut the crap," said Judge Allgood.

His mouth twisted about in odd, fascinating contortions because of his new braces.

The jury found her guilty.

The sentence: Cleanup of the class bathroom for three days.

While tension and resentment separated Laura and Tessa

more than ever, necessity was bringing them together. Their friendship was based largely on the fact that their parents had been friends, as well as next-door neighbors, since before the kids' births. Tessa's parents divorced and her father moved out of the house. With Tessa's mother depressed as she filled out job applications and made arrangements for an invigorated social life, Tessa was more and more thrown into contact with Laura's family. Not only was Laura's family by all appearances picture-perfect, or at least that's the way Laura depicted it in class counseling sessions, but also now Tessa had to *depend* on it—on Laura's mother largely—for rides to school, ballet classes, often meals.

Furious and envious, her life a mess, Tessa lashed out at the only family (target) available to her. She belittled Laura's family as Laura earlier had belittled her. To their friends and classmates she renamed Laura's parents Ozzie and Harriet. She parodied their infinite cheer and good will. Their family dinners she referred to as "Cleaver Time."

Once she even phoned Laura to ask what the Cleavers were having for dinner—a dinner to which she was invited—that evening.

Laura covered her wounds with laughter, and the more together they were, the more alien they became.

Until the literature class in which we began reading and discussing the virtuoso of the put-down himself, Holden Caulfield, the classic American teenager dedicating himself to rooting out the phoniness of conventional society wherever he might find it.

Cynical as she had become since the breakup of her family, Tessa loved Holden. She selected passage after passage, all of them hilarious sendups of everything conventional in America—from family values to the work ethic to higher education—laughing uproariously, carrying the class along as she did so.

Meanwhile, Laura fumed.

She covered up her anger with academic criticism. "There's no plot," she complained.

"So what," said Tessa.

With that, Laura exploded. Not the idealized version, but Laura herself.

"Holden's the biggest phony of them all," she said. "He hates everyone. They're all working, raising families, at least trying to live a positive life and all he can do is make fun of them and put them down."

"In our class he'd probably be charged by the DA," said Tessa, who had no idea she'd been acting just like him.

"He's afraid," said Laura. *"He's* the one who's unreal. Everyone else, according to him, is phony, but he spends an entire novel so afraid of real love and yet so desperate for it that he ignores people he loves and instead tries to make friends with strangers off the street. Why doesn't he just phone Jane Gallagher? He loves her! Maybe *that's* why."

"He's afraid to love?" I asked her.

All eyes were on her. Hers, at the approach of truth, looked away.

"Laura?"

She nodded. Yes. He was afraid to love.

"Why?"

A few hands were raised tentatively but I waved them away, the attention was on her. She had courageously and defiantly staked her claim, and if she could handle it, the territory was hers. I'd been waiting for this.

"Because he's right," she said. "They're not real."

"Are you angry with him for telling you that? Were you reluctant to say it, or am I missing something? You were squirming and fidgeting a bit. How do you feel about him telling you that people are unreal?"

She was embarrassed, uncomfortable.

"You were angry with him?"

She nodded, her eyes on her pencil. The class was rapt, the highest encomium a student can achieve.

"Why?"

You could barely hear her, but finally Laura spoke, wounded, barely above a whisper.

"My relationships aren't real either," Laura said.

Tessa burst into tears.

That's when it all came out, the jealousy, the competitiveness, underneath which, popping out of the hat like magic, were admiration, open envy, and affection.

"You *admired* me?" said Tessa. "My social life, my stories? But that's why I put down *your* family. Mine was a mess."

Laura smiled.

"*Who's* afraid to love?" I asked them.

The laws of progress, however, are as unpredictable and idiosyncratic as human nature. The word that would eventually liberate Laura she had not yet truly found. So only weeks later, in my creative writing class, more directly personal than the literature class, resistance appeared to dictate her posture, her carriage. She sat as if she were awaiting tea and crumpets in any parlor in Yorkshire, blithely denying amid her classmates' stories of first kisses, runaway fathers, unrequited love, and thwarted ambitions that she had ever had any tension or conflict in her life at all. She couldn't write about her relationship with Tessa because she hadn't had enough time and distance from it to achieve perspective (which was true). But were there other Tessas in her life, Tessas before Tessa? asked a classmate. Oh no, she said, that had never happened before. She'd never competed in a relationship before? I wondered. This was the first time? If I asked your classmates at your former school whether you bragged about your grades there, what would they say? I didn't need to do it there, she told us, we all knew each other.

Really? I said, a touch of Caulfield in my tone. How well?

No, she insisted, we did, really.

You've never had a problem in your entire life?

"Look," she said firmly, "I think the problem here is I'm, well, normal. Well, there you have it. It's why Tessa was jealous of my family. I mean, am I right, Tessa?"

Tessa looked at her. "Am I *abnormal*?" she said.

"Oh no, heavens no, no, no, no. I didn't mean that at all."

"What is going on here?" I asked the class.

"You're making excuses, Laura," said Tessa, not without fondness.

"Okay," she said.

Perfectly poised and composed, her hands demurely in her lap, speaking as my fifth-grade teacher must have spoken to my mother when informing her that I was failing math, Laura Daye addressed us.

"I had difficulty," she said, "accepting the death of my grandmother."

"Okay. Good, Laura. That's true. You're expressing it," I said, "but you're expressing it as a cliché. You're in your head. Do you see what I mean? No thinking now. Just let yourself feel. Do you understand?"

She nodded. "I think so."

"Okay. No headwork, just heartwork. Just relax and allow your feelings to surface. I promise you, they'll be a welcome relief, not nearly so frightening as what you've been avoiding."

"Do it, Laura," said Tessa. "Please."

Laura's eyes fell, and I thought I saw her tremble. She looked, in a barely perceptible fashion, as if she were coming apart. Her features softened. Only when you come apart can you come together.

When she looked up she spoke through tears, and without realizing it, she offered what would turn out to be the first line of her story.

"For hours I would brush her hair…"

"Go write," I told her. "Do as much as you can tonight. It'll write itself. We'll hear your draft in the morning."

I didn't usually read or hear first drafts, but I thought this would probably save time in the long run. I thought also it would encourage her.

The next morning she was excited, but she confessed she didn't fully have the story. Something, she told the class, was missing. She began reading.

Her hair was long and so white and pure and fine. It draped all the way to her waist and she had beautiful silver antique combs and brushes and it was so peaceful standing behind her, in front of her mirror, letting the brush run all the way down. She was always so beautiful to me, and I admired her more than anyone in the world.

I wanted to *be* her, or to become her. So elegant and refined. I never once heard her raise her voice. We read poetry in her garden and painted together by candlelight in the evenings and had cider or hot chocolate by the fireplace. "Can I get your combs and brushes, Grandma?" Often it was there, both of us in our nightgowns ready for bed, that she let me brush her hair.

One day my parents told me she had cancer and she was in the hospital. I couldn't wait to see her. I was going by myself, my parents dropping me off, coming up later. They didn't tell me though what cancer was, what it meant, how horrible and disgusting…or maybe I didn't want to hear…I entered the room like a surprise. I wanted to surprise her. I had flowers which I'd picked myself and a poem for her and I knew we'd play cards like we did when I was little, when she made such perfect little character cookies. She was sitting in a chair by the window. She looked up, a blanket and shawl over her shoulders. She was so ugly, so old and wrinkled, she couldn't have been my grandmother, she just couldn't. Don't you see? My grandmother was beautiful, so elegant and refined and pleasant. *She* was bald.

I ran from her room and never went back. When my parents visited her I made excuses not to go. I refused to think about her. I feel so guilty. I left her in that room to die.

At her funeral I couldn't cry. All my relatives, my uncles and aunts and cousins, everyone was crying but me. I felt their eyes on me, judging me, boring holes through me. Who was this little girl so unfeeling as not to cry at her grandmother's funeral?"

"But you're crying now," I offered, when she'd finished reading.

"Yes," she said, "I feel so ashamed, so guilty."

"Do you know why?" I asked.

"She's my grandmother," she said, mildly irritated.

"So?"

"I loved her, Bernie," she said, surprising herself.

"Oh."

And then she smiled. Radiantly, through tears.

"It's a love story, Laura, between you and your grand-mother. Now do you know why you avoided her?"

"I couldn't stand to see her that way."

"You loved her too much, it was too painful."

"Yes. I did. I did. I do!"

"Can you write it fully now?" I asked. "Scenes, details, the whole works…"

She nodded.

"Feel better?"

"*Much* better. Gosh."

"Do you really feel your relatives were judging you at the funeral, or were you really just judging yourself?"

"I was judging myself."

"And how do you feel about Laura," I asked the class, "after this story?"

"I *love* her," said Tessa. She couldn't take her eyes off Laura. "You're so, so…*human*."

LISA OVERTON

Lisa Overton was a precociously bright, dark-eyed, dark-haired cherub; her mouth was full and sensual, her cheeks in full bloom. A veritable rose, she nevertheless remained in my class-room basically inexpressive, as unknown and unrevealing as an unmarked tombstone. In her conventional academic cours-es, like Laura Daye, she made straight A's. Her hand always at the ready, she answered the teachers' questions in a robotic monotone, after which a satisfied, if not superior smile played fleetingly across the otherwise undistinguished marquee of her persona. As precocious as her mind was, her heart was a sealed vault, her personality boarded up for the winter, the shutters latched on her soul. Yet if she was not part of the troupe she was part of the audience. Spontaneity and fun were viewed as interesting phenomena, enjoyed only from a distance. Emotionally she was strait-jacketed and she could not break through, she could not let go. Naturally she was lonely, adrift outside the social periphery, her stories and attempts at self-expression a confused amalgam of spurious internal logic, her political speeches flat and uninspired, her perceptions in literature classes safe and uninteresting.

Where was her fire, her soul; did she in the innermost reaches of her heart—a distance she could not even fathom, much less traverse—yearn and long for inspiration and intimacy, for art and friendship?

I had no doubt. She was a human being, and she was ambitious. In a subtle way the class had its back to her; she gave them, after all, little choice, but I observed her observe.

"To get, Lisa, you have to give," I told her.

"I don't know how," she said.

The plea of ignorance is as classic a defense psychologically as it is legally.

Of course she didn't know how. How does one make oneself interesting? There are no techniques. There is an answer, of course: by revealing oneself.

She was running for court officer, the safest, most conservative position in the court system, and she was practicing her speech in front of the class. Her delivery was, as you might expect, mechanical. The kids were fidgety and probably a little embarrassed, except for Lester Hardwicke, who was running against her. She probably made him feel great about his speech. I wanted them both to win.

Clearly the class was bored, and elections, the time when the speeches counted, was only a week away. Lisa had been in my class a year and a half. She was an eighth grader, and she was fundamentally no different now from the day she entered. She hadn't come out. I still didn't know who she was.

She was behind the lectern, at the front of the classroom. The class was facing her, like an audience, with me seated toward the rear.

"There's no emotion, Lisa," I told her. "Scream. At the top of your lungs. From the diaphragm, not from the throat."

She smiled.

"Frighten the hell out of us. Send us scurrying off like mice. Show us what kind of power you've got."

She took a deep breath, almost choking on it. She appeared resigned to an awful fate, the one I had in mind for her, but after ten minutes of encouragement, she squeaked.

A clipped, abrupt, parsimonious squeak.

"Jesus, Lisa, why can't you let go? Haven't you ever been mad at anyone? Without the growl and the roar, even if we never hear them, there's no melody."

"I know."

"Do you want to create that melody?"

"Yes."

"Okay, let's talk for a minute. Tell me: why are you running for court officer?"

"I think it will be interesting, and I think I can do the job well. The purpose of the court officer is to be available to press, write up, and file charges, and to organize and present them in court. As I said in my speech, I'm organized. I organize the food in my refrigerator. My room is spotless."

"Your life is spotless—your speech is spotless; that's what's wrong with it. Anyway, that's why you're running. But that's not necessarily why they should vote for you. Can you answer that? What's in it for them? Why should they care whether or not the cases are organized?"

"Cases were misplaced, disorganized, and actually lost last term."

"So?"

"That's not fair."

"Not just?"

"Right."

"Why not?"

She couldn't answer.

It'll be a mess, she repeated. It wouldn't be fair. She couldn't personalize the issue.

"Can anyone help her?"

Her classmates couldn't help.

"Why not?" I asked them.

Maury Michaels said: "We don't know her well enough."

At this Lisa blanched; it was barely perceptible, but I saw it.

"If nothing bad has ever happened to you—nothing unfair or unjust—then why would you care whether cases are lost or misplaced or forgotten?" I asked. "Where does your drive, your motivation, come from? That answer—if you have one—could be the source of your passion. I mean, do you really care about what happens to other people in this classroom, since you don't seem to really know them?"

"No," Lisa said.

"No?"

"I suppose I don't care what happens to people in here."

"So why run for office? Why should they vote for you? Relax, Lisa. Let it come. Please. We've got time."

"I want power," she said.

"Over whom?"

She stared at her shoes.

I waited for a message, however slight and incipient, from her heart that I knew from faith and experience she would deliver.

Emotionally and artistically, at this point in her life, Lisa is a slow learner.

It's only because, at this point, she is afraid. We will begin slowly.

"Last term..." she was having trouble speaking; she was tearing up and blubbering and blew her nose. "Every day in science class Betsy would ask to see my notes; I thought she just wanted to copy them to study for the tests later. They were answers to questions I anticipated the teacher was going to ask in class that day. Class participation counted half of the overall grade. She cheated. Every night I'd do the work, and every day she'd holler out my answers."

"How do you feel, Lisa?"

"Pissed off."

"At whom?"

"I'm pissed off at you, Betsy," she said looking directly at her. Then she took a good, healthy deep breath, and she took the entire room in with her eyes. She looked radiant.

"If you elect me court officer," she said, "I'll promise you this—or anything like it—will never happen again."

The class was with her now; still, they were waiting.

"To anybody," she said.

"That," she said, "is why I'm running."

Unrequited Love
Lisa Overton

It was third period, sometime near the end of seventh grade. None of us seventh graders had class, so we all sat around in the study area. We were supposed to be doing writing, but nobody was. In fact, nobody was even working. We were all whispering and writing notes to each other, but with some semblance of work in our laps that we could pick up in case Bernie walked in.

I was starting a note to Helen when Anna, who had been bugging me for days about who I liked, leaned over and scribbled on my paper. "Hey Lisa, who do you like?"

"Nobody," I wrote back.

"Come on, tell me."

"I don't like anyone. Isn't that possible?"

"Well, people usually have their eye on someone."

"I don't...

"Do you like Robbie?"

"No."

"Lanny?"

"Nope."

"Jeff?"

"Guess again."

"Checker?"

"No."

She kept writing down names and I alternated between shaking my head, clutching my throat, and writing assorted negative answers.

After naming most of the boys in the middle school, Anna wrote, "Josh?"

"Try again," I wrote.

"You used to love Josh, didn't you?"

"Yeah. . ." I had. For almost an entire school year. It had all started in the fall...

It was the beginning of seventh grade. In a few days

would be the first middle school dance. I was talking on the phone with Kathleen Rabinowitz, my best friend at the time.

"Who do you like?" I asked.

"Ryan. Who do you like?"

"I don't know. Ryan, I guess..." I didn't really like him or anybody else, but I decided I might as well like somebody. And I didn't really know who to like, so I decided to take Kathleen's word for it that it was good to like Ryan.

I invited Angela, a friend from my old school, to come to the dance with me. After being dropped off, we stood around talking with a group of girls all waiting for Jane, the chaperone, to open the door. When she did, we walked into the high school building, paid, and went upstairs to the commons, where we stood around talking to people. The guys were at one end of the room, either standing up or sitting on the benches that lined two walls.

Fast music was playing, and the strobe lights were blinking wildly. After several songs, people started to dance. The first slow songs of the dance came over the speakers to carry the bravest of middle school couples onto the floor. More songs played, and the number of people dancing slowly increased.

I wasn't dancing. I wanted to ask somebody, but I was too chicken. Finally I asked Angela and Kathleen to fix me up with somebody.

"Who?" they asked.

"I don't know, Josh or someone," I said. Ryan was dancing with Ruthie Wiseman, and I didn't really like him anyhow, so I had just decided to pick a name. Angela and Kathleen ran off toward the clump of guys standing in the corner. A few minutes later they returned.

"He says the next slow song."

"Okay." I waited nervously through three fast songs. The first strains of a slow song came over the speakers. Josh walked over to where I was sitting, and I followed him out to the middle of the room. We started to dance. I could feel his breath softly on my face and I was aware of our feet bumping gently. I looked at him. It was so thrilling to be this close to a boy. Not that I was an incredibly close dancer. I had just slow danced about three times in my whole life, so this was a big deal. In actuality, you could have fit a ruler between us, but even that was incredible for me.

I enjoyed it so much that I started asking other people to dance, too. The butterflies in my stomach seemed to have migrated: After that first dance, it wasn't hard at all. But I danced with Josh more, and enjoyed dancing with him more, than anyone else. I'm not sure why. All I know is, somewhere between that first dance with him and the Monday three days later, I started to like him.

Actually, that puts it mildly. By Wednesday, I was madly in like. Me, who had never really liked a boy before.

I didn't think about why I liked him that much. Whenever I did think about him, he was just so intoxicatingly wonderful that it overwhelmed me and I couldn't break it down into specific parts. But I'm pretty sure that a lot of it was his thoughtful, quiet manner, and the way he seemed, at least to me, really sensitive. Also, I admired the hell out of him. He was good in school, like I was; we were the two best in science—he had recently joined me at the top there—and even though Susan's math class wasn't very competitive, I'm pretty sure we were in the top few there, too. But he was better in creative writing and pre-law than I was, and he was good at things like basketball and soccer, things I could never get the hang of. I'm not sure if anyone else considered the things he did great, but to me, they all were.

I know I didn't like him for his looks. Don't get me wrong, he wasn't ugly—in fact, he looked pretty good, but then I never really thought about people's looks, and I thought it was really stupid when people said things like, "He's so fine. I love him so much," or "He has such a good butt. I want his bod."

I thought about Josh all the time. I thought about how nice he was, and how funny he could be—even though everybody else considered that side of him obnoxious—and how smart...in short, he could do no wrong. Most of this wasn't backed up by any evidence. It was just the image I conjured up whenever I thought of Josh. I liked him so much that I took no care to keep it a secret. Anytime anybody said, "Who do you like?" I answered immediately, "Josh." Anytime I had a question about schoolwork, I called him just so I could hear his voice. One time he called me about a mock trial in pre-law. I was in bed and mostly asleep, but when I heard who it was, I ran for the phone. Never before had I found a phone call so imperative that it couldn't wait for the next day, and I doubt it'll ever happen again. But then I hurriedly grabbed the receiver and answered all of his questions, talking slowly and pausing often so that I could enjoy the pure thrill of having Josh on the other end of the line.

Finally the call ended. I waited for him to hang up first and then I replaced the receiver in its cradle. I went back into my room, singing "Johnny Angel" and making the necessary adjustments so that I could include Josh's name.

In class, I worshiped him from afar, each day praying that he would decide to sit by me in math or pre-law. But the only time I got lucky was once when Bernie, the writing teacher, was reading a story to the class, and Josh came in late. He took the last seat available: The one next to me. He was wearing the outfit I liked best—light blue Levi's jeans, a white turtle-neck, and an orange and navy blue Auburn sweatshirt. I looked over at him as he sat down. I loved the way his light red hair fell into his face. I loved his deep, thoughtful brown eyes. I suddenly realized that he had caught me staring. I quickly turned away, my face unnaturally hot.

All of my internal organs were about to jump right out of me and fly across the room in rapid succession. It was so wonderful being next to him. Part of me wanted to fly right out of the classroom and into the wild blue yonder, but part of me didn't because then I wouldn't be sitting next to him.

Bernie started reading the story. Josh and I were both resting our feet on the legs of the chairs in front of us, so our knees were touching. I was so happy about this that I was about to jump out of my seat and fly around the room like a bottle rocket. The whole time, I marveled over the aura of pure electricity that surrounded Josh, and the volts that went from his knee to my knee in the form of wonderful anxiety. I was worried that I was leaning on his knee too much or something, so I kept moving mine just a little bit away. But then he might not like me moving my knee so much. I rested it on his again, only to worry if maybe I was putting too much pressure on it. I jerked it away once more, then I eased it back again. He shifted, and I thought he was moving his leg because he was annoyed with me leaning on his knee. I quickly moved away. He settled and I was relieved to discover that he wasn't moving his leg. I carefully rested my knee on his. I kept moving my knee when I thought he didn't like me doing it and then putting it back because I loved the sensation of it all. This went on the whole hour, and I gloated over it for days afterward. I had actually sat next to him! O Great One! I was so happy. It was like catching a falling star. And to this day, I still don't know anything about the story Bernie read that day.

We were sitting in court one Friday afternoon. The front of the room was active, but the back of the room was about as motionless as stagnant pond water. I was sitting in the back row. Josh was one row ahead of me. I was staring dreamily at him. It was very boring in court and I had nothing better to do, but even if I had, I don't know if I would've directed my attention elsewhere, for I was pretty much caught up in Josh. Even staring at the back of his head almost overwhelmed me. It was like a sugar rush.

He was wearing his winter coat. It was black and blue, two of my favorite colors, and I loved it. (As you can imagine, though, my liking the coat may have had something to do with my feelings for its owner). Suddenly, I got this incredible urge to jump up and hug him and his coat too. I could not have thought about anything else even if I had wanted to. I just wanted to get up and throw my arms around him. I loved him so much. All I could think about was getting right up in the middle of court and hugging him. It took fifteen minutes and all the strength I had to keep from doing so.

Once, during a free period, Bernie walked into the room. He leaned languidly against the doorframe, surveying us. "Josh, who do you like?" he asked. Picking someone at random and asking them who they liked was a habit of Bernie's.

"Jimmi," Josh said. Jimmi wasn't in the room, or Bernie would've asked her if she liked Josh.

I wasn't worried that he didn't like me. He was just

immature and hadn't come to his senses yet. When he did, of course, he'd fall head over heels in love with me.

But in the meantime, I sure was in love with him. I looked down at my notebook. On top was what my friends and I had dubbed a "masterpiece." "I love Josh," written over and over in bubble letters, covering the whole paper. Underneath was one that said, "Lisa loves Josh." He was always in my thoughts and doodles.

I stared at Josh during all my classes. I asked him every time I had a question about homework. I thought about him all the time. Whenever I looked at him I had to visibly employ a great deal of effort to pull my eyes away from his face and concentrate on something besides him. If I didn't, I would keep staring at him and thinking about how wonderful he was, and never do anything else. That was fine with me, but, well, the circumstances always demanded the activation of at least some thought processes, or at least some semblance thereof.

Even with all this, I still thought Josh had no idea I liked him. But even if it hadn't been through me, he would've found out.

Everyone who asked me got the same truthful answer, and all of those people couldn't really be expected to keep their mouths shut. I discovered by general hearsay that all of those people not only did the usual. "Hey, Josh, do you like Lisa?" but, after receiving a negative answer, continued with, "She's really nice when you get to know her…" I heard stories of all of them ganging up on him at lunch and trying to get him to like me. I didn't think Josh would notice anything. I don't know why, I just assumed he wouldn't. But unless Josh was incredibly dense, he must've suspected something by then.

He didn't like me back. He wasn't rude to me though. Looking back, I found him incredibly tolerant of what must have been a great annoyance. The only time he ever asked me to dance at one of the dances was the time Robbie, Josh's best friend, called me, Kathleen, and Ruthie up at my house, asked me if I liked Josh (to which I replied, "Why do you want to know," acting like I had no idea how he could think that), and then, after receiving a positive answer of sorts, told me that Josh would ask me to dance. He did, and I was positively ecstatic even though I knew Robbie had told him to ask me and Josh didn't really like me.

It was about that time of year that Josh started going with Marisa, who was in Jane's class. In short, Marisa was the social queen of the middle school. Most of the boys in seventh grade would've given their eyeteeth to go with her. This included Josh. But I kept on liking him. I wasn't even bitter toward Marisa. I was so intoxicated with Josh that I convinced myself he would like me if I waited long enough, and so I considered his and Marisa's relationship an immature fling, a phase that would end soon when Josh came to his senses. It did end within a week or so, but by Marisa's doing, not Josh's.

All through this, I was sure Josh would like me. I just knew that if I waited long enough, sometime he would like me. I could not be discouraged, I could not fall out of love, and I could not convince myself that Josh had never liked me, did not like me now, and wasn't going to like me. Every day that he didn't like me, I assumed that he was going to come around sooner or later and that it was inevitable that sooner or later we would be going together. It was destiny. I knew it was.

I felt almost amused by it all: I was the one who knew

what was going to happen, and he was the one who was going through a short bout of immaturity that would eventually end with him falling madly in love with me, asking me out, and us growing up and getting married.

I daydreamed about what it would be like when Josh came to his senses. I didn't know if people went to the movies before or after they were going together, so when I daydreamed I just used whichever order fit best with the rest of the context. One of my favorite daydreams went like this:

We would all be at the dance. I would be thinking it was going to be like any other one, but then Josh would start asking me to dance. I would keep saying yes and really have a great time. The next day Robbie would call me up. "Hi, Lisa, this is Robbie. Josh wants to know—hold on." I would hear talking in the background, and then Robbie would come back on. "Josh wants to know if you'll go with him."

"Umm…tell him, uh tell him…yes," I would say, taking a long time to answer so they wouldn't think I was really eager or anything.

"Hold on again," Robbie would say. I would hear talking in the background, and then Robbie would say, "Josh wants to talk to you."

Josh would come on then, and he would be laughing, that kind of laughing when you're so happy that you can't stop smiling and you just laugh every now and then.

"Hi," Josh would say.

"Hi," I would say.

"Well, um, do you want to go to the movies?"

"Um, sure, when?"

"Tomorrow."

"Okay." We would talk for a little while and then say goodbye. He would say I love you first and then I would.

When we went to the movies, there would be a whole bunch of other people there. We would sit kind of close to them, but not too close. The movie would start, and Josh would put his arm around me when it was half over. (Of course he'd want to do it sooner, but he'd be too nervous.) Close to the end, he'd say, "Do you want to kiss?"

"I don't know," I'd reply.

"Well, do you not want to kiss?" he'd ask.

"No," I'd answer.

"Then you want to kiss," Josh would say.

"I guess so..." and then we'd kiss.

That was when I just kind of had a temporary blank in my fantasy, because I had no idea what it was like to kiss a boy as I had never done so before. But my daydream would pick up again during school. We'd sit together in all of our classes. We'd talk on the phone for hours every night, and tell each other everything. People would tease us, and sometimes we'd get a little embarrassed, but mostly we would like it because we were happily ever after in love.

At the time I thought it was very realistic. I think that it goes without saying that I was mistaken.

For a while it was fun being in love. You know, when the sky is always blue and the birds are always singing and the world is full of hope and joy—you know, like cartoon love. But after a while, staring at Josh and daydreaming about him became painful. It was painful because I was so in love with him, and he didn't like me. All of my day-dreaming was in vain, all my wishing futile. I believed that, or at least thought I did, but I still couldn't fall out of love. I would look at Josh and see him looking at some other girl, and be totally miserable.

My daydreams still persisted, but they had changed

some. I had decided that since my previous daydreams weren't very realistic because Josh didn't like me, that I might as well make them as fantastic as possible. We now lived in a castle in the clouds—Queen Lisa and King Josh. We invited all our friends—mere mortals, they were—up to the cloud cinema every Friday night. We kissed at the movies, and Josh always put his arm around me. I was free to hug him and his coat both anytime I wanted and he would naturally hug me back.

The Saga of Queen Lisa and King Josh continued through spring. I was sick of liking Josh but I couldn't stop. I wanted to ask him out even though I knew he'd say no. I wanted to because I knew that if we went out it would end this one-sided infatuation of mine. Finally I decided to find out what would happen if I did ask him out.

It was a Tuesday night. I was doing my science homework. I reached over and picked up the phone to call Kathleen. "Kathleen," I said, "will you do me a favor?"

"What?"

"Call Josh and ask him what he would say if I asked him."

"Okay."

"Now. And make sure he doesn't think I told you to ask."

"I'll call you right back, okay?"

"Yeah, right after you call him."

"All right, bye."

I flopped on my bed. "He is soooo gorgeous," I thought. "And I have no idea why he doesn't like me…I love him I love him I love him but I wish I didn't because he doesn't love me but I do…" I waited impatiently for Kathleen to call back. Twenty minutes later, I called her. "Hi," she said calmly.

"Kathleen! What the heck were you doing, teaching him foreign languages?"

"No...we were just talking about school and stuff..."

"Did you ask him?" I interrupted.

"Yeah."

"What'd he say? I mean I already know but tell me anyway."

"No." I tried to tell myself I'd known it all along, but I was still a little bit disappointed. I realized this meant that I had still been holding out hope that Josh would like me, even though I had thought otherwise.

I returned to my homework. I was resigned to me always liking him and him never liking me. I wished I could either stop liking him or he could like me.

For two more days he monopolized my thoughts. But some of the thoughts were indecision about whether I liked him or not. Do I like him? I would think. The reasons I had already collected for liking him were there, but I couldn't come up with any specifics on why I shouldn't like him. Still, I felt indecisive. Several ten-minute bouts of this ended in me deciding that of course I liked him, as unfortunate as it may have been. And then, on the third day, things changed.

I walked into school. He was wearing the outfit I liked best: white turtle-neck, Auburn sweatshirt, Levi's, and his winter coat. I looked over at him, looked away, and went on about my business.

Wait a minute. I turned and stared. He was talking to someone else and didn't notice me.

My eyes were not locked to his face. I didn't have to employ a great deal of effort to keep my mind on track.

Wow. This was a surprise. I could not believe that I

was not in love anymore. That was what it meant, wasn't it. Hadn't I, thanks to Kathleen and a certain phone call, finally gotten it through my thick skull that Josh didn't like me. Hadn't I finally given up.

I was not sure how to behave out of love. It had been at least six months since I had had any practice. My insecurity about this, and also curiosity, caused me to wonder if I could make myself love him again. Several times through first and second period that day, I thought about how wonderful he was. Some of it came back to me, but not all of it. I kept this up until I realized that I was playing with fire: What the hell was I doing, trying to make myself like him when I had wished I don't know how many times that I would fall out of love?

During the days after that, I felt free and happy. I didn't think about Josh anymore. It was almost like my life for most of school had been Josh Josh Josh, and now I could think about other things. I was incredibly relieved. I also discovered new insight into the whole thing.

Looking back, I found all of my, shall we say, affectionate behavior towards Josh really funny and I hadn't even thought he'd noticed. I must have really annoyed the hell out of him. I wondered if it would all happen again in eighth grade. God, I hoped not. I didn't want to go through it all again.

In eighth grade I became a lot more outgoing than in seventh. I started talking to boys. I wasn't really close to any of them, but I didn't feel almost scared of them, like I had to keep my distance, either.

But I was always careful around Josh so he wouldn't think I liked him. I knew he'd be on the lookout after what had happened the year before. The truth was that I really didn't like him, except maybe as a friend. I was pretty sure I was permanently over him. But I was still wary: I really didn't want to like him again.

I avoided Josh most of the time. I would try not to think about him. At the dances, I would ask other boys that I didn't necessarily like to dance, but not Josh. If I had a question about homework, I would go out of my way to ask someone else. I didn't talk to him even though I rarely hesitated to talk to other boys. All of this was for two reasons. One, I didn't want to like him, and if I had too much to do with him I might. And two, I didn't want him to think I liked him. But soon, I began to realize how ridiculous that was. I couldn't go around avoiding him for the rest of my life just because I had had a huge crush on him one year. If I was going to like him again, there wasn't much I could do about it. Whether I avoided him or not wasn't going to make a difference in how I felt about it. And as for him thinking I liked him—so what? It was his business what he thought. If he was wrong, it would show sooner or later. If he was going to assume I liked him just because I was friendly towards him, then he could assume that. But he'd have to notice that I was friendly to other boys too.

Also I couldn't keep worrying about what had gone on last year. This was a new school year, and if everybody worried about who liked who last year, we weren't going to get very far, were we?

I didn't know what would happen. Anything could, really. Maybe Josh and I would become really good friends. Maybe we would become even more academically competitive and end up arch rivals. Maybe we would automatically hate each other and be enemies for the rest of our lives. Or maybe—just maybe—I would like him again. Only this time he really would fall madly in love with me, and we really would grow up and get married. Maybe.

ALBERT HERMAN AND MARIE ZELGADO

"Spontaneity," wrote Albert Herman, "takes me years of planning."

And he was right. It did. In social situations the boy just choked. Even in a classroom situation, as badly as he wanted to, he was too self-conscious to freely speak his mind.

All day long he smoldered. His paralysis burned inside. He was quietly contemptuous of anyone else's success. "I learn from no one," he wrote. "I simply resent them for having learned it." If I showed you a class photograph, you would spot him immediately, recognizing him as one of the most bitter, morose, angry kids you have ever seen.

I used to hold the photograph up in front of the class, point to his picture, and say: "Tell me a man's character is not revealed in his face."

Albert liked that. It would always make him smile. He got attention. His problem got attention. And he could bask in the attention without having to speak.

He was intelligent and bright; what he suffered from was the paralysis of obsessive self-analysis. By the time he thought out everything he was going to say, no one was left in the room.

He wanted to be like his father, who loved him deeply and who sang Beatles songs in crowded elevators. He would stare at the portrait of his grandfather, who spent his leisure time flying airplanes upside down, and he would ask himself, "Why can't I be like that? Why can't I take a risk?"

His mother, who also loved him very much, constantly

fussed over him and at the age of five, contemplating what he would say to a potential friend in kindergarten that day, knowing even at that young age he would never say it, he said: "Mom, why do I have to be me?"

Of course, what he really meant, and what I think, at bottom, we all mean, is, "Why *can't* I be me?"

Only in his writing could he be a wild man, as he liked to put it. His writing is, in fact, what provides me the details I'm offering you. There, spontaneity ruled and prevailed, and there, and only there, was he happy.

He wrote about masturbation:

It confirmed my worst fear: I was abnormal. Why, whenever I began, did I hear the front door open and my mother's voice: "Albert, are you home?" I had trouble, as Bernie would say, following through. I could not talk with my dad about it: certainly he had never done it. The only person left was Bernie. I walked in and stared at my shoes for what seemed like an eternity.

I knew I was boring him. I bored everybody.

"What's the problem?" he said, looking up from his papers. "You playing with your pecker?"

Bernie was joking, of course. But do you think, as obsessed as I was with my "problem," I realized that? Of course not. I was shocked that he could so easily see through me.

So I said, looking up: "Why yes, as a matter of fact, I am."

Even his loneliness and self-consciousness he made funny. On his best friend: "He was the most boring person I ever knew; we were meant for each other. We would invite each other over for the afternoon and sit there, staring into space."

On sex and girls: "Joseph dreams of patrician kisses on moonstruck terraces. I dream of ripping their clothes off."

The class loved his stories.

Onstage, in the spotlight, however, as in real life, he was a mess. His pretentious oratory and histrionic gestures seemed taut and mechanical. His voice boomed. I felt as if I were being lectured *at*. He liked to act, and thought he was great; he'd been in local musicals and was even in a movie once. But Albert never *spoke* to anyone onstage; he simply waved his arms and addressed the whole world.

Our stage was our classroom. With the tables folded and put away and the chairs arranged in a circle around the walls, the classroom was converted into a theater-in-the-round.

We were rehearsing *The Children's Hour* by Lillian Hellman. He was playing the character of Joseph Cardin, the local doctor, trying to get the truth out of a malicious, precocious thirteen-year-old who has slandered her teachers in a small New England town in the 1930's. "I don't feel like he's talking to me," said the student playing the thirteen-year-old.

He can't, I thought to myself. Why should I expect otherwise?

But I also thought that some drama coach had unintentionally exploited his weakness—his flight from himself—by asking him to leave his personality in the wings.

I asked him who had taught him that when he walked onstage he was supposed to leave himself behind.

"Every drama teacher I have ever had, and all of them, Bernie, are better than you."

"If that were true, you wouldn't be boring us out of our gourds. You're...you're operatic up there, all voice and arms, making speeches."

"So? What's wrong with that?"

"You're supposed to be talking with *me*," said the girl. "We're supposed to be having a conversation."

"You've got to get her to confess the truth or your fiancée, who happens to be the headmistress, will be ruined. Her school, for which she's saved every penny, will be closed. Your impending marriage will inevitably be in danger. She's been labeled a lesbian by this wicked thirteen-year-old, back when it wasn't exactly kosher in mainstream America. Do you understand your motivation? Look Albert, you're a lover of classical music. Right?"

He nodded. He had written in one of his stories that he jogged to Beethoven and contemplated suicide to Wagner.

"If you were to hear for the first time," I asked him, "a particular composition by Beethoven and yet had no way of knowing it was by him, would you nevertheless recognize it as his? Beethoven was a great composer because he was a great man. He is *in* his music. He is his music. His music is him. That is why you hear him. Show us who *you* are, rather than your *idea* of a great actor. Then you'll be a wonderful actor. Okay? Relax..."

Albert quietly sat down across from the girl and without histrionics did his damndest to persuade her to tell the truth. At one point he admitted with a touching candor that he had lied many times in his life, but that he had always felt better when finally he told the truth. It was as if he were trying to help her.

When the scene was over, the class burst into applause and one kid blurted out: "Albert, you're a nice guy."

I agreed.

He smiled.

A year later, as a ninth grader whom I continued to counsel and teach creative writing privately in my home office, Albert wrote a story about a boy too fearful and apprehensive to ask a girl out. The girl in question was the actress; Albert had come to like her in person. The story was about courage and risk-taking. It was unfinished, of course, because he hadn't phoned the girl. I assigned him to do so.

He came to the next session all smiles, totally pleased with himself, perhaps even a bit smug, and plopped down on the sofa.

"She accepted?" I asked.

"No," he said.

I was confused. "Why are you so happy?"

"I did it!" he screamed, and he threw up his arms in the air and danced a soft shoe on the sofa. "I did it."

Marie Zelgado was an exquisitely featured child with a figure as taut as a pencil. Every feeling she had was expressed through dance; it was her dream and her escape. But when people were attracted to her, she deflected them with put-downs. When Marianne approached, excited that she had a boyfriend, Marie responded that boyfriends seemed to be "the fad." She needed a friend, of course, and later would wonder why Marianne avoided her. She needed friends, but chose dance. One was alone while dancing, and one was respected. Intimacy, as much as she needed it, frightened her. Reveal nothing, show nothing, and if necessary, resort to the put-down.

Marie was in the same drama class as Albert, where we were analyzing and practicing *The Children's Hour*. Wicked, precocious thirteen-year-old Mary, as suggested earlier, has viciously spread the rumor that Karen, the headmistress, and Martha, Karen's lifelong friend and co-teacher, had a lesbian relationship. She "…heard noises," she had said, "and saw strange, frightening things," all of which were untrue. By this time in the play, however, Karen's fiancée has left her, her school is destroyed, her reputation ruined. Sitting in Karen's room, Martha confesses: The child had been right, though she had had no way of knowing it. She did have sexual feelings for Karen; nightly she prayed to the Lord to rid her of them. But she did have them, she blurted out with a terrible shame and guilt, and she always had.

This is the play's pivotal scene. How is Karen to feel? Betrayed? Tainted? Lost? Is the despair and irony so great that she bursts into laughter?

I don't know, but I know this: the way Marie played her I couldn't feel anything.

I was both surprised and disappointed. The relationships with her parents and her friends revealed in her stories were superficial and flat—that's why the stories themselves, like her acting, seemed mechanical. But I had seen her dance, and then I saw tension and passion. And she was emotional, exciting, sensitive, perceptive—the quickest to laugh at Hellman's wit, to discern a character's motivation—when we discussed and analyzed the play.

The paradox of drama is that you can play no character truly and honestly if you can't express your own.

This is why Marie was lonely. This is why she couldn't write. It was all right there before me: she couldn't give. Why, I asked her, was she so boring? Why was she afraid to express herself? Why was she afraid to be vulnerable?

When one is frightened, I told her, one retreats to mechanics.

She glanced at Anna Rossini—exciting, aggressive, extremely talented—who played Martha. I did not understand the glance. They'd both attended Paideia since early elementary school, Anna having enrolled after her parents' divorce; they'd always been classmates, but they weren't close friends.

It was a frightened glance.

I asked Marie if she was embarrassed that Anna had given so much, and she had given so little.

She sat in one of the chairs against the wall, shaking her head, and when she began talking I had no idea, quite frankly, that she was talking about Anna.

"In third grade a new girl entered our school. She was so beautiful and so close to me. Everyone loved her. All of us wanted to be her best friend, and I was so excited when she chose me. I don't know how to describe her. She was always the first to volunteer for anything. Her stories were always the most colorful and interesting. We were so close. When we were alone—spending the night together—we told each other secrets that we'd never told anyone before.

"I've never told those secrets since. I'm afraid of secrets. I don't even tell them to myself, but I enjoy them in books. I can know them, the people, without them knowing me. I won't permit anyone knowing me. I am afraid to be vulnerable.

"I began to become confused. Alone, we had such fun together and I loved her so much and she seemed to love me so much. Could I have been wrong?"

"No," I told her.

"But around our other friends and classmates she began taunting and teasing me. I couldn't understand. Alone, she told me things she would tell no one else; she seemed to like me so much, and once back at school, around our classmates, she would begin the teasing.

"You asked me why I was afraid to be vulnerable."

"Yes."

"One day I made a mistake. I began to cry. And the more I wept, the more she began to tease me. And the more she jeered and taunted, the more all of her other friends joined in. I ran and hid behind a yellow partition that separated the reading area from the rest of the room. They thought I'd run outside, so they continued talking about me behind my back, and for twenty minutes I hid behind the partition in the reading area, listening to their contempt and jeers and taunts."

"Why did you do it to me, Anna?"

"I was afraid," Anna said, the tears stinging her eyes. "I loved you so much. It's what always happens. I get scared..."

"Had someone done to you what you did to me?"

"My father," she said. "He left us that fall."

They returned to the scene and this time Martha poured out her love in a terrifying, frustrating, humiliating anguish to a Karen who was at first skeptical, then denied it, and finally understood and accepted it.

"Anna, Marie," I offered, "this scene, as you know, is about friendship and love, the only one this emotional. You could have signed up for a dozen other scenes, yet you both chose this one. Coincidence?"

Marie smiled shyly, then looked over at Anna. "I signed up for Karen only when I saw Anna signing up for Martha."

Anna smiled.

"Me too," she said, giggling.

RAQUEL MILLSEY, JOSEPH COHEN, AND CHECKER BLUMENTHAL

Neuroses are the closet-feelings of society. The greater the shame and guilt the more intense the seclusion. Kids, like adults, are basically irrational and emotional; nowhere is this truer and more palpably demonstrable, however, than what is for a child the ultimate tragedy, the death of a parent.

Seance at a Tombstone
Raquel Millsey

When I was little, every morning I used to crawl into my mom and dad's bed, shove myself in between them, and wake them up. Sneaking in, I remember it always still dark out and the only lights in the room were the small beams of light coming in through the slats on the closet doors and the one big ray of light coming from the bathroom door. I thought it was some kind of monster, which didn't seem very unlikely, seeing how there were monsters in my room. I used the same method that I had used for the other haunted rooms in the house: I leapt over the light so that the monsters couldn't see that I had human feet and maybe then they would think I was a monster too and would leave me alone. I also remember the way my parents snored. It sounded like they were trying to out-snore each other because every time one of them snored, the other would snore louder. Maybe that was just their way of keeping the monsters away. Anyway, every morning when I went in and woke them up Dad would say "Raquel, I'm gonna have to beard you now!" and I would pretend to try to stop him.

"No, no Dad, don't beard me!" But he always did. He would rub his unshaved, stubby face on my cheek, and when he was done my face would be all red and I could hardly breathe from laughing so hard. Despite how much it may have hurt, I loved it. I also loved it when he took me to Huey's. The two of us would sneak away and not tell anyone where we were going. It was usually closed, but that didn't really seem to matter much. Most of the fun was just getting away with my dad. It was even better though when it was open. We would always order beignets with lots of powdered sugar. The whole time we would sit and eat and laugh, and when we were done we would have powdered sugar all over the place. Another thing that I loved was lying on the bed in North Carolina "snuggled" up next to my dad while he told me Raquel of the Millsey clan stories.

"Once upon a time there was a girl named Raquel of the Millsey clan who flew around on her pterodactyl named Pet..." He would go on and on and I would just lie there and listen. Most of the time we got along great, but every once in a while we had fights: actually, we had them pretty frequently and they almost always were provoked by me. If there was a game or a toy that I wanted that he wouldn't get me or if I wanted him to take me to a movie or a friend's house and he wouldn't take me, I would have a tantrum. Every one of these fits ended the same.

"Dad, I hate you! I wish you would die."

Jesus, why in the hell did I say that.

Four years ago my father died of cancer. I was only ten years old and it was the most devastating thing that had ever happened to me. I remember when I first found out about it. My parents had just come home from some three-week trip that they had taken. They hadn't told me or my brother why they had gone but we knew something was wrong when they wouldn't say. Anyway, my father called me and my brother into the living room and said, "Alex, Raquel..." He sighed and then there was a short silence. "The trip we just took to Miami was for me. I went to see a very good doctor because we've found a tumor in my liver and we didn't know what it was." There was another silence that felt like it lasted years. "I have cancer. Now this may kill me in a year, it may kill me within months, or this may never kill me at all." That was it. Those words created an unknowing feeling for the next six months of If and When and Where he would die. We all just sat there hugging and crying and thinking. I had so many thoughts and questions going through my mind then that I couldn't even get them into words. The rest of that day, all I did was cry. I think it was more the not knowing and hoping part than it was the fact that he actually had cancer that made me cry. For a long time after that I didn't notice anything too different than usual except that he was losing a lot of weight and was always tired. The first time it really hit me was when we got the automatic chair put on our steps. At first I thought it was really cool that we had this chair that just took you up and down the stairs but then I thought about it. Dad was getting too weak to walk up and down the stairs by himself.

From then on Dad kept getting weaker and weaker and it really scared me. I remember coming home from school and Mom would tell me to go back and say Hi to Dad, but I rarely did because I was scared of him. After school wasn't the only time I avoided him. I avoided him almost all of the time. During meals, on the week-ends. The reason was because the less I saw him, the less I would think about him and the less it would hurt.

I didn't think about him all of the time, and that's the way my parents planned it. They had found out that my dad was going to die sometime soon for sure. They had already told everyone except for me and Alex, so whenever anyone was around him, they acted as if they were already in mourning and Dad didn't want me or Alex to act like that. He wanted us to have normal, happy lives. Once I was sitting in the hallway saying to myself "Dad's going to die" over and over again to see how it would feel if someone really said it to me but nothing happened. I didn't cry or anything. While I was sitting there talking to myself my parents called me in their room. When I went in, I remember feeling good about the way I had reacted to my dramatic phrase, thinking that I wouldn't overreact if someone told it to me for real. So I went in and crawled up on the bed and shoved myself in between my parents. I said in a cheerful voice, "What's up?"

"Raquel…"

I knew something was wrong because they said my name first, the same way they did every time something was wrong.

"You remember what I said about my cancer a few months ago…"

Please let this be good news, I thought.

"It's fatal."

"What?"

"It's going to kill me."

"What?"

That was all I could say.

"We've known about it for a while, but we didn't want to tell you because—"

"Why not? You should have told me. God!"

I couldn't believe they hadn't told me, their own daughter! Why would they hold something like this from me. I didn't think about it then but it was for my own sake. I stormed off. While I was slamming the door behind me they tried to talk to me about why, but I wouldn't listen, all I knew was that I was mad as hell. It was that they hadn't told me at first, but then it hit hard. Dad was going to die and it was real. It wasn't just some stupid phrase to see how I would react: it was very real, too real, almost more than I could take.

Later I thought about it and went in to talk to dad. I apologized, and then: "Dad, when?" I said nervously.

He knew what I was talking about. "Raquel, honey, I don't know exactly, but fairly soon."

"How soon is fairly soon?" I asked, wanting to know everything.

"Well, probably within a few months."

"But I don't want you to die, you can't die, Dad."

"I know, sweetie, I know," he said as he stroked my bangs out of my face and kissed me on my forehead.

I just lay there next to him for some time until I got very uncomfortable with the whole situation and made up some excuse like "I have to go finish my homework now" so I wouldn't have to say anything. I think Dad knew what I was doing but he let me do it anyway. I think he was very uncomfortable about the situation too, but he was prepared for it and ready to answer any questions that would come up.

After that I had all of the answers. He had cancer, he was going to die, and he was going to die soon. Actually these weren't all of the answers; these were the obvious, easy questions. Not that they weren't important, they were, but I had other questions, too. Like what did I do to make God be so mean to me, and why, out of all of the people in the world, did my dad have to get cancer. These were the hard questions that no one could answer.

Dad was getting very thin, very weak, very tired, very sick and very, very scary. To see your father going around the house in a wheelchair when you are only ten years old is very frightening. It would be frightening at any age. He also had machines everywhere. Dad said the last thing he wanted was to go to the hospital. He couldn't stand hospitals. So we brought everything to him. The nurses, the machines, the special food. It was all really depressing.

My best friend was afraid to go to my house because of my father, most of my friends felt the same way. One time I had a friend over at my house and we needed something from the breakfast room. When I went in to get it Dad said: "Raquel, please leave."

"Wait a minute, Dad. I need something," I said, being the stubborn, curious person I am. I decided to take a very long time getting whatever it was I was supposed to be getting so I could stay and see what was going on.

"Raquel, leave!" Dad said again, this time in a very stern voice.

"Dad, wait a minute!" I yelled back. I was determined to find out what was going on, and I did. Next thing I knew, Dad had thrown up. I felt awful about having stayed when he told me to leave. Now he had lost his last drop of dignity and it was my fault.

About a month later, he was in awful shape. He could barely move his head from side to side and he could hardly talk. The machines were on loud and clear twenty-four hours a day and we always had nurses here. One night it just got too bad and I spent the night at my best friend's house whose mom just happened to be one of our nurses. That night my friend Karen and I decided to hit the mall and go shopping to relieve some of my stress. While I was there I got Dad this huge Snoopy card. On the front it said "Get Better Soon" (that's what you call wishful thinking) and on the inside I wrote "I LOVE YOU THIS MUCH DAD" about fifty times; it was bordered with X's and O's. When I brought it home to Dad that night little did I know that that would be the last time that I would ever see him. I went in his room where he was lying in his hospital bed. All day he had been going in and out of consciousness and, at the time, he was out. It was dark in his room, and there were about eight people sitting around him, not saying a word, just staring and crying. I saw my uncle so I gave him my card to show Dad just in case he became conscious again. I went over to the bed and just looked at him for a second. He was yellow and very thin. His eyes just sagged down and he didn't move at all. You could tell he was on his way. I gave him a kiss and left.

That night I woke up at about 12:30 and had an awful feeling something had happened to Dad, so I woke up Karen.

"Karen, don't think I'm stupid, okay?"

"Okay."

"Promise?"

"I promise, now what?"

"Well, I think something happened to Dad, nothing probably happened, but I'm scared."

"Raquel, you should be scared. I'm scared, but if anything happened, they would have called, go back to sleep."

"I can't, I need some water."

"Okay, Raquel, but then let's go back to sleep."

"Fine, but will you give me a back rub first?"

"Sure."

We did just that and I slept the rest of the night. The next morning I told Karen I was sorry for waking her and that it was stupid of me to think that. She told me it was fine with her. When we were done getting ready for school, her parents sat me down on the couch.

"Raquel, your dad died last night." I didn't say a word.

I didn't move, I didn't cry, nothing. I was in shock. I didn't feel anything. I had so much pain inside that I couldn't take it, so I just got rid of all of my feelings and felt nothing at all. No loneliness, no sadness, no madness, no guilt, nothing, nothing at all. I know that sounds heartless and cruel, but even though this nothingness only lasted until I got home, I don't know how I could have borne this crisis without it. No matter how much I went through beforehand, all of the nurses at our house all the time and the loud beeping from all of the different kinds of machines, watching my Dad throwing up, losing weight, getting weak, dying, there is nothing that could have prepared me for his death.

Right after they told me I remember saying to myself, "Raquel, your Dad is dead, your dad is dead." I kept trying to make myself cry. The whole way home that's all I did was try to make myself cry, but it didn't work. What would people think, what would Dad think if I didn't cry. Everyone would think I didn't love him. Of course I loved him so why wasn't I crying? If I really loved him I would be crying right now, but I did really love him. I loved him so much that I couldn't cry. If I let myself cry it would hurt too much right then. But nobody else knew that.

When I got home and saw all of Dad's machines being picked up in trucks, that's when I really felt it. I walked into my house and saw my brother and my mother standing there eyes red from crying with tears still filling their eyes. I came up to my mom without saying a word and I cried and hugged her. As I saw Dad's machines go by us I slowly started to realize that he was really gone.

Starting right about the minute I got home, I started to feel so guilty for so many things that I had done. The way my fucking curiosity took away his last drop of dignity. The way that when he told me that he was dying, all I could do was yell at him for not telling me sooner. Or how I spent his last night alive away because I couldn't get any sleep, maybe he thought I did it because I just didn't care that he was dying. Here he was about to die and all I could do was be a selfish little bitch. But the worst part, the part that I will probably never get over, is remembering back to our fights: "Dad, I hate you I wish you would die." Jesus, why in the hell did I say that. That is one of the worst feelings a person could have and I swear, for as long as I live, I will never, ever say that to anybody again. There were so many times that I could have gone and lain down next to him and just said, "Dad, I love you. I love you, and I didn't ever really want you to die. I want you to live. Dad, I love you." There were so many times I could have, but why didn't I? Maybe if I had told him that I loved him more often or that I didn't mean any of that stuff about him dying, maybe he would have lived longer, and been happier. Why didn't I ever ask him how he was, instead of telling him how mad I was. I know realistically that his death had nothing to do with me but I just can't fully accept it because I had been so heartless. Even now, four years later, when I go to the cemetery and am lying next to his gravestone I still try to tell him I'm sorry and that I didn't mean it. There is no way to tell if he hears me or not. But it helps me to think that he might.

We had Dad's funeral that Friday. I have completely blocked it out of my memories. There is only one small part that I can remember. I am standing outside and the ceremony has just ended. I am right behind the hearse looking through the back window down at my dad's casket thinking to myself, "Dad, I'm really gonna miss you." Then the hearse drove away, taking a part of my life with it.

Raquel was depressed and overweight. Academically, she was lethargic and her grades suffered. Socially she did well. When there were social conflicts, however, between her and her friends, she tended to be analytical about them rather than revealing herself. It was all "You, you, you." "I think you..." feel this way or that way. She was sensitive, but she inevitably attempted to shift the focus away from herself. In a calm, pleasant voice she blamed. The possibility of her own culpability frightened her.

This did not improve after she wrote her story. She did seem more loving and a bit happier, perhaps because of her realization that she had avoided grief because it hurt too much, not because it wasn't there. This is important: it confirmed her love for him.

As brave and lovely as her story was, however, she failed to absolve herself of her guilt over his death, her feeling of responsibility for it. Never, she resolved, would she ever say to another person that she wished them dead. That was fine for them, but it only confirmed for the reader the sad, irrational guilt and responsibility she still felt for her father's death. Unresolved in her life, it remained unresolved in her story.

That is obviously too much responsibility for a child—or anyone for that matter—to bear. So naturally elsewhere in her life, in her social conflicts, for example, she attempted to shift responsibility on to others. Already she had too much to handle. To resolve the guilt she would have had to acknowledge it, and the fear was too overwhelming at that point. Responsibility was something she does not want. Already, she felt, she had killed her father. No more, please.

So academically she barely hung on, she gained weight, her friends she enjoyed at a superficial level, and she clung to me.

Liberation would occur with self-absolution and the final,

real (for her) burial of her father.

Too much pain at once, however, before she was ready, could have caused her to kill herself.

Joseph Cohen, whose story follows, suffered not from his father's death, but rather from his painful, grotesque convalescence following an automobile accident. Joseph's pain is particularly localized, as opposed to Rachel's, which affected every aspect of her life. He was open-hearted, self-deprecating, academically successful, artistically successful, and socially happy. He simply could neither speak nor write articulately about his father's accident for a full year and a half after his recovery.

He was too scared and too guilty.

He too had to recover.

A Kiss for My Father
Joseph Cohen

I walked cautiously down the stairs, scared, and unsure if I should've come down in the first place. I tiptoed into the kitchen deciding whether or not I should make breakfast. I thought maybe it would make too much noise, and wake him up. And if he was awake, and he heard me awake he would call me in there, and I would have to be with him, and… I decided against breakfast and crept into the den and flicked on the television. The Smurfs were on. I was sitting tense on the edge of my seat with the volume barely on when I heard his metal bed creak.

"Oh shit," I breathed heavily.

"Who's there?" A cold sick voice came from behind a closed door. I turned off the TV and held my breath and pretended I wasn't there.

The anguished voice sounded off again.

"Hello?"

I couldn't ignore it this time.

"It's me."

I corrected myself.

"Joseph."

"Come here, Joseph."

Oh god, I knew it. I shuffled through the kitchen and pushed open the heavy, swinging door which led into the dining room. Dad had to sleep in the dining room because he couldn't get upstairs to his bedroom. In fact, not only couldn't he get upstairs into his bedroom, but he couldn't do much else either. He could barely move, seldom spoke, and almost never ate.

Three weeks ago dad was jogging in Piedmont Park when he was hit by a car. He was in the hospital for over two weeks and for the longest time the doctors were unsure whether he'd live. But he pulled through. I was never given the chance to visit him in the hospital. Mom said that she wasn't sure if I could handle it. But after a few weeks he came home, he still wasn't well, in fact, they had to transport him from the hospital to our house in a hospital bed because he wasn't well enough to get out of bed. And when I saw him for the first I couldn't handle it. His face was cut and swollen. There were scabs on his cheek, and a red stained bandage was wrapped around his forehead. His black wavy hair was uncombed and thin, and his usual dark complexion looked pale and empty. The rest of his body was bony, weak and gross. Patches of hair were missing from his arms where shots had been injected. On the part of his right leg that was not covered up by a cast you could see stitches and scars where doctors had operated. He looked gross and disfigured and helpless. *My* dad. I had never seen my dad that way before. The only way I used to picture my dad was being playful and lively, and then all of a sudden, he was lying in a hospital bed all dead-looking and helpless. Not even barely able to move. It scared me. And seeing him lying there made me afraid of him, and afraid of what happened to him. And I grew so afraid of him that I couldn't be in the same room with him without trembling or crying. I couldn't be with him because I was so afraid, so I tried to shut him out of my life.

The swinging door closed behind me and my eyes lay on the cold metal bed. I considered leaving but that idea vanished when once more he croaked, "Hello?"

My eyes focused on his hand which was flopped over one of the safety bars on the bed. It had dried blood on the end of the thumb and each knuckle was skinned.

I walked over to his bedside. He was only half awake. While both eyes were swollen shut I could tell he was looking at me. He shifted his cast in a hopeless effort to remove itching. His limp body was so immobile and torn.

"Give me a hug." His hand pulled off the safety bar and motioned me to him.

Jesus Christ, I didn't want to give him a hug. I didn't even want to be in the same room with him. He scared me so much. I wanted to leave but his hand was still out for me. So I gave him a little hug on the hand.

"I got to go." I let go of his hand and hurried out of the dining room and away from calling distance.

The next day mom had to go pick up my sister at a friend's house and she asked me to look after Dad, and listen out for if he needs anything. Once she left I turned on the TV and rested my tired body on the sofa. It was getting late and I could smell dinner cooking in the oven. It smelled like the food was burning. I got up and walked over to the oven humming a song I had previously heard on the radio. I stood dumbly staring at the control panel on the oven, trying to figure out what to do, when dad's feeble voice sounded.

"Who's there?"

I abruptly quit humming and stood completely still, not moving a muscle.

"It's time for my pills, could someone bring me a glass of water?"

I didn't even breathe. My eyes glazed over and I stood totally still staring at the control panel on the oven. I could feel the sweat in my hands. He said something else, but I didn't catch it. I couldn't go in there and have to see dad. I just couldn't do that to myself. I would get scared and upset. I felt terrible leaving him there helpless, not able to get his own water, but I couldn't make myself go in there. I turned away from the oven and tiptoed upstairs to my room and closed the door behind me.

Almost every night mom would tell me how I needed to pay so much extra attention to dad. How he needed love and support and encouragement to help him through this ordeal. She would tell me how I needed to go in the dining room a couple times a day and just talk to him. I couldn't tell mom how I was scared of dad, I was afraid that she wouldn't understand. So I kept it to myself, and just stayed away from Dad.

Each afternoon after school my sisters would go into

the dining room to talk to him and tell him about their days at school. While I would race up to my room as if dad wasn't even there. And at dinner, I would either eat quickly or sometimes not eat at all, only to avoid Dad.

A week or two continued like this, me deliberately staying away from the person I was supposed to love and help so much.

After a few weeks Dad was really recovering. He looked a whole lot better, and he was getting his senses back. He was becoming aware of what was going on around him. I was becoming less frightened of him the more he recovered. When I was around him, I wasn't very tense anymore. Everything was going pretty good. It was about the time when Dad graduated from a wheelchair to crutches when things went bad. Whenever I was around Dad I would feel as if he were mad at me. He would push me aside and ignore me. And I thought he needed *me*! I figured he realized I had been staying away from him when he needed me, and that must've made him angry. I didn't think it was fair of him to be angry at me. I mean, it's not like I didn't have a reason to be with him when he was hurt. I was scared. Can't he understand that I was scared? But then I began to question if that was a legitimate reason to treat him the way I did. I mean, maybe that wasn't a good reason to treat him so bad. Maybe I was a bad person to act the way I acted towards him. Maybe Dad had every right in the world to be mad at me. Or maybe a thirteen-year-old boy should be able to overcome that kind of fear, and look beyond it. And I began to feel guilty. I felt guilty for treating him so poorly. I felt guilty for not being around when he needed me. And I felt guilty for all of the times I ignored his call, or left him alone and helpless. And the guilt really fell on me heavy, and I felt awful. I wished I could have gone back in time and forced myself to be with him when he needed it. But it was too late.

Dad was really getting well now and he was almost back to his old self. He was working full-time again and he walked a lot without his crutches. Dad and I didn't talk much. I was pretty sure he was still mad at me, and I was too busy feeling guilty to talk to him anyway.

After a while I think Dad noticed how bad I felt, and he wasn't as mad at me anymore. I guess he kind of forgave me for what I did. And as days and days passed, the guilt slowly went away.

It's now one half of a year since all of this happened. It's just recently when Dad has fully recovered. I don't think about his accident much anymore, because whenever I do a small wave of guilt and sorrow floods my body. But, just last night I was lying in bed thinking, and I thought about all that had happened to Dad, and to me. And I wondered if Dad ever knew the true reason that I didn't give him the love and support that he needed when he was hurt. I was wondering if I wrote him a note saying why I treated him like I did, what would that note be like. And I figured it would be something like this:

"Dear Dad,

I wasn't sure if you ever knew the true reason why I treated you like I did when you were hurt, it was because I was scared of you. I had never seen you that hurt, and you can imagine how much it scared me. I couldn't be around you and give you the kind of love you needed from me because I was scared of you. Sorry. I hope you understand. That is the only reason I didn't tell you or mom how I felt, I didn't think you'd understand. But between then and now I've felt a whole lot of guilt for the way I treated you. I'm not sure if I deserved all of it, but it's in the past now. I just wanted to get things straight.

    Love,
    Joseph

After I was through reciting what I'd say in my mind, I thought about it a minute. I liked it. I jotted it down on a piece of paper and thought to myself, some day I might actually give this to him. I then folded it up real small, stashed it in the top drawer of my dresser, clicked off the lamp, and went to sleep.

THE WATER OAK

Checker Blumenthal's mother died of cancer when he was five years old. For a long time all he could say about it was that it had made him sad. The story he attempted was frankly a bore, glib and untruthful, evasive, though I was uncertain as to exactly what he was avoiding. Finally one day he announced to the class: "Sometimes I wish I had a mother to complain about."

Then he glanced about, embarrassed.

Approximately a month later, referring to his father's marriage to his stepmother, he said: "I burned her wedding dress."

"I'd say that's registering a complaint, Checker."

"I wanted a real mother to complain about, not a woman named Betsy."

Then finally, after Raquel Millsey's story was read to the class, Checker announced: "I killed her."

The card that Raquel had bought her father...

Checker's mother had come home from the hospital for her final few days. He remembered that he and his older brother had had to tiptoe, avoid tussling and fighting, and to be very quiet and respectful so as not to disturb her. His older brother had punched him and normally he would have lit right into him but not now, he was very careful not to cause his mother further decline and maybe even...he didn't want to imagine it.

When his mother suggested that he draw her a picture he eagerly collected his crayons and drew until a water oak, her tree, came alive. He was certain that she would become as happy and alive as his water oak—his pictures made her "feel better," she had told him; he would save his mother's life.

He took it into her bedroom and she lifted a weak hand to look at it and she smiled and thanked him but that night she died anyway.

"It wasn't good enough," he said.

My classroom held the authentic sadness and palpable grief of a funeral.

"She told me," he said crying uncontrollably, "that it'd make her feel better. That's what she said. It always had. It had always made her happy. She lied...She *lied* to me...It didn't work..."

"You didn't kill her, Checker," Raquel said, and she spoke as if she were discovering herself: "You loved her. Just like I loved my father. That's probably why you feel so guilty. It's why I do. It's just taken me a long time to understand it."

Checker couldn't look at her, he couldn't look at anyone. He nodded.

"I just realized," she said smiling, "that drawings and words don't cause cancer. You know? Our parents just died, Checker. That's all. They just died. It didn't have anything to do with us. They died of cancer."

"It just feels so bad…"

"I know. It's sad."

"Yeah," Checker said.

"It's just sad, I guess."

And it was, and so we buried them, that afternoon, in my classroom.

CARRIE ENRIGHT AND AMY LEVENSON

Carrie Enright is a pale, thin, thirteen-year-old; frankly, the most boring, frustrating child I have ever taught. Unable to reveal the abuse inflicted by her baby sitter, a trusted friend of the family, for a period of a year when she was six years old, she was unable to make a direct statement about anything. Neglected by her parents, conferences with whom seemed fruitless, she craved attention and was constantly signing up for class conferences and counseling sessions, only to begin a flat, needy monologue that was so timid and disconnected that everyone went nuts just trying to follow it.

Still, once she did reveal the abuse and vent her anger toward the former baby sitter with her classmates right there with her, she became socially and creatively, in areas unrelated to the abuse, a more direct, interesting person. Her face became more animated; she looked healthier, and teachers would stop me in the hall to comment on the change.

She no longer compulsively washed her hands.

Still, such work is rarely over. What she enjoyed about the abuse (and initially felt guilty about) was the attention it gave her. Naturally then at the age of thirteen her strategy for getting attention was again sexual: she would instigate suggestive rumors about herself, only to be taken advantage of by an older high school boy, once again leaving herself open to betrayal.

She made the same comment about the high school boy as she had made about her baby sitter, the family friend: "I trusted him."

"What really disturbs me, Bernie, is that as much as I hate him and as angry as I am with him, if he were to walk in this room right now I'd be the first one to jump up, smile, walk over to him and say 'Hi.'"

How had she felt?

Dirty, she said. Uncomfortable.

As if she had invited it, just as she had felt with the abusive baby sitter.

She invited Faye Brown to the mountains for the weekend with her father and a male friend of his from boyhood days. During the course of their time together, she continuously pulled Faye off into a corner with suggestive insinuations. Referring to her father's friend, a man approaching forty, she would say, "Boy, Faye, you can tell, he's really got his eye on you.

"He likes you.

"He thinks you're cool, I can tell. It's so obvious."

And how did Faye feel?

Dirty.

Uncomfortable.

As if she had invited it.

"Why was a forty-year-old interested in me?" Faye wondered, fingering the top button of her blouse. "Was my blouse not properly buttoned?"

"He wasn't," Carrie admitted to her, and she truly had been unaware of her motivation and the consequences; she surprised herself as soon as she opened her mouth: "I wanted you to feel as I had."

Amy Levenson is a fourteen-year-old Jewish girl who wears a cross, sometimes surreptitiously fingering it in class, to ward off the sexual advances of her father, a chemist who lives in Idaho. Amy's residual image of him is Dracula disappearing into the mist, his attack dogs behind him; according to Amy, he can raise a finger and the attack dogs, having lunged, will cease their attack in midflight. Any man can be him, particularly one who shows affection.

Love shows itself then in the form of her father, a wealthy, intelligent man, a Yale graduate, a man who began by "renting" his daughter's "butt" as if it were a vacant motel room when she was five years old in exchange for her favorite candy—"He knew I had a sweet tooth"—and brutally raping her for the next five years. She was his "favorite little girl," he told her, and after she reached for the loaded gun he kept under his pillow he began to regularly place the pillow over her face until she could barely breathe, leaving visible only her open, gasping mouth in which to deposit his sex.

Once she asked her best friend in third grade, Ruthie Wiseman, how it felt when her father rented her butt. Having no other father, Amy naturally assumed all fathers were like hers.

Amy frustrated her teachers—until recently she was a chronic liar and even now she remains too anxious to complete most of her schoolwork—and she creates havoc in her home. Her mother is unable to love her, and having no other parent, Amy is wrecking the home in order to get the attention she needs. She screams and yells, rebelling at every opportunity; she breaks and throws things; she beats up her younger brother, who also cannot see his father. Her mother is afraid to invite friends over for fear that her daughter will embarrass her.

The first lie she told was to her mother, and the bet is that her father was very pleased. She was five.

"Do I get to see Daddy this weekend? Do I?"

"Honey, you're asking me over and over. I've told you. Yes."

"Goody. I can't wait. I can't wait."

Amy lied about everything; now that she tells the truth, her father, while estranged from her physically, is still too dominant a force in her imagination for her to fully pay attention in class or to complete her schoolwork in a satisfactory fashion; so in class she contemplates the cross, keeping him away, still trying, though, to be a good student.

At home she squeezes her brother's arm extra hard, making him cry: she is angry.

Nightly in her dreams she retrieves her father's loaded pistol from under his pillow and as he forces himself upon her she aims and fires once, twice, three times, whispering each time a truth that even he could not destroy, "I love you, I love you, I love you…"

As much as she despises him, such an expression of tenderness toward her father shocks, frightens, and alienates her mother. She is ashamed; she does not want to be reminded. She hates this man who "fucked" her daughter; she despises him. She never loved him, she repeats emphatically, never, she was young, she wanted to get out of her house, away from her parents, she didn't know what she was doing when she married him.

Does Amy's mother wonder if she were an accomplice, and if so, why? Was she a coward, as she is now? Why did she remain unaware of the protest in the repetition: "Do I get to see Daddy this weekend? Do I? Do I?…Do I…"

Amy's very presence is too painful a reminder.

Her mother is ashamed of her daughter, for whom she must once have imagined wonderful things.

And so she rejects her.

Thus the love that Amy feels for her father, for the man who both loved and raped her, is as necessary and truthful and honest as is her terror and loathing of him. Yet her mother's attitude toward her former husband makes Amy ashamed even of that.

Amy keeps asking; she is persistent, it comes from desperation. "Didn't you ever love him? Ever, Mom? You must have, you married him? At first?"

"No," her mother replies coldly. "Never. And don't you ever ask that question again."

And with that response she unknowingly and unintentionally reaches for her own pillow and places it over her child's face, stifling and suffocating a child's last gasp for goodness, for quality.

We must not judge Amy's mother harshly: she is receiving therapy, she wants desperately for her daughter to triumph over her trauma.

I think I understand Amy's mother: Amy is a painful reminder to us all.

The truth hurts.

But expressed openly and judiciously, it helps; it is the only hope we have.

The abuse of Amy Levenson, after all, is no longer happening. Carrie Enright no longer compulsively washes her hands. Faye Brown is not checking the top button of her blouse.

The Trial

F AYE'S MOM

Faye's mom called.

"Bernie, she's hysterical over her case. She's driving us crazy."

"Really? She's doing great at school."

"God, is she disorganized!"

"Really? I never see that."

"No, we see it at home. Her teachers never see it. What that child goes through to be perfect. I just don't know how long she can take it."

"Well, she does get hysterical at school. And she *is* obsessive. We like watching her. Then afterwards she's fine."

"You mean, just *let* her go crazy?"

"Why not?"

"Why?"

"Well, she is a little crazy. There's nothing you can do about it. Trying to curb her just intensifies it. Just let her do it.

Besides, the result is wonderful work. That's her way. It's her *only* way. Just close the door and let her do it. If she badgers you and starts obsessing all over the place, let's face it, by then she's so self-involved, so tied up with herself, just pretend to listen. That's what I do. Sometimes I've left the room and she hasn't even known it."

"And you don't think it's the pressure?"

"Look, she thrives on it. It gives her something important to go crazy over. With or without it, she's obsessive. Just let her be that way, since that's the way she is anyway. Develop a sense of humor about it. Let yourself laugh. I mean, it *is* funny. I mean, who else, taking a test, spreads two dollar bills and rabbit's feet all over the table? Just remind her she needs them, she'll bring them anyway, but she'll see the absurdity of it."

"It *is* absurd."

"So? Her philosophy, though I doubt she'd articulate it like this yet, is that *life* is. Let her treat it that way. Listen, she might be right."

"Okay Bernie. We'll just let her be. Okay?"

"Yeah. Bye, Charlene, call me if you need me. You'll be relieved, if not happier, trying this."

Norman Stewart

"No, Norman, you can't have the court case take the place of your story."

"Bernie, I don't have enough time. Do you want me to end up doing a bad job on both?"

"Is the story too painful? Do you get scared?"

"Yes."

"Do you know what you're scared of?"

"Not exactly. When I start to remember I feel creepy all over."

"Do you feel like it's loneliness?"

"No."

"Norman."

"I don't want to feel it. It's scary."

"Okay, Norman. Don't write that one yet. Write about stealing everybody's money and destroying their property and putting everybody down and destroying your friendships."

"But it leads to the same thing."

"The abandonment. And violence?"

"Maybe."

"Okay. Here's your story. The fear of rejection causes you to be rejected. Never mind, same problem. Abandonment caused that fear."

"When I deal with it I go crazy. I want to hurt myself, or somebody."

"Okay. Hang on. Relax. Do the court case, and when it's all over and you're ready, we'll work on the story. Okay? Do you eventually want to do the story?"

"I *have* to."

"Okay."

THE TRIAL

In the formally arranged courtroom, the judge sits at a table, on which is his gavel, facing the prosecution and defense attorneys (and the defendant herself), each of whom sit at tables a few feet apart. Behind the attorneys sit the spectators, the remainder of the class. As in a normal courtroom, the jurors, of whom there are six, sit in chairs directly to the left of the judge, where they can see both him and the prosecuting and defense attorneys.

Presiding over the trial of Betsy Robinson, gavel in hand, Judge Dwight Allgood is relaxed, attentive, confident, and determined. This is his element; this is where he wants to be. He is there, as he promised, to protect the rights of the defendant and the rights of the accused and to see that the trial is fair and that justice is done.

This is no small task, particularly with two aggressive lawyers who will do almost anything to win. Their political reputations are on the line here; how well they fare in front of the class will determine not only their future clientele, but also to some degree, the future fulfillment of their political ambitions in the classroom.

Norman, leaving no room for chance, pressed for a mostly girl jury peppered with several of Betsy's castaway boyfriends.

"Your honor," said Faye, "not only do I object to every juror Norman has put forward, since they all have reason to either envy or resent my client, but the fact is, according to the constitution jurors must be members of this class, and every member of this class, I can prove, has been privy to rumor and gossip. Therefore I'm asking for a dismissal. There can obviously be no fair trial here. Too much pre-trial publicity. No juror is going to be without bias. Everyone will have heard about this case."

"Your honor," said Norman, "they could have heard about the case without having a bias, and if there's no bias, what difference does it make?"

"Are you asking for a dismissal, Faye, or a set of jurors without bias?" asked Dwight.

"A dismissal, your honor. That's the only fair thing to do."

"Overruled. It wouldn't be fair to Maury. Also, your client wouldn't have the opportunity to prove her innocence. Besides, knowledge of the case doesn't necessarily mean bias. Present your jurors."

Faye called six twelve-year-old boys to the stand, a social clique unto themselves. All were much littler than their classmates, none had pimples or incipient mustaches, and all regarded girls as little more than curiosities.

She asked each of them three questions: Have you ever liked or disliked either the plaintiff or the defendant? Have you ever kissed a girl? Have you ever had a girlfriend?

The answers were all no.

Norman asked, "If a girl wore a padded bra, how would you feel about her?"

They shrugged: how were they to know? The answer was total indifference.

"If someone spread a rumor that she wore one, how would you feel about the person who spread the rumor?"

"Objection, your honor. He's beginning his opening statement. He's suggesting a conclusion to the jurors who may serve on this case."

"Withdrawn," said Norman, smiling. He'd already begun his case.

"Strike that from your minds," Dwight instructed the potential jurors. "All right, Norman, can you accept these jurors or not? Don't try that again."

"I can, your honor. They look very reasonable and intelligent to me." Of course, Norman had no choice but to accept them if he wanted his case to go to trial. Everyone else, he knew, Faye could show to have too much interest in the case. His were struck, and only the six twelve-year-olds remained, all wide-eyed and freshly scrubbed. They weren't yet teenagers, and didn't look like it. They were, however, intelligent, logical, and sensitive.

"Anything you might have heard about this case you must dismiss from your minds," instructed Dwight. "Your verdict is based only on the evidence you will hear today. Do you understand that?"

The jurors nodded.

"The prosecution," he said, "may present his opening statement."

Norman stood before the jury, opening statement in hand. When he turned it in to me for criticism, it was already clear, logical, and persuasive. What it lacked was passion. Still wary of fully trusting, Norman was more methodical and meticulous—controlling, in other words—than emotional and spontaneous. Still, not only did the jury need to be persuaded, I told him, it needed to be moved to be persuaded.

"You just need a bit at the end," I told him. "Something to leave them with."

I was curious to see what he'd added.

"Betsy," he began, "told a lie to her classmates about Maury. Betsy told them that Maury wore a padded bra. The lie was circulated as a rumor all through our classroom. Most of Maury's classmates heard it, either thought it was true or wondered if it was true, and thought less of her. Why did Betsy do such a dastardly, despicable thing? Why would she go to such lengths to hurt an innocent classmate? Very simple. Very simple, ladies and gentlemen—excuse me, gentlemen—of the jury, she was jealous of Maury. Having gone through five boyfriends in five months—"

"Objection! Objection, your honor. Irrelevant."

"Character," asked Norman with a smile, "is irrelevant in a *slander* case? Please."

"Overruled," said Dwight. "Go on, Norman."

Norman had been prepared for that particular objection. He had made a list of every objection Faye might make and his alternative responses.

"Having run through five boys in five months, Betsy still wasn't satisfied."

"Objection. *Satisfied?* Speculation."

"Sustained."

"Having gone through five boys in five months—"

"Your honor, he's manipulating the jury. We get the drift. I object to this repetition."

"Go on, Norman. We got it."

"Having gone through five boys in five months—"

Faye sighed deeply.

"—she set her sights on Maury's boyfriend, Charlie, whose necklace Maury wore."

"Objection. 'Set her sights on…?' Speculation again."

"Two witnesses, your honor, will testify that Betsy told them she loved Charlie. Those two witnesses also just happen to be Betsy's closest friends."

"Overruled, Faye. Sit down."

"They will testify that she loved Charlie and hated Maury, his girlfriend. It doesn't take a rocket scientist to make the connection here. She was jealous and envious and resentful."

"Objection. Your honor, he's drawing conclusions I assumed that was the jury's job."

"Slander has to be malicious, your honor. I am showing her motive. I *have* to prove that."

"Overruled."

"Her motive therefore," continued Norman to the jury, "was jealousy and vengefulness.

"Slander must be an oral statement that is false, mean-spirited, and harmful to a person's reputation. Betsy made oral statements to her two closest friends that Maury stuffed her bra. These people told classmates, who told other classmates. Maury, as she will testify, does *not* wear a padded bra and has never worn one. Betsy's statement was a lie. It was 'false.' It was also malicious and mean-spirited. Her motive was jealousy and resentment, as the testimony of her two closest friends will show. Twenty of her classmates either thought less of Maury or wondered about her because of Betsy's lie."

"Objection. Drawing a conclusion."

"Overruled. He's just listing the points he wants to prove."

"Her reputation therefore was harmed.

"Betsy spread the rumor that Maury wore a padded bra. It was embarrassing. It hurt her reputation. It was a mean lie.

"It could happen to you.

"Find her guilty."

"Faye, your opening statement?"

"Thank you, your honor," Faye said as she rose, stumbled over the table's leg, and faced the jury, just as if she had no idea what she was doing up there. Perhaps, her expression seemed to indicate, they might help her?

In my critique of Faye's opening statement I felt she was arguing against way too much. All she had to do, I said, was to mount enough evidence to create a "reasonable" doubt in the minds of the jurors. Argue only where you're strong, I told her. If two people didn't think less of Maury and eighteen did, concede the point by not mentioning it. My only question was this: Would her obsessive-compulsiveness focus her, or would her hysteria scatter her?

The more helpless she appeared, I knew, the more confident she was.

She'd be fine.

"Members of the jury, this case is actually even simpler than the prosecution suggests. Very simple indeed. Why, if we all got charged with slander because we *disliked* certain people and then were so *bold* as to actually *confess* and *admit* to such human emotions, why, there'd be little freedom of speech, almost no honest expressions of emotion, and we'd all be running around with these phony fixed grins on our faces. I mean, you know? God! I mean, watch out, folks, be careful what you write in your stories. Big Brother—excuse me, Norman—is watching. Be careful what you say, even if it might be, God help us, true.

"Now what exactly do I mean here? What if I look at Jamey

and I say to Anna, 'He's got a big one, I can tell.' What if I'm wrong? Did I tell a lie? No, it was an *opinion*, which according to the constitution, I'm free to express, even if it's wrong. Betsy was of the opinion that Maury's breasts are smaller than they might appear. She thought Maury stuffed her bra, so she said it. Maury can tell us she doesn't, we can believe whom we choose, and we can get out of here. Betsy honestly thought that Maury stuffed her bra. She expressed that thought, a right incidentally granted her in the constitution. If you find her guilty, you yourselves will be guilty of Failing to Uphold the Class Constitution by failing to uphold the right of Freedom of Thought and Expression. Shoot Big Brother, let my client remain free, so you and I can be free.

"So my first point: Betsy, like the rest of us—indeed, like Maury—is free to express a thought, even if it's tacky, which it was. The prosecution also says her motive was jealousy and revenge. They have to prove this beyond a reasonable doubt. There is reasonable doubt. She disliked Maury. She liked Charlie. She said Maury wore a padded bra. She did not, however, say it because she disliked her. She said it because she thought it was true. It was her opinion, however tacky it may have been. She may even have been *glad* that Maury wore a padded bra, if she did, but hostility was not her motive for saying it. It was an observation. Again, she has the right to be wrong. She disliked Maury, she readily concedes. She likes Charlie, she readily concedes. She's honest. She will also tell you honestly, were you to ask her, that her contempt for Maury and affection for Charlie had nothing to do with her comment. She was being objective, as you no doubt are at this very moment.

"My last and most earth shaking point that will surely acquit my client is simple: the prosecution must prove that the statement was false. They can't. Certainly not beyond a reasonable doubt. They say Maury will tell us she's never worn a padded bra. Wow! Surprise, surprise? If she wears a padded bra, presenting herself falsely to the boys, including the one my client likes, in this classroom, do you think she's going to hop up to the stand and announce it?

"I don't think so. I mean, give me a break, man.

"Look. Let's be reasonable. My client thought it, she said it. She has that right. Her motive was not malicious, it was an observation. The prosecution can't really prove Maury doesn't wear a padded bra, that the statement is false.

"Uphold the constitution, the right of freedom of expression, particularly when Betsy may have been right. There's enough reasonable doubt here to protect us all.

"Protect Betsy. Find her innocent."

Norman was apparently so stunned and emotionally disfigured by her final point—that Maury's testimony would not suffice to prove that her bra was unpadded—that he seemed to sit there in shock as Faye completed her opening statement.

"Your honor, I object to her third and final point," he said. "The only witness in this courtroom who can testify with first-hand knowledge that Maury does not wear a padded bra is Maury herself. Faye is characterizing Maury, my client, my witness, the plaintiff, as a liar. Faye is discrediting her as a witness before she even takes the stand."

"I daresay she'll manage that on her own," said Faye.

"Next time, Faye, it's contempt. Shut up."

"Sorree," said Faye, to the amusement of the jurors.

"Norman," said Dwight, "you've already given the jury her testimony, and she hasn't yet taken the stand. Faye can respond to what you offer. I'm going to have to overrule the objection. I remind you jurors that the plaintiff's testimony has yet to be offered, by her, on the stand, where you can judge it."

"Your honor, what's she supposed to do?" asked Norman.

"Bare her breasts before the jury?"

"The prosecution," said Dwight, "may call its first witness."

"Anna Rossini, please."

Anna approached the stand.

"Do you swear to tell the truth, the whole truth, and nothing but the truth so help you?"

"I do," she said, and she sat down in the witness chair.

"How would you characterize your relationship with Betsy?" asked Norman.

"We're best friends."

"Do you have any reason to resent her? To be angry with her?"

"No."

"Did you offer to testify here?"

"No."

"You were subpoenaed?"

"Yes."

"Why didn't you offer?"

"She's my friend. I didn't want to hurt her."

"And if you hadn't testified, responded to the subpoena, in other words?"

"*I'd* have been punished."

"So you testify reluctantly, since you're her friend, and you don't want to hurt her case?"

"Yes."

"You're loyal to your friends then?"

"Your honor...we get the point. This is repetitious," said Faye. "Objection."

"Sustained."

"On February eighteenth, Thursday morning during recess, did Betsy say anything to you about Maury's bra?"

"She said Maury wore a padded bra."

"Were those her exact words?"

"She said, 'She stuffs her bra, you know.'"

"She said, 'She stuffs her bra.' How did you know who 'she' was?"

"She was talking about her before that."

"During recess, on the same day?"

"Yes."

"What did she say before she made the comment that Maury stuffed her bra?"

"She said—"

"Give us the words precisely as you remember them, if you don't mind."

She nodded. "She said, 'God, I love Charlie, he's so cute.' Then she said, 'What does he see in Maury. She stuffs her bra, you know.'"

"Are you telling us that one statement immediately followed the other? 'God, I love Charlie, he's so cute. What does he see in Maury? She stuffs her bra, you know?'"

"Yes."

"So her motive was clearly jealousy and resentment?"

"Objection!"

But Norman had already sat down, and the jury had already heard him.

"Sustained," said Dwight. "Jurors, strike the last question from your minds."

They were scribbling furiously, taking notes, since there was no stenographer.

"Wait, your honor. Excuse me." Norman was checking his notes. "Before the witness is dismissed, may I ask one more question?"

Dwight nodded.

"How many people did you repeat the statement, 'Maury

wears a padded bra,' or 'Maury stuffs her bra' to?"

"Leading," said Faye. "Objection."

"Sustained."

"Did you repeat the statements to anyone?"

"Yes."

"To how many people?"

"Three or four."

"At least three?"

"Yes."

"Did you believe it?"

"I didn't question it, I just figured somehow Betsy knew."

"So?"

Yes, I guess I did believe it."

"You guess?"

"Yes, I did."

"How did it make you feel about Maury?"

"You know, like why would someone want to do that, like she was insecure or something."

"Did you think more of her, less of her, or the same?"

"Objection. Leading. Too simple."

"Overruled."

"Anna?" prodded Norman.

"I probably thought less of her."

"Probably?"

"I thought less of her."

"Thank you."

Norman sat down at the prosecutor's table. "Your witness, Faye," said Dwight.

"You believed her?" asked Faye.

"Yes."

"Why?"

"She's my friend."

"You trust her?"

"Yes."

"Good. So do I."

"Objection," said Norman. "Irrelevant."

"Sustained."

"Your testimony is that she described Charlie as cute, that she said she loved him, that she wondered what he saw in Maury, and that she said that Maury stuffs her bra?"

"Yes."

"If you believed and trusted what she said, isn't it true that you believed and trusted her motive for saying it? Believing it to be sincere and honest?"

"Objection!"

"What does he see in her? She stuffs her bra? What could be more innocent than that question?"

"Objection!"

"She's not real, so what could he see in her?"

"Objection, your honor, this is speculative, rhetorical."

"No further questions, your honor."

"This is a warning, Faye. The last one. If you have a question, ask it, and wait for the answer. If you want to make a statement, save it for the closing argument or keep it to yourself. In other words, stuff it."

"Sure. Thank you, your honor."

Norman glanced at Faye as if she were crazy, just long enough for the jury to notice him.

"On the day in question," Norman asked Frannie McGee, who was in the witness chair, "what did you hear, if anything, Betsy say about Maury?"

"'God, I love Charlie, he's so cute. What does he see in Maury? She stuffs her bra, you know?'"

"And did she make these comments, one after the other,

during recess on the day in question?"

"Yes."

"And again, one comment followed immediately and directly the other?"

"Yes."

"Did you comment in between any of them?"

"Yes."

"You did? What did you say?"

"When she said 'he's so cute,' I said 'I know, he's really fine.'"

The audience tittered.

"Anything else?"

"No."

"Then she immediately said, 'What does he see in Maury? She stuffs her bra, you know.'"

"Yes."

"So her comments, one after another, interrupted only with your 'I know,' were 'God, I love Charlie, he's so cute. What does he see in Maury? She stuffs her bra, you know?'"

"Right. Yes."

"Did you repeat the statement 'Maury stuffs her bra' or 'Maury wears a padded bra' to others in this class?"

"Yes."

"To how many people?"

"Three."

"How did you feel about Maury after you heard this comment from Betsy and while you were repeating it to others?"

"I just thought, God, you know, I mean, she must be desperate or something. *I* wouldn't do that."

"Did it make you think more or less of her or the same as you'd always felt?"

"It made me wonder if she was, well, slutty or something. Less. Less. Yes."

"Thank you. No further questions."

"So you believed Betsy?" asked Faye.

"Yes," said Frannie. "I suppose I did. I didn't question it when I repeated it."

"You're certain?"

"Why not? Betsy's a good friend. Why would I not believe her?"

"So when she made the statements to you, you didn't question her motivation?"

"No."

"No further questions, your honor."

"Your honor," said Norman, "I would like to recall Frannie to the stand."

"Objection, your honor. He did not reserve the right to recall her."

"She's right, Norman."

"Your honor, Faye's shown that *at the time* Frannie didn't question Betsy's motivation. That question was cleverly phrased. I would like to ask Frannie if she questioned Betsy's motivation later, when she thought about it."

"Sustained."

Very clever. Norman had gotten the question in front of the jurors without assuming the risk of getting the wrong answer.

Norman called twenty witnesses to the stand, and asked each of them the same set of questions.

"Did you hear a rumor about Maury?"

"Yes."

"What was it?"

"That she stuffed her bra."

"Did you think more of her, less of her, or the same as you

always had after you heard the comment?"

Fourteen said they thought less of her. Six said it made them wonder about her. To those six Norman asked, "Did it make you have doubts about her or no doubts about her?"

All six responded that it made them doubt her.

Faye didn't bother to cross-examine, essentially conceding that point. The only students whose answers would have been indifferent were seated on the jury. She had consciously, she told me when preparing the case, made that tradeoff. The rumor, after all, *had* hurt Maury's reputation. The questions were: Was Betsy motivated by malice, which in my mind Norman had pretty much proven, Faye's cross-examination notwithstanding; and Was the statement false, which I never even questioned.

Maury was in the witness chair.

Norman asked, "Have you ever in your entire life stuffed or padded your bra? Remember, you are under oath. Perjury calls for the most severe punishment of any crime in our classroom and would ruin anyone's reputation."

"Absolutely not."

"You're certain?"

"Completely certain."

"How would you feel if Betsy were to be acquitted?"

"Sick. Disgusted. Betrayed by the system."

"Could you elaborate?"

"Yes, I would feel that people in this class thought less of me and doubted me because of a lie."

"And?"

"Anyone in this classroom could have her reputation destroyed by jealousy and envy. It's sick."

"Objection, your honor. 'Anyone' in this classroom is not on trial here. Irrelevant and speculative."

"Overruled, Faye. It's the plaintiff's opinion. "

"As long," said Faye, "as it's not seen by the jury as evidence."

"It's the plaintiff's opinion," repeated the judge to the jury.

"No further questions, your honor."

"Maury," asked Faye, "how badly has your reputation been hurt by the comments in question?"

"Badly."

"How does it make you feel?"

"Awful. Sick to my stomach. Disgusted. Angry."

"As bad as—"

"As anything you could mention. How would you feel? It's terrible to have people thinking something like this."

"So terrible that rather than accept the truth and be done with it you'd lie about it in order to correct the impression and make my client instead look like a liar? Isn't that right, Maury? Admit it. Tell the court who the real liar is here. No further questions, your honor."

"That's ridiculous. That's laughable, I'm not lying. You know it. Betsy is. She's jealous. She's a bitch."

"Because she likes your boyfriend? Is she threatened, or were you? Is *that* why you filed these ridiculous charges?"

"I'm telling the truth."

"As badly as the truth has hurt you, would I expect you to say otherwise?"

Maury looked stunned. So did Norman.

"No further questions, your honor."

Maury left the witness chair and walked back to the prosecutor's table with a grim, determined smile. She scribbled a note to Norman, who looked at her desperately.

The Jurors

DANNY FIELDS

Danny Fields was twelve years old when he wrote "A Creature Called Attention." He was emotional, exuberant, and exciting, and his parents adored him and worried about him because he did suffer from an attention deficit disorder. Classes in which there was a great deal of talking sent him into wildly imaginative daydreams in which he was a Viking, a Roman gladiator, or a cavalry major, naturally the last one standing, holding the fort. If incidentally his attention was caught, suddenly he was brilliantly illuminated, and often I wondered whether all that he missed was somehow for a greater purpose.

When he wasn't listening to the teacher, his imagination was nevertheless working, and what an imagination he had.

Also, when something did compel his attention, no student was more thoroughly focused and analytical. One day at recess the fire drill sounded. Everyone lined up outside the middle school building. No Danny.

"Where's Danny?" I screamed.

We were out there five minutes.

"Where the hell's Danny?" I repeated.

"Last time I saw him," said Lester, "he was in the building, just like the rest of us."

I ran in the building, into my classroom.

There was Danny, seated at a table, laboring over his work.

I was flabbergasted. "There's a fire!" I screamed. Of course there was no fire, but he didn't know it. "Danny, there's a god-damn fire! It's all over the building!"

"Look," he said, "can you wait just a minute? I'm trying to finish my French assignment."

A Creature Called Attention

Danny Fields

When I was five years old, a mighty creature of awe-some power entered this world. This mystic creature bore the commanding power of "Attention." I myself dreaded the overpowering rule of this deity otherwise known as… my little brother.

My mom used to hold me and carry me everywhere. She would read me stories and watch me draw little pic-tures. My dad would always play baseball with me and play games with me and do board games. From the age of one to four those are the best things in life. I loved my parents, and as far as I knew they would always love me. They were the greatest. I even had plans to live with them until I died, and they would always carry me and play with me. I would cry when they left me with a baby sitter because I missed them even if it was just for a couple of hours. Life was always sugar-plum happy and good.

"Come here, sweetie," my mom yelled from the dining room.

"Why?" I asked, not wanting to stop playing with my transformers.

"Come and I'll tell you, honey," my mom said.

"Please tell me from there," I replied, all the while bashing my transformer against the couch in my living room till his head fell off.

"Come on dear."

"Okay," I said, only because my toy had temporarily kicked the bucket.

"What is it?"

"Well sugar, your father and I have some good news."

"Yes," my dad said, "um, son, we are having another baby."

"WOW," I said with my eyes open as wide as two big plates. I was excited, you know the kind of excitement you get when your parents take you out for ice cream for no reason. "Really, my own baby for me to play with? This is better than ice cream, this is better than transformers, this is going to move by itself." I was smiling from ear to ear. My mom looked at my transformer dangling from my hand, head hanging by a wire.

"Um, well, the baby can't be treated like, um, your toys. You can only hold him and you can only do that with my permission."

"Fine, then I will teach it stuff and it has to be a girl and we will have fun together."

"Honey, what if it's not a girl?"

"Oh it will be, we already have a boy, Meeeeee!" I yelled with glee, pointing to myself.

Finally the day came when my sister was born. Back at the house me and a baby sitter were playing Chutes and Ladders when we received a phone call.

"Hi, really? Oh my god, that's wonderful, that's great, here's Danny."

"Hi Mommy! How's my new sister?"

"Brother," she corrected.

"What?"

"Sorry honey, it's a boy."

"But we already have one, you made a mistake, get rid of him and try again."

"We had a boy and we can't change it."

"Okay, fine, I guess that's pretty neat," I said reluctantly. I was happy and innocent like a rat going for the cheese, not knowing that farmer Phil was hiding behind the hay with a Twelve-Gauge Shot Gun.

On the day my brother came home I don't remember what I was doing, all I remember was my tiny brother, Jeff. I watched him come up the driveway in my mother's arms. His head was like one of those solar panels with the sun shining off it. His little eyes were half open and were like small brown marbles, and his mouth was half expressionless, half frown. His nose was small and resembled a button. His small body was hidden by a blanket and so were his feet which were encased by two large casts. When he was born he had club feet and had to have an operation to fix them. Basically he looked miserable. If he could have said something at the time he probably would have said, "What the Hell is this. I was fine in the lady, warm, comfortable, with good free food. But no, I had to be taken out, cut up, and then have some hard oatmeal crap smeared on my legs. And to top if off I'm at some damn house with two redheads and some friggin guy with a beard. So far, Life Sucks!" But he couldn't talk, so he just sat there.

The first week was fun and exciting. Especially the first time I got to hold him. My mom gently put him in my lap and I stroked his head and noticed a small soft spot in the back of his head where I could just poke it in, you know, the place where you're not supposed to push. So I then proceeded to push it in, smiling innocently at my mom. She instantly, after seeing what I was doing, grabbed him away from me. "No, Danny, never press that part of his head." She looked at him and in a baby voice said, "Is my smuckums wuckums okay?"

I thought he was fun and cute. Until we went to Lenox Mall to go shopping. When we got there we started walking around, Jeff in the stroller, I walking alongside, and my parents walking on the other side. I began to notice a change in the regular mall routine. Normally we came and about five people would say, "Your red hair is so cute." Or, "Look at your beautiful hair," and I would be embarrassed and hate it, but really enjoy the compliments. Instead this time they were saying, "Oh, look at the baby," or, "Is it a boy or a girl?" Jeff would still have a depressed look and was probably thinking, "First they ruin my life and now they take me out to a big stupid place to be made fun of, by blind bastards who can't even tell if I'm a boy or a girl." I was getting jealous because I liked getting mad about getting told that I was cute, because really I enjoyed it. And the depressing part was that Jeff was smiling, which he had never really done before. I could tell he was thinking, "This is not that bad. At least I get to watch the kid with the red 'fro get mad because the people aren't making fun of him. What a nerd." I was very mad by this time but we went home and I cooled down.

"Dad, will you come outside and play ball with me?"

"Not right now, I'm reading to Jeff."

"Mom, how about you, will you come play?"

Maybe later, I have to make Jeff's bed and when your father's done reading change his diaper."

Jeff was thinking all the while, "I am beginning to like this. The two big ones are treating me like a king and I get to watch the little weirdo throw fits when I get attention."

"Nobody wants to play, fine, I don't need ya." I whispered under my breath to myself, as I left the house to go play with myself. It all became so clear now, I had gotten too big so my parents got a replacement. And were now just hoping I would go away.

I thought my parents hated me because they weren't paying any attention to me since my replacement came. So I decided to run away to make my mom and dad, who I still loved dearly, happy. This is what they wanted. I got my backpack and filled it with…nothing, actually I just kind of brought it along. I walked out of my house and started down my block. As I walked I thought about how my parents did not love me anymore, how they got a replacement and would always play with him and never with me. I thought about the people at the mall and about how they complimented him but never me. I loved my parents but they weren't loving back. They hated me, I was lonely. On the outside I kept a straight face and kept walking. But on the inside I felt like a young, defenseless Weeping Willow. With unending, fragile branches, dangling lifelessly. With leaves that were feelings and all sorrow and loneliness growing firmly on branches that held my soul in place. And all love, caring and security were lost and dead brown, lying randomly around my crooked, tired trunk. Basically I was lonely and unloved to tears. I felt so bad I almost forgot to watch where I was going, and I noticed that I was right back in front of my house. Where else could I have gone but around the corner, I wasn't allowed to cross the street. But hey, I was thirsty anyway. So I, sad and unloved, walk reluctantly into my house.

Time passed, and Jeff started preschool, but he did not like it much. I could imagine him saying, "What the hell did I do so wrong to deserve this?" He was not at home as much anymore and I came home before him so I had a little time with my parents. My mom would read or play with me for a while, and then go to get Jeff, and leave me with my dad. And in the time between when my Mom left to get Jeff and when he came home I played with my Dad. It was getting better, but really, they were just playing with me as a "stunt double," I was just there for them when Jeff wasn't, I was satisfying their boredom, while the one they really wanted was away. But at least I was liking Jeff a little more. I guess you could say I was "growing" to like him, I had finally realized that he was not going to leave. And I couldn't leave because I was not allowed to cross the street. I started to have fun with him because I realized he would do anything I did. If I walked he would crawl after me, if I clapped he would too. I realized my parents only liked him, and not me. But Jeff liked me and we're friends now. He wasn't much but he was all I had. I imagined my parents would keep Jeff and kick me out but I would secretly stay and live in the walls and my brother would slip me food. So now instead of my parents and my brother being the enemy it was just my parents.

I went through a really weird two week phase where I thought my parents were robbers. It was a quick phase, but very scary as well. I thought they were tired of waiting for me to leave, so to fix the problem they were just simply going to slaughter me. That way they could be with their favorite, Jeff, and not have to worry about me. So every night when they came in to kiss me good night I would have a fight with myself and start crying. It would go something like this: "Mo-om I-I'm scared, and I want y-you to make me feel better." Then I would think, Danny, Don't, if she gets too close she'll kill you. "Stop, no, you can't touch me because you're a robber, wait Mom hug me, help me. Wait, don't. It's you I'm afraid of, you, you're going to kill me." Then I would start to cry. I don't remember how that ended but it was confusing and scary when it happened. My parents really weren't all that bad; I realized that after my robber phase when I saw that my parents really did care. Near the end of the phase I remember one time when, well, just listen:

"Mom, I am scared and I want you to help me but it's you I'm afraid of and you're going to kill me."

"Danny, I don't understand what's going on, but I will do anything to make you feel better. I don't like it when you feel bad either because then I feel bad, I don't like to feel bad…"

I thought about what she said, and I realized that she did care because she was trying to make me feel better. And she was trying to be nice and she loved me. That made me feel better, and I figured that it was not that Jeff was a replacement. It was that they needed to pay a little more attention to him when he was younger because he was a baby. I learned this from watching the expressions on their faces, the tired "I want to sit and relax" look, it wasn't a happy hoarding face at all. I realized that they were paying attention because he needed it not because they loved him more. My life was fixed, Jeff was big enough for both of us to be treated the same, except I got more privileges because I was the big boy, my mom said. Jeff even smiled more now and looked more happy now than before. I don't know what happened, maybe he was just making baby faces and I was interpreting them into bad vibes because I did not like him and everything he did was bad to me. But then, since I began to like him, my eyes were opened and I saw him for what he really was, a happy innocent baby. I was happy and everything was fine, I wasn't lonely anymore. I felt good and happy. Now instead of a Weeping Willow I felt like a young, cheery Apple tree full of deep, red apples, surrounded by light green leaves of joy and a trunk that was the world. With a family of loving caring apple trees at my side.

Danny knew the soft spots in which to push.

The paradox compounds itself: he fights for love. Danny was mad only because this intruder who was initially uninteresting had managed, without saying a word or any way Holding Them Up, to burglarize his parents' hearts. The fact is Danny felt he was no longer needed. He is emotionally, as he is physically, a healthy, happy robust twelve-year-old, which is attributable to his healthy, loving parents. His feelings are clear, simple, honest, and without the equivocation, qualification, and even commentary of self-doubt and neurosis. I'm leaving. I'm not permitted to cross the street. I'm coming back.

Wallowing in misery, disobedience is never even a question.

It is his authenticity which is so appealing, his perceptiveness that is so clear. Equally impressive, however, strikingly illuminated in all of his stories, is his imagination, a liberated kite on a gorgeous Sunday afternoon.

Danny is on Ritalin for an attention deficit disorder. How wonderfully, however, he sees and hears. How attentive, in his own way, he is.

What he has taught me, as a teacher, is how important it is for me to see *him*.

He misses the fire for a French lesson?

Imagine that.

There is plenty of room for him and his very fortunate younger brother, and he saw that far earlier than most of us. Isn't that attentiveness?

Pasha's Story

Pasha Zybinski is a short, skinny Jewish kid, a Russian immigrant. Owl-eyed, knobby-kneed, feisty and intellectual, Pasha so bursts with vitality and exuberance that you wonder if any one country, America included, can contain him. He thrives on engagement, he loves to mix it up. Fighting—even physically— is fun. Whatever he does he comes out swinging. Naturally the class bullies defer to him as to no one else. In the land of the free and the home of the brave, Pasha, I often muse, is the freest and the bravest of them all. His campaign speeches in class are so passionate and lively that afterward kids chant Pasha, Pasha, Pasha and carry him around the room on their shoulders.

This strength, of course, was also his weakness, and a failure of courage will show up in one's writing as it will nowhere else.

In a conference about his story I said, "Pasha, your exuberance is wonderful. It runs rampant for twenty pages. But you leave Russia, your past, your friend, your grandmother, the park in which you played—all these people and places you loved—and simply, without any sense of sadness or loss, emerge exuberantly into the present."

What did I get in the next draft?

More exuberance.

"Pasha! No conflict, no story. You don't really leave."

"I left," he suddenly realized, "so that I could bring it with me."

"Show *that*," I said.

Listen to this: Pasha knew no English until fourth grade.

Roses for Grandma

Pasha Zybinski

I slid down the muddy hill, covering myself with black earth so aromatically scented with summer violets and roses. Hearing a slight rip break the silence, I began to systematically check my body parts, looking for open wounds gushing with blood. I heard yet another tear interrupt the chirping of the swallows and the sparrows. A horrible realization came to my primitive mind. My bruised hand slowly made its way around my hip to my behind. "Oh, no," I thought. I pinched myself to wake up, to end that horrid nightmare, but it was real. Swinging my oversized head to the extreme left, I looked down at my brand new Lee jeans, now cleanly split down the middle. "It can't get any worse," I thought to myself. Just then I heard a final pop, and the muddy rags that used to be my favorite pair of pants, fell, exposing my sparkling white Fruit-of-the-Looms at the top of my chicken-thin legs. The park was filled with hundreds of people enjoying a warm summer afternoon, forming a tight barrier blocking the front gate. My face turned blotchy red, and tears of hopelessness began to mar it. I blamed myself for sliding down that damned hill. I blamed my mom for buying Lees instead of Levis. I blamed the laws of physics and the gravity of the earth for pulling my rotten jeans apart, in exactly the wrong place and time.

I slapped myself and took control of my wandering mind. Pulling down my Ocean Pacific T-shirt, I tied the remnants of my jeans around my underwear, forming a strange mixture between a Scottish kilt and the latest bare clothing models of Karl Lagerfeld. Trying to keep my back to the wall, I ran to the back exit, away from humiliating hills populated by wide-eyed people, and towards the unbroken, immovable place of assurance and safety, home.

I breathed relief as I reached my front door, only to be met by Sylvia, the house witch. Sylvia was one of the scariest and ugliest people I knew. Her wart-covered, crooked nose cast a dark shadow on her bountiful moustache, so elegantly curving around a mouthful of decaying teeth. "Boris Karloff's" long, gray hair was always hidden by an 18th century traveling cap, and her dark monotonous dresses made from rich velvet dragged behind her in the dust.

"Good afternoon, young boy," she greeted me. Sylvia classified people into three groups, young boys and girls, young persons, and young men and women, depending on their age. I was a young boy, my dad a young person, and Sylvia herself was a young woman, even though by my calculations, she was 143 years old.

"Answer when being spoken to," bellowed the witch in a groggy voice. "Hello Aunt Sylvia," I answered staring into the asphalt. "Aunt" Sylvia looked me over, head to toe. Her bulging eyes stopped and widened at the sight of a dirty cloth wrapped around my waist.

"Is it not improper for a young boy such as yourself to dress in female skirts and kilts of this fashion?"

"I don't usually wear clothes like this. There's been an accident in the park, Aunt Sylvia."

"Bah, accident-shmaccident, these kids and their rock'n roll. You oughta get sent to boarding school, they'll fix you straight."

While Sylvia went on, madly rambling about the disrespect of the new generation and their rudeness to the elder members of our society, I snuck past her into the house and ran up the brick steps leading to the second story and swung open the door to my home.

After taking a long shower and changing into a fresh pair of pants (Levis this time) I walked into my room. Ah, my room. A solid, safe place. A place to hide from the disturbances of common life like a monk, and a place to have the wildest birthday party a seven year old could have. I was the sole occupant of this gracious castle since birth, due to the absence of younger siblings who I hoped would never come. My room was mine and mine only. The yellow king sized bed, which I inherited from my parents after they purchased an imported Sealy posturepedic. The tiny crib in which I slept until the age of six stood by my favorite blue velvet armchair. I often climbed and slept in my former bed, when feeling nostalgic for those distant days when Mommy tucked me in with a bedtime story or song. The sky-blue wallpaper, which Daddy bought for me when I turned five. The solid oak table, marred by endless pen marks, still smelled of freshly cut wood. The glass display case portraying the family heirlooms stood shining from the weekly polishes Mom had given it. The pine bookcase slumped in the middle of the room, held the classical literature my parents thought would be inspiring to my brain.

A family portrait hung above my bed. I looked so many times at it, yet every time brought a new experience, a new feeling. There is Mom, smiling as usual. Her brown curls encompassing her ivory face, "cut" to the brink of perfection by the finest jewel cutters in heaven. Her ruby lips, stretched to the limits, revealed her diamond white teeth, softly warming the room. There is Dad, in a checkered wool suit and black rimmed glasses, serious as he'll ever be. You might think Dad was one of those boring business academics, who consider three hour meetings fun. But Dad was a barrel of laughs with bad teeth, and his dentist was working on him the day the picture was taken. If you were perceptive enough, you'd see little bonfires that lit up his eyes, the fires responsible for all the incredibly crazy fun that Dad contained. In front of Mommy and Daddy stands a rather ugly example of a three year old in dark brown shorts and blue T-shirt, his bony arms raised high in the air. That plucked turkey of a kid is myself, in all my might. There is Grandpa in a detective hat of the 1940's. Grandpa was obviously the coolest and most muscularly built person in my family. His powerful biceps had not been touched by the merciless angel of old age, and he retained that vigorous youthfulness that let us roam around amusement parks as if Grandpa was a kid again.

Just above my bed hung a black encased picture of Grandma Polly: Grandma had her usual golden smile beautifying her face. Grandma always smiled when she looked at me. She had the same brown curls that Mommy had. And those same chocolate brown eyes, that Mommy inherited from her, lit up Grandma's pearly white face. On a pine table, next to my bed, stood a five gallon aquarium that my Grandmother presented to me on my fifth birthday. Chalky white fish remains swam atop the swampy green water, which had never been changed. Those fish met their deaths from suffocation within the first minutes of their arrival to my bedroom. I mean, how was I supposed to know that fish can't live out of the water? That aquarium had begun to smell very badly, after a while, but I wouldn't get rid of it because Grandma gave it to me. We had a lot of good times with Grandma, you know. I remember it clear as the day when we were in Central Park on sunny spring afternoons. Grandma just talked to her senior-citizen friends, and I hopped around the little green field doing all the cute kid stuff, squishing bugs and peeing in restricted areas. But then when the clock ticked "eleven," and the flower booth opened, I ran there to spend my last dollar on roses. Grandma Polly loved roses. All different kinds, crimson glory, charlotte, tallyho, or rubaiyat. Grandma loved all of them. And just as I ran towards her, with a single red rose clutched in my five year old hand, I saw Grandma's heart melt with love for me. Every time I'd given her that rose, Grandma would hug me and raise me to the skies, while I chuckled in elation. Boy, I loved Grandma Polly a lot. Cried for a long time when she died too. Still, it seemed like she was always there, always looking at me, guarding me with her chocolate eyes from a black framed picture just above my bed.

Snapping out of my trance, I walked over to my green/black phone and dialed Eddie's phone number. Eddie and I had always been friends. Since birth we were partners, hand in hand. I even had a picture of us at the age of nine months, learning how to walk together, holding hands. Eddie and I both knew each other's deepest darkest secrets. My friend told me that the reason he wore a geeky beach hat for the past two weeks was because of a blue stain in his dark brown hair he got playing with his dad's brand new chemistry set. I entrusted Eddie with my most strongly guarded secret, the secret that if discovered, would lead me into the world of geeks and nerds—I was getting glasses. I've never given away Eddie's secrets and he never told mine. I waited for Eddie to pick up the phone.

"Hello?" a high pitched voice, very similar to mine answered.

"Hey, Eddie, guess what just happened?"

"What?"

"I was sliding down a hill in Central Park and split my jeans right down the middle!"

"Did anybody see you?"

"Oh not a soul, or a human soul at least," I said.

"Sylvia caught you, didn't she?"

"Yeah," I answered.

"Hey Eddie, let's go to the park and play around with

Scorlupsky."

"Okay. You bring the capes. See ya in ten minutes."

"Bye."

Mr. Scorlupsky was the park gardener. He was madly in love with his azaleas, roses, tulips, and asters. Scorlupsky spent hours pruning, fertilizing and watering his precious creations until they were on the brink of mortal perfection. He gave as much affection to his thinly scented violets as a short balding man in his early fifties could give. His vegetation were considered to be works of art, and he had been named the artist of the year by the Chernovtsy Cultural Society, and a barbarian of the month by Eddie and myself.

Any time we would take our BMX bikes for a ride in Central Park, out of nowhere would leap Mr. Scorlupsky, ready to ram his five foot broom through our wheel spokes, calling us ruffians if we came anywhere near his exquisite beauties. Eddie and I were by no means ruffians, we were super-heroes. Eddie was E-MAN, and I was SUPER-V. V stood for vengeance and E stood for electricity. We owned an identical pair of BMX bikes. Eddie named his "Lightning," and I named mine "The Spirit of Vengeance." We rode around the asphalt alleys of Central Park dressed in mysterious vampire capes and notorious masks, scaring decent citizens. The sun shone into our rebellious eyes, and the warm summer wind brushed past our unbrushed hair. We were indeed James Dean juniors, the rebels without a cause.

It was an unfortunate turn of events that memorable day, when Super-V and E-Man were chasing vicious crime lords and ruthless convicts, and happened to trample across a few tall daisies, all for a good cause of apprehending dangerous criminals, of course. We should have been rewarded for our noble deeds, but instead what happened to us next exceeded all of our expectations. It was Scorlupsky coming at us, his broom pointed at our wheels like a bayonet. He was Doomsday and we were Supermen. As if in slow motion, the gardener rammed through our brand new gum-wall tire wheels. Metal spokes flew in the air and Super-V along with E-Man lost the battle. But by no means were we defeated. Not admitting our loss, we gave each other high fives and stuck out our tongues to show that we were victorious and always would be.

Eddie and I were held together by a friendship bond that would last forever. Nothing could break it apart. Nothing. Not the storms and tornadoes of life. Not wild animals clawing at our flesh. Nothing. Super-V and E-Man were on this earth together, and together they would be.

As I entered the dining room, the delicious smell of freshly grilled chicken hit me in the face and traveled up my nostrils. Mom, Dad, and Grandpa were already seated around the round table, when I, King Arthur, walked in. There were five chairs and five sets of silverware set up, one for each member of the family, and the fifth for Mikey, my teddy bear. When I was born, Grandma bought him as a gift for me. Mikey was six feet tall, dark brown with a bright blue ribbon tied around his six inch neck, and all stuffed with cotton. My teddy bear was my first friend, first playmate, first hero. When we would go to the movies, Mikey had to be taken along. When we went on a long vacation, Mikey had to be dragged behind. When we had breakfast, lunch, or dinner, I would not touch my food if Mikey wasn't "eating." There was always another set of silverware on the table, so Mikey wouldn't be hungry. Mikey's plate never got dusty, because I washed it twice a day, just like my Grandma Polly told me to. She said that even stuffed bears cared about their personal hygiene, and little boys like myself should too. That's how Grandma got me to take showers, you know, using that good-little-boy personal hygiene stuff. Anyway, even though I was too old to play with stuffed animals, Mikey always had a special place in my heart and around the dinner table.

I took quick bites out of my chicken sandwich, while cautiously glancing at Dad. Dad was wearing a blue shirt. He always wore blue shirts. Grandma told him it brings out his eyes. My parents were arguing again.

An avid discussion among my family members was by no means rare. Since I was a tiny tot, my parents led lengthy discussions on all different topics, ranging from the world chess championship to the new prime minister of Turkey. But I didn't like this conversation. Dad had this mad look on his face. I'd seen that look before, when Dad had been rejected for another promotion at the firm. Or when the quota at the medical university suddenly became full when Mom tried to apply. Or when certain gravestones at the city cemetery were found shattered on cold winter mornings, just because the deceased went by the names of Horowitz, Rabinovich, or Fleishman. That's the kind of mad look Dad had that day.

After twenty minutes of intense yelling, my wise father rose from his mighty throne and banging his huge palm against our mahogany table, Dad whispered in a soft voice, "It happened again."

You didn't have to tell me what "it" was. I already knew. "It"—was the evil spirit that always dwelled around us. "It"—was the devil that followed us everywhere we went.

"It"—was the monster that turned homes into enclaves of barbed wire, sent hordes of killers to draw the blood of the innocent, and held us in its satanish grip for centuries. We hated "it."

"And I'm not going to take this any longer. The tickets are for September twenty-fourth," Dad continued.

"But that gives us only a month to take care of everything. We can't just leave at an instant," Mom yelled back.

"We're leaving for America in four weeks and that's final."

"Whatever you say," Mommy answered, returning to her calm voice.

America. I'd heard of that great continent in the western hemisphere so many times before. America, the land of opportunity, golden roads and annual money showers. America, the country of Rambos, Rockies, and cheeseburgers. America, the place where all the handsome people with Clairol hair lived. America…

The next month was filled with rapid selling and spending. The state Inspection Agency limited the amount of money brought out of the country to $360 dollars per family. Besides valuables, we were allowed to take anything we could carry, and send an additional luggage to the U.S. Everything we could pack went with us. Anything we couldn't, was either sold or given away. Since valuables couldn't be taken out, my parents' remaining life savings had to be spent on worthless junk none of us needed. Dad suddenly became a photo fanatic, and purchased an $860 dollar photo-gun. The "gun" was really an extremely large camera with three million lenses mounted on it. The box in which the camera was resting, claimed that "PHOTO-GUN" could catch an image of an ant from a ten story building.

Mommy, however, found the gun to be more useful as an automatic onion slicer.

Our sent-away luggage was composed of rather interesting materials. Twenty-two bottles of shampoo, thirty-seven boxes of corn puffs, ninety-eight bars of Ivory soap, seventeen pillow cases, one Japanese stereo system (later stolen by the immigration officials), two crates of raunchy Seventies records, 368 volumes of various literary books, three Persian rugs (later used to bribe a drunk cabbie in New York), one window sized picture of Grandma Polly, and finally photo-gun, the only automatic onion dicer and slicer with a zoom.

Hoping to get a piece of our property, a vast array of never-before-known-to-us relatives popped up. Aunt Rosa got our wooden cabinet T.V. Uncle Rudolph inherited the eighty year old refrigerator. Vanya, the town alcoholic, picked a moldy bottle of vodka, with the inscription "Happy New Year, 1963!"

We had to sell the mortgage to our home and had a limited amount of time left. After Dad had placed an advertisement in the city newspaper, customers started coming in by the dozens. One day this couple with a three year old kid stopped by to take a look around. They introduced themselves as Mike and Jane Ivan. Their kid's name was Robby. They were television kind of people. Jane had a terrific smile splattered across her disfigured face. Her make-up was painted on in dozens of levels, completely hiding her meaty nose. Jane's vocabulary consisted of two expressions, "really" and "how charming." Mike' was the chip off the old "Revenge of the Nerds" movie. He was normal most of the time, but wait till you hear his laugh. That disgustingly loud mixture of rapid hiccups and belches really grossed me out. I won't even begin to tell you about his halitosis. Robby seemed as if he was fathered by the Three Stooges. He was short, fat, and had a brain the size of a Mongolian pea. His main attraction, however, was the tangled mass of curly blond hair towering above his pimpled head. With that hairdo, Robby closely resembled a poriferan, or a sponge. I was itching to ask him if his head was extra absorbent, but remembering what Dad mentioned about being courteous and all to potential customers, I backed off.

The Ivans' stay was pretty uneventful. Mike and Jane exclaimed "really," and "how charming," every step of the way from my room to the kitchen. Finally after bypassing the bathroom which had already been gassed up by Mike, we entered the dining room. Mikey was still slumped in his honorary chair, a fresh set of silverware in front of him. Robby glanced around the room in sheer boredom. Suddenly, his eyes lit up. Moving his chubby legs, the junior Ivan ran towards my favorite teddy bear and embracing him Robby yelled out, "Iggy! Iggy?" Who the hell is he calling Iggy? That was my teddy in that oak chair, and his name was Mikey. Mikey, not some nerdy name like Iggy! Robby was still hugging "Iggy," even drooling on teddy's furry body. My teddy's body!

"We'll take the house if the bear comes with it," breathed out Mike. It was only a week before leaving. I knew we had to sell the house now, or never. Dad gave me a questioning glance. He would never dare give away Mikey without my consent. Breaking the deathly silence, I answered Mike myself. "That old cotton rat? Oh sure take him. I was gonna throw him away anyways!" Oh, they took him, all right. Robby was still hugging teddy, and slobbering all over him.

At that moment, I wanted to break the "sponge's" filthy neck and trample all over his bloody windpipe, sucking all the breath from that poriferan's body. Only I couldn't do that. Robby was a customer, and I had to be nice.

After the Ivans had left, Mommy gave me a hug. "I know it hurts. I know you'll miss Mikey. But I'm proud of you. Do you understand?" I nodded. "You know why we have to leave don't you?" I nodded again, bowing my head down to hide my tears.

It was September twenty-third, and our family went to the city cemetery, to pay final respects to Grandma. It was unusually cold that September day. The wind was blowing into our backs with an angry taint. The trees had lost their green coats in exchange for orange, yellow and brown ones. The charred barren sticks, which used to be flower bushes, stuck out of the ground like torched Sabbath candles. Somewhere far away on the coast, a wretched sea gull gave a painful cry as the construction bulldozers ripped his nest apart. Somewhere, someone laughed, cried, and fought. But it was all quiet here. Just the wind whistling among the oaks, and the rabbit rustling a few brown leaves in its step. We reached Grandma's resting place, and knelt down in front of it. Grandma's chocolate eyes stared at me from the engraving on the granite stone in the same manner as her picture did in my bedroom. I reached into the plastic bag by my side, and took out a small rose cutting. I dug out a small hole at the head of the gravestone. I knew the seedling would probably die in the cold harsh winter, but Grandma loved roses. All different kinds. I knew she'd take care of my rose. Slowly, I planted the little seed into the ground, and covered it with the rich black earth, so aromatically scented with fall pines and oaks. I stood up and cried out loud. Somewhere inside me I knew I would never "visit" Grandma again. Dad was heaving another bribe to the cemetery personnel in return for looking after the grave. Money. It's the only thing that could stop "those" barbarians. Mommy was crying again. She always did when we "visited" Grandma. Grandpa just wore a sad solemn look on his face. When we were about to leave, I raised my eyes into the gray sky and then at Grandma's grave. I poured a bit of warm water over the flower, so it wouldn't freeze. Then, wiping my tears, I thought about the flower booth in Central Park, and turning slightly around, whispered "Bye, Grandma." I never "saw" her again.

It was the day. September twenty fourth. Everything we owned was already packed or sold. The house was all empty, except for one cocktail table covered by foods of all sorts for the final party we were throwing, and the big black piano in the corner of the living room. Pretty soon people started coming in, giving presents, hugging, laughing, crying. Eddie came. We tried to horse around a bit. I remember we dropped a rotten egg on Scorlupsky's shiny head, from my balcony. And mooned Sylvia, while the latter came out for a walk. It wasn't the same anymore. For the first time in our lives, we weren't Super-V and E-Man. Eddie and I were just best friends. Not the terrorists who ruled Central Park. But just friends. Friends that didn't want to say goodbye, but had to. Eddie must've heard of Mikey's fate, and gave me his own teddy, whom he loved and adored. His name was Peter, and he was Eddie's most valuable possession. In return, I gave Eddie my prized Pentax camera. When the final goodbyes came, I just said as I always did, "See ya, Eddie."

"Take care of Peter," he answered. Just as Eddie was

exiting, he turned around. Then we gave each other high fives and stuck out our tongues, to show that we were victorious and always would be. Even when Super-V and E-Man lost the battle.

Finally, all the guests were gone. Little candy and gum wrappers were spread all over the polished brown floor, turning it into an exotically colorful carpet. I walked over to the big, black piano. I took piano lessons for quite a while, but I never became the Horowitz my parents hoped I would be. Every time I played it, the piano did not make beautiful flowing sounds. Instead, these disgusting, croaking noises poured out of the big black box called the piano. I slaved over my music for hours hoping to get just one piece straight. It was no use though. That piano hated me. Over the years however, we had grown to love each other, heart in heart. I came up to it, that last day, and began to play the piece I never got straight, the "Love Story." For the first time, since I began to play that melody, really beautiful sounds came out. Their rich tone vibrated with a kind of sadness in my mind, that one can never explain. My whole family gathered around me, just sort of listening. I looked at them. Oh, how different it all was. We all were no longer the same people as we were four weeks ago. Mommy's hair was streaked with gray, a color I had not seen in her curled locks before. Her face radiated sadness and fatigue. The bonfires that lit up Dad's eyes were gone somewhere, never to return again. The demon of age had finally caught up with Grandpa. For the first time he looked old. For the first time I realized what was happening. We were leaving our home. Our precious home where every one of us was born and lived all our lives in. No longer would I ride my bike around the asphalt alleys of Central Park, and feel the soft breeze run through my hair. No longer would I slide down muddy hills, make fun of Scorlupsky or moon Sylvia. Never again would I run towards a flower booth with my last dollar clutched in my hand. Never again would I hear Eddie's high pitched voice asking me to go to the park. Never again would I see the land where I was born. Never again.

"We have to go. The bus will leave without us," said Dad. I quit playing in the middle of the final chord and closed the piano. Looking around the empty rooms that used to be my home, a sad thought inspired my soul.

"Everything is gone," I said. "Nothing to tell we were ever here." That's when I broke down and started crying. I didn't try to stop myself. It was okay to cry. Mommy and Daddy cried too, and I saw Grandpa wipe away a tear. We stood outside our door, just looking at the empty hallway, crying. Finally, a cold wind blew from the opened window and closed shut the large pine door to our past.

Daddy turned the key, and we trudged off facing the future and the unknown. One thing was certain. We would never return.

I woke up the next day to the chugging of the train and the bawling of the drunks in the next compartment. My face still bore the lines of yesterday's tears. I felt like sleeping for ten more hours, and never waking up. I felt like one of those guys who got drunk the night before, and then woke up in the morning. I felt really lousy all over. Putting my pants on, I walked out of my sleeping suite into the hallway. Boy, it was a beautiful day out. The sun sent its rays to playfully cuddle my face. The very first ray just bounced around the hall, as if looking for a friend. Then the next one came, and they joined. Then another ray, and another and another. I opened the window, feeling the minty fall air rush in and surround the caboose. Then, I looked out at the sun-drenched valley spreading before me. The birds were tweeting, and the cows were mooing, only seldom interrupted by a herder's cry for his sheep.

"It sure is beautiful today," Dad called out.

"Yes," Mom said, dreamily staring into a young oak where two ravens were repairing their nest from yesterday's thunder.

"I haven't seen a finer day in weeks," Grandpa added, while swallowing another expectorate pill.

I quickly darted back into our quarters to get something. There, I unzipped my duffle bag and came up with a picture of Grandma Polly. Then, I ran back into the hallway and took my place closer to Mommy. She ruffled my hair as she has always done and gave me another one of her diamond smiles. I put Grandma's picture closer to the window so she could enjoy the view. It was a hell of a day out. Suddenly, I felt like doing something crazy, you know. I felt like flicking off the conductor, mooning the lady across from us and peeing out of the window. I would do it too, if Mom wasn't there. For some reason I felt so good on the inside. That good feeling spread out, reaching every part of my body until a grin emerged. I squeezed between Mom and Dad, spreading my grin around. Everything was not gone. My home, Central Park, Eddie. The gentle breeze, the muddy hill, the rose flower booth. My room, my bike, Mikey. The spark that drove me to insult Sylvia and trample Scorlupsky's azaleas. It was all here, with me. It would always be with me. Wherever life's turmoils would take me, I would always have it. The park, Eddie, Grandma.

They are all mine. They always will be…

JEREMY SINCLAIR

Jeremy Sinclair had one of the saddest smiles I have ever seen. It was a smile that illuminated nothing so much as vulnerability.

When Jeremy was eight years old, his stepfather, Bob Sinclair, and his mother, Natalie, took him to the courthouse in Fulton County, Atlanta, Georgia, and against Jeremy's wishes, had him adopted by his stepfather, and had his last name changed from Langdon to Sinclair. At the time he was very confused, but he loved his real father very much, and he did not want this to happen.

"Why did it happen, Jeremy?"

"I'm not sure. All I remember is that my stepfather overheard me tell my father I loved him in a telephone conversation."

"Why do you suppose that mattered so much to him?"

"I don't know. He has no children of his own. I don't have any brothers or sisters. I suppose he was jealous."

"How do you feel about your stepfather?"

"I hate him. He took away my father. He won't let me see him."

"You haven't seen him since you were eight?"

"No. Except for every once in a while, when Bob is out of town. Then my father will rent a motel room and my mother will let me sneak and see him. As long as Bob doesn't find out."

"Jesus, Jeremy, this is awful. Terrible."

"Yes. Yes it is. It is. I can't talk to him when he calls on the phone, and they even go through the letters he sends me. I can tell. He sent me photographs of his cars. He loves old cars, and he knows I love them, and my parents removed them from the envelope. I knew, because the last time I saw him he asked me what I'd thought of them."

"This is the worst goddamn thing I've ever heard of in my life."

"I'm going to get my father back. He's told me. We just

have to be patient. He's going to take them to court."

"It's been how long since the adoption?"

"Six years."

"Does your mom know how you feel?"

"No."

"Why not?"

"I'm afraid of hurting her."

"You're afraid of hurting her?"

"Yes."

"Why?"

"I love her. There's nothing she can do. It would destroy her marriage."

Which is, of course, why she hadn't done anything. I would imagine she'd felt the same way.

"When you go home tonight, Jeremy, tell her that. Tell her how much you miss your father, how much you need him, and that you haven't told her because you love her so much you were afraid of hurting her."

"It won't do any good."

"Yeah. Right. Do it anyway."

"How about if I write a note?"

"Fine. But let me see it before you leave school. Okay?"

"Do I have to?"

"Yeah, Jeremy, you have to. You have nothing to lose. You're miserable now, and if it doesn't work out, you'll be miserable later. But I think you'll be surprised. Tell me about Bob. All this began with an overheard phone conversation?"

"Yes."

"He must care about you a lot. Right? That's the problem?"

"Yes. But he's nice to me too. We do stuff together."

"Like what?"

"Well, we play basketball."

"Really? Just the two of you?"

"Yes."

"How often?"

"Every afternoon."

"Really? Goddamn, Jeremy. He's old, isn't he? Isn't Bob close to sixty?"

"I think so."

"I'll be damned. And every afternoon he gets out there and plays basketball."

Jeremy smiled. "Yeah."

"Is he good?"

He laughed. "Not very, but it's fun."

"You like that."

"Right."

"What else do you do together? Anything else? Just the two of you?"

"Oh yeah. We go out to dinner, and to movies."

"Who selects the restaurants?"

"I do."

"And the movies?"

"Oh, he picks those."

"He picks them?"

"Yeah. We always go to horror movies."

"Why horror movies?"

"Because those are my favorites."

"Jeremy, how would you feel about Bob if he permitted you to see your father?"

"I'd love him," he said, and he shocked himself.

"Put that in your note too, Jeremy, okay?"

"Okay," he said, "okay."

The class was present during this exchange, chipping in now and then, as they usually did.

When Jeremy returned to school the following day, I saw

his true, genuine smile.

"She took me out to dinner," he said. "Boy, she was really worried."

"How'd that feel?"

"Great."

"So what happened? What happened?" The entire class was waiting, and when he told us that not only could he see his father, but that he could see him openly, and that not only she but Bob was now completely behind it, and not only that—wait, wait, there's more—but he got to call his father and tell him, the entire class broke into a cheer.

"My father wanted me to give you a message," he said. "He said to tell Bernie Schein this: 'Thank you for my son.'"

MARVIN PAZOL, EMILE DELONG, AND OLIVER PEALE

Marvin Pazol was short, Jewish, brilliant, tense, and unhappy because, like many teenagers, he was living the wrong life. Marvin suffered the wrong ambition, pursued the wrong friends, and even assumed the wrong personality. At thirteen, he was the age a Jewish boy traditionally becomes a man, yet Marvin was so meager of stature, so physically unendowed and ignored, so tiny and diminutive that people were always scanning rooms for him only to find he was right there, immediately before them, and had been there the whole time. Marvin himself at least had a sense of humor about it. He wrote in a story once that when he was introduced to people they didn't ask Who are you? or What is your name? Instead they organized a search party.

His voice was no help. Small, thin, and high-pitched, parsimonious of tone, it mirrored his physique.

At home in his bedroom he scoured his chest with a magnifying glass, searching in vain for hair. He wasn't expecting a forest, a fullback's torso, the chest of a lumberjack. Just one hair.

At night, he wrote, he knelt beside his bed and prayed for hair.

That's how Marvin Pazol discovered there was no God.

At all costs he shunned and avoided the academic kids, those like himself, long on brains and short on brawn, and with struggle and determination he managed to keep his grades and his schoolwork short of excellent. His approach to his schoolwork I could most aptly characterize as quality prevention. Nobody had to work harder at it than Marvin because naturally and potentially at anything academic—particularly mathematics—Marvin was a wizard.

Mathematics, in fact, is what deep in his heart he most enjoyed and truly loved.

What he did, however, was to hurl his foundation for success and self-fulfillment, i.e., his slide rule and calculator, to the winds, and then to the utter and complete dismay of the middle school coaches he joined the basketball team. Here he strove to dominate and excel. Through basketball would burst forth his manhood, or so he believed. He persisted mercilessly, and yet he did not improve. To me it was painful, like watching someone running around in circles, never getting anywhere. He was all hustle, grit, and determination—normally a coach's pride—and the result was unequivocal failure. In fact, the harder he played the more he hurt the team. One coach characterized him on the court as in a perpetual "hyperactive frenzy." "He seems always to have his finger in some invisible electrical outlet."

Marvin made his teammates resentful and guilty. "A pass to Marvin," said Checker Blumenthal, "is a basket for the other team. I mean, what am I supposed to do, prop up Marvin or play for the team?"

I thought about his question. "Play for the team?" I asked him, "Or play to win?"

"Okay, Bernie. Do I make Marvin feel good about himself or play to win?"

"'Feel good about himself'? That's psychobabble. It's

insincere. Fuck him. I'd play to win."

"Right," he said. He was happy.

Marvin, however, wasn't.

He was always running to catch up, ramming his head against the wall. Every game he'd have the ball stolen from him, charge after the thief like a one-man army, only to slam full force into the gymnasium wall, his opponent cruising in casually for a layup.

He was falling behind in everything: life, school work, friendships, even in the preparation for his upcoming Bar Mitzvah, which his father complained he no longer wanted.

"Why not?" I asked Marvin.

"I'm not a man," he said simply.

"Do you want to be?"

"Yes."

"Why can't he hold onto the ball?" I asked the coach. The coach was a black, middle-aged man, a former college star.

"He don't want it," said the coach.

Why didn't he socialize with the academics? I wondered. Emile DeLong, Emmet Stern, Oliver Peale, kids short on brawn but long on brains, kids like himself with whom he could be real friends, instead of abusing the jocks all recess by calling them fags.

Why didn't he give himself to his math equations, essays, and classroom debates, all of which might have truly inspired him? Why was he so ruthlessly and zealously sabotaging himself?

"Marvin," I finally asked, "are you going a bit nuts or is it my imagination? If you're unhappy, tell me."

"I'm alone," he said.

And he was. Fleeing himself he inadvertently fled the pack, his friends, classmates, his teammates, coach, and teachers.

Marvin suffered a universal American dilemma: he had

lost his authentic voice, which was too frightening and painful for him to hear.

To find it, courage was required.

"I'm afraid I'm gay," he told the class.

Seated in a large circle, in one of our biweekly, marathon counseling sessions, all were present, as they almost always are, because all, in one way or another, would be affected.

Shame robbed Marvin Pazol of further speech. His face was red, tears flowed down his cheeks, and this magician with words, confronted with a simple, courageous truth—*I'm afraid I'm gay*—was reduced, as was the entire classroom, to an expectant silence. For the first time, Marvin Pazol had the respect and attention of the entire class.

Earlier, when he told the class that he was alone, Emile DeLong and Oliver Peale were infuriated. "You snubbed us," they had told him. "For the jocks," said Emile, as if Marvin were a child who should have known better. "The popular kids," jeered Oliver.

"Hey, come on man, we can't help who we are. Okay?" said Checker Blumenthal.

Now, however, there was only understanding, empathy, and tension.

Clearly Emile wanted to help—it was all over his face—but didn't know how. Lester Hardwicke, the class busybody, himself effeminate, normally openly disdainful and contemptuous of Marvin, suddenly grew pensive. The girls were attentive, curious, and the more mature almost maternal in their demeanor. Jimmy Ryan, tall, gingerly freckled, with a flattop, one of the most likable kids I have ever known, said: "Gosh. Really?"

Marvin nodded.

"Can I ask why?" asked Jimmy. "Is that okay? Do you mind? I mean—"

"Well," he said, "I don't like girls, I mean, the way you do and most of the other boys—" he glanced at Lester.

"I saw that look, Marvin. I'm not gay. Okay?"

"I'm sensitive," Marvin continued. "My feelings get hurt real easily."

"But you've been running around calling us fags," said Checker Blumenthal.

"But don't you understand *why* I called you all fags? I might *be* one. Don't you understand that? *I might be one.*"

They understood. Still, everyone was waiting. There had to be more. Why would Marvin think he was gay? Sensitivity alone was too easy. What was the precipitating factor? What was it he couldn't tell us?

He could not tell us, he said. Why were we having this counseling session anyway? It wasn't doing any good. It wasn't that big a deal anyway, he wasn't even worried about "all this gay stuff" until I brought it up—it wasn't a problem, he emphasized—it was a waste of everybody's time.

"Marvin," I asked him, "Would you like to die?"

He looked away, the shame returning.

"I can promise you one thing. The quicker you get to the truth, and the more fully you express it, the better you'll feel."

"Okay, but I've got to turn around."

"What?"

"I'm ashamed. I can't face people with this."

"Okay. Turn around."

He turned his chair around and began talking to the wall.

"When I was little," he began, "halfway through elementary school even, my best friend and I, Keith Derrick, well..."

"Keep going."

"We kissed and all."

"You kissed?"

He nodded.

We waited.

"We'd take turns being the girl. And kiss and stuff…"

"Oh God," said Jimmy Ryan, "I remember doing that with Billy Paultz. Gosh, I'd forgotten. We'd kiss and smooch and stuff and say, 'Okay, now you turn over and be the girl.'"

"Did you think you were gay?" asked Marvin. He had turned around, looking up at Jimmy.

"No," said Jimmy. "I just loved him. He was my best friend. We were really close."

"You were?" said Marvin.

"Yeah. It was fun. We just loved each other, that's all. Why's everybody staring at me?"

But they weren't staring. They were smiling. The room had never been so relaxed. Clearly Jimmy had become a figure of admiration. Marvin was radiant.

"That was really sweet," said Anna Rossini.

"It was," said Checker Blumenthal.

"You got balls," said Lester Hardwicke.

The next day Marvin Pazol quit the basketball team.

"I don't really want it," he told the coach.

"No shit, Marvin," said the coach.

At recess he played chess with Emile DeLong and Oliver Peale.

That afternoon he caught me as I was leaving. "My story's going to be great," he said, grinning. "It's about me and Keith Derrick, about friendship, but I mean, you know, real friendship. I started it last night."

"That's great, Marvin. That's great. This story could be great. You're right. You know why?"

"I've got something to write about. Finally."

"You always have. It didn't just suddenly come knockin' at your door."

"True," he said. "True."

In the next whole-class counseling session so many homophobic kids came flying out of the woodwork that Joseph Cohen said, "You mean it's *normal* to wonder if you're gay? I mean, if I thought a guy was good-looking, say a movie star—"

"Or even, you know, somebody in school, a friend or something…" said Checker.

"I mean," said Joseph, "I'd always look at the guy next to me and say, 'You're a fag, man.'"

"Me too. I feel a little guilty about that now, you know?" said Checker.

"I've wondered about it for myself," said Anna, "just like a lot of other people in here. It's like we weren't really talking to each other. I mean, if there's something this big to hide…"

"The irony?" I asked.

"It took the loneliest kid in the class," said Anna, "to bring us together. In a way Marvin wasn't the only one who was alone. He was the only one who knew it."

Marvin smiled beneficently upon his work. Throwing a crumb to humility, he said, "Well, I do owe something to Jimmy over here."

Jimmy blushed. "Thanks."

The Verdict

The Surprise Witness

"Your honor," said Norman, "I would like to call Charlie Webb to the stand."

The class was abuzz. People stared at each other in astonishment and whispered. Faye was shocked. Maury fingered Charlie's necklace as if it were a rosary.

"Order. Order." Dwight pounded his gavel. "Shut up back there. Bailiff, the next person who opens his mouth, throw him out."

"Objection, your honor. Objection." Faye was standing.

"On what grounds?"

"According to the class constitution the defense must be notified of all prosecution witnesses forty-eight hours in advance of the trial. I was not notified. To allow him to testify would be unconstitutional."

"The constitution," argued Norman, "also guarantees a fair trial. What Faye is talking about is a technicality, a procedure she desperately wants to use as a loophole. That's *not* why that procedure was put in the constitution. The issue here is what's fair. What's fair, your honor. Charlie's testimony is important. It gets to the truth we've all been looking for. This case shouldn't be won or lost on a technicality."

"The constitution," argued Faye, "provides justice for everybody. If you let Charlie testify, surprise witnesses will be sprung on the next defense attorney, and the one after that. The technicality, as you call it, Norman, allows the defense time to *prepare* its case, to *answer* the accusations. You let him testify, your honor, and that sets a scary precedent that is unconstitutional."

Dwight looked like he didn't know what the hell to do, so he adjourned court for ten minutes and retired to his "chambers"—my office—to think it over.

"The court will come to order," announced the court officer. "Judge Allgood presiding. Please stand and rise."

Judge Allgood entered the courtroom, pounded the gavel, and sat down behind his table at the front of the courtroom.

"Look, this is hard. I asked myself, 'In the evaluation session after the trial, what will people say? Will they say, the verdict was decided on a technicality, we'll never know the truth, or will they say, Dwight was fair, we know the truth. He did his best to be fair.'

"I know personally, from my own experience with my father, who was an asshole, what abuse of authority means. Bernie taught us in the preparatory course to think deeply. 'Don't be superficial.' Remember? At the end, ask yourself, 'Was I fair?' 'What's fair?'

"If I don't allow Charlie to testify, I abuse justice, fairness, the most basic right in the constitution. Try to understand this, Faye. I abuse a 'right.' Norman, I think, is right about that. If I *allow* Charlie to testify, I abuse a procedure, one that does happen to be important, as they all are. Faye, I think, is right about that.

"This is not to be seen as a precedent, it's not likely that this ruling will ever be made again by me or any other judge. Is that clear?"

Norman nodded his assent.

Faye did not.

"Charlie can testify, but beforehand Faye can have forty-eight hours to review his testimony and prepare her cross-examination."

Faye whispered something to Betsy, who nodded. To tell you the truth, I thought, for the first time in months, that Betsy looked relieved.

"I waive the right to a delay, your honor, and would like the court to acknowledge our interest in quick and efficient justice. We have no desire to waste the court's time. If there is a need for cross-examination, I would like a few minutes to prepare for it, if I may."

"If you need it," said Dwight, "you'll have it."

"Thank you, your honor."

"Norman," said Dwight, "call your witness."

After establishing Charlie's relationship with the plaintiff, including a description of the dates they'd been on, the parties they'd gone to, and the number of opportunities they'd found to be alone together, Norman asked him a simple question.

"Are her tits real?"

Charlie smiled.

Every juror leaned forward.

Faye drummed her pencil on the table in front of her. I could see her writing out an argument for a reduced sentence.

"You better believe it," he said.

And the prosecutor's table went nuts. Maury threw her hands in the air. She and Norman slapped skin.

"Order! Order!" yelled Dwight, pounding his gavel. "This

trial's not over."

He looked at Faye; she acknowledged Norman with a brief conciliatory smile.

It took the jury less than five minutes to return to the courtroom.

The verdict: guilty.

The sentence: twenty-five days of cleaning out the toilet.

The punishment, announced the judge, fit the crime.

BETSY ROBINSON

The question in the post-trial discussion and analysis session is always the same: What have you learned?

The class stood and applauded both lawyers; too, they admired Dwight's intelligence and judiciousness. He could have prevented both lawyers' constant drawing of conclusions, speculative and rhetorical questions, and statements to witnesses a bit earlier, but as he said, how could he have known that that was indeed their intention? Besides, he said, he gave both lawyers plenty of latitude, so it evened out.

Faye was brilliant, everyone agreed, but the truth just wasn't on her side.

"And Norman?" I asked.

"He did great," said Frannie McGee. "I mean, he seemed to have an answer for everything."

"Except for one thing. And only Maury had an answer for that. She saved me. Thank you, Maury," Norman said to her. Then he turned to Faye. "You really caught me by surprise. I had thought Maury's testimony would hold up because there was no testimony to rebut it."

"You were right," I said. "There wasn't. Only Faye's outrageous chiding and badgering. You let her drive you nuts. You started off, I thought, handling it fine, because your instincts flared."

"What would you have her do, bare her breasts before the jury?" Faye reminded him. "That was funny, and effective."

"Because it showed the outrageousness of your argument," I offered.

"Exactly."

"Then fear got in the way?"

Norman grinned. "Yes. I was surprised."

"You weren't prepared for that."

"No, but I couldn't have, I don't think."

"So your criticism of yourself?"

"Follow my instincts. Trust my feelings more. Go nuts, like Faye."

"But you did wonderfully and you were well-prepared."

"Thanks."

"Hey, Maury." It was Betsy.

"Yeah?"

"I'm really sorry. Okay? I really am."

Maury smiled at her. "It's okay."

"You sure?"

"I'm sure."

"I learned something, too, Bernie," Betsy said, looking at me with an ironic smile.

"What's that?"

"I learned not to make a fool of myself anymore."

"Good. I'm sure every girl in the class will be relieved."

"Bernie!"

"Just kidding. Do you know what to do?"

"Yeah. But I'm scared."

"That he'll be mad? That he'll go even farther away? Incidentally, are you through punishing him?"

"I think so."

"You're just scared. What's so bad about losing him?"

"I've told you, he's my father."

"So?"

"I need him. I love him. I miss him."

She began to cry.

"Go ahead. Cry. It'll make you feel better. Make it a good cry."

We let her have that good cry, and then I said, "Write him a note. Begin with I need you, I love you, I miss you. Okay? Put it on my desk. Try not to sound like Elvis."

Betsy's note:

> Dad,
>
> The reason I took the pills was because I was mad at you. You left me. I wanted to get you back. That's also why I avoided you and why I was nasty to you. I didn't know all this at the time. But I know it now. It's also why I made a fool of myself and acted stupid with all those boys. I wanted you to hurt for leaving me. I'm really not sorry I hurt you because I think you deserved it for leaving me because I loved you so much and you just left, Daddy. And you didn't tell me anything. But I didn't tell you anything either. I was afraid and mad. So I guess I hurt myself. But what I want to say that sounds crazy is that I did all this because I need you. I need you. I miss you, Daddy, and I'm not mad anymore. Please love me so I won't be crazy.
>
> Your daughter,
> Betsy
>
> P.S. Bernie says you're probably scared to death

of *me. That* sounds crazy to me, but if you *are*, don't
be. I'm not mad. Please don't be mad at me.

P.P.S. Do not show Mom this note.

"Gosh," Betsy told me a week or so later, "he won't leave
me alone. I want to spend *some* time with my friends."

"Tell him."

"Nah, he'd pout and sulk and make me feel sorry for
him."

"Betsy?"

"He wouldn't, I'd just feel guilty. He needs to get a life,
Bernie!"

"I know what you mean."

The trial of Betsy Robinson was over, and despite her sentence—or perhaps because of it—she was free. Now—now she
could finish her story, since it was over.

For Teachers

THE FIRST DAY

What I tell kids the first day of school is that basically I only want to hear what they don't want to tell me, that if they want to be smart and happy and respected and have real friendships and good relationships with their parents and siblings, "Don't tell us what you think we want to hear, but what you really, truly feel." Do they know what they feel, deep down? No, I tell them, but if they're brave and honest and try, we can bring them out. I will learn, I tell them, from them. I also promise them that once they do express themselves honestly, they'll feel better.

My sense of humor usually seems to pop up as soon as they began filing into the classroom. To parents who hear about it, I fall back on the old tried and true: "You had to have been there..." Kids like it because, in their words, it's "stupid."

I'm also, the first day, unusually direct in my opening remarks.

My point here is that though your message may be similar

to mine, it must fit your personality: If by nature you enjoy humor but are not particularly a hoot yourself, don't try to be. If you're basically a fairly direct person, fine, but if not, be more subtle and indirect. If you aren't yet ready to coax all the demons out of Pandora's Box, don't pretend you are. If you want kids to be true to themselves, you must be true to yourself.

"What you do in this classroom, to a surprising degree, will decide your social life, your love life, your family life, your artistic, creative life, your intellectual life. Open your eyes wide—WIDE—that's it. Betsy, you're not opening wide. Your eyes, stupid, not your mouth."

She sighed. "Okay, Bernie. How's this?"

"Fine. Keep them open until you get uncomfortable, then open them even wider. That's it. Let them hurt. Good, Betsy, much better. It hurts to see. Ultimately, however, it will bring you joy and respect, it will enrich your lives because it will enable you to see what you've never seen before. And because you'll be able to see far more than anyone else your age, and be able to express what you see, it will make you smarter than you could ever imagine, smarter, for example, than them. It'll make you the smartest kids in the world: socially, artistically, and intellectually. Just please don't give me 'school.' I hate school. I've always hated school, ever since I was a kid. Don't give me school. Give me your heart, your soul, and you'll be able to give to your world anything, everything.

"Don't give me what you think I want. Don't tell me what you think I want to hear. If you want to be successful in this classroom—in the class court system as a lawyer, judge, congressperson; in creative writing; in debates and discussions; in counseling sessions—if you want happiness, respect, and the awe and admiration of everyone in here—tell me only one thing: that which you've never told anyone, that which you would never want anyone—least of all me—to know, that which is so frightening and dark that you can barely, if at all, tell yourself, even—or particularly—if it sounds stupid. I love stupidity. Only stupid people can become smart. They learn. Courage is intelligence. Who would like to begin? Who would like to be the best student in here first? The best writer, for example, first? Who's willing to risk his butt? Who's the bravest?

"Don't raise your hands. Be obnoxious and blurt out. Be yourselves."

STARTING FROM SCRATCH

When I began teaching at Paideia in the early seventies, revolution and reform were everywhere. Free schools and open classrooms flourished and floundered. Architects designed classrooms without walls. Ivan Illich, arguing that schools themselves were walls, advocated "de-schooling" society. A.S. Neill preached freedom, not license, in his small school in England called Summerhill. Jonathan Kozol depicted inner-city kids intellectually and artistically dying at an early age. Yet inner-city kids and teachers were at least conscious of their collaborative failure. In our more sophisticated and elite schools, argued John Holt in *How Children Fail*, America's best and brightest were outsmarting themselves as they outsmarted the system.

The disapproval and disavowal of American education was so widespread and universal that if you left the stacks and seminars of the elite graduate schools of education, ventured out into the system, and returned to the ivied halls a success, you were vilified and condemned as an accomplice to an evil system.

Education itself, as it was, was a non-winnable war, a no-win situation.

So what did I do?

I left the public school system to join in the creation of yet another school, one that not only survives, but also prospers.

Autonomy was a given, since as headmaster Paul Bianchi point-ed out, none of us knew what we were doing anyway. We were pretty much starting from scratch.

The pre- and early adolescents in my classroom are sur-prise-a-minute kids, most ricocheting like billiard balls between child, adolescent, and adult, a few withdrawing into a corner pocket, all, however, aggressively and defiantly pursuing their true spirit, their genuine personality and soul, their social, mor-al, artistic, and intellectual values, all screaming, in one form or another, to be heard, to be seen, to come out.

When they do truly come out—and it is my job to bring them out—they have surprising things to say, as you've seen in this book—things that surprise them as much as me and their classmates.

Is the world ready for such surprises? Certainly, if pop-ping out of the box is truth, beauty, and wisdom, but the world doesn't know this if the lid is on, just as the kids don't.

Politically middle school is more susceptible and conducive to change than either elementary or secondary grades because traditionally the world has turned its back to it. Indifference leaves a vacuum: if nobody cares, you can. Middle school has been called the cesspool of American education. Nobody knows what to do with the pre- and early adolescent because nobody knows who he is. Few have dared ask. Certainly he is larger than life, easily outsizing the conventional lens through which we obstinately pursue him; grander, subtler, and more passion-ate than the conventional mirror we stubbornly hold up to him. He shatters our image only because we refuse to see him as he truly is. So little is written about him: if we cannot teach him to make sense of himself, how can we make sense of him? Teachers clamor for the elementary or high school grades. Parents dream of furloughs or leaves of absence.

To know him, however, is indeed a pleasant surprise, and

the purpose of *If Holden Caulfield Were in My Classroom* has been to reveal him to you as you have never seen him before. More than any particular techniques, the more promising of which I have shared with you, your own will develop naturally from your knowledge of him, as mine have, and as those of other teachers I have known. To have their souls, their hearts, and their minds illuminated before your very eyes is to have your own repertoire of approaches and responses broadened and deepened.

I teach what might best be characterized in conventional terms as English and social studies to twenty-six seventh and eighth graders in a multi-aged classroom. I am also considered their counselor or advisor.

Their varying math levels dictate varying schedules. Still, I have the kids new to my classroom, mostly seventh graders, nine periods weekly. I have the eighth graders four periods weekly. I have the whole class, both seventh and eighth graders together, an additional five periods weekly, several of them back to back. I can also work with kids individually or in small groups during their study/work periods; each student has from three to five study/work periods per week. Since I designed my own curriculum, naturally I am free, as you've seen, to use and adjust my time with my students as I see fit.

They visit other teachers for math (five periods per week), science (four periods per week), art (three periods per week), music and physical education (two periods each per week).

The school day is divided into seven periods, each period approximately fifty minutes long.

The revolution going on in American education was in reality an excuse, not a motivation, to use my time with my students to bring them out in every possible way. My own education, if you remember, was a sterile, dreary bore, and I wanted, initially at least, to create for my students what had been absent in my own education—art, emotion, life, personality, meaning.

I had something to say as a student, but because my teachers didn't know it, I didn't either. I was a teenager. Certainly I had something to say about death—I had lost all four grandparents and a rival classmate (to a coronary thrombosis). About unrequited love. About first love. About sexual yearnings. About friendship and betrayal. About bullying and victimization. I grew up a Jewish southerner in a small town; certainly I had something to say about identity and alienation. About sibling rivalry—I had two brothers. About status and popularity—in high school it was all I *thought* I cared about. About courage and ambition—running for elected office, trying for a spot on the basketball team. About rebellion and power—my God, I had two parents and was a teenager. About government and civility—there really wasn't any government that I thought affected me; the student government was a surrogate mouthpiece for the faculty. About social exclusion and discrimination—no one fought either for principle or intimacy, only to be popular. About class—if your family was aristocratic (or at least rich) it meant you came from a "nice" family; wealth and aristocracy were equated with goodness.

We studied these themes, of course, since they are the basis of any classical curriculum; we studied them, however, in a remote and abstract fashion, as if they had nothing to do with us.

And so they didn't.

I became a teacher because I hated school. If education was largely dissociated from my life, my emotions, my personality, then it's fairly obvious, in retrospect, that I wasn't there.

I was surprised to discover, upon graduating from school, that education, despite society's stricture, is ultimately *personal*.

Liberated from society's taboo, I discovered myself—and consequently my immediate and greater world—in my reading and writing. At a small rural school in Yemassee, South Carolina, where I began after graduating from college as a teaching principal, I began to see in my middle school students the forbidden themes of my earlier years. If the discussion was about sex, romance, love, death, violence, relations between family and friends, suddenly the room caught fire. With my own friends, one of whom became a prominent writer, all of whom were teaching in nearby counties, I talked about what mattered to me and listened to what seemed interesting or inviting, a far cry from my student days.

Through reading, writing, and talking with my friends about what truly mattered—a self-education, if you will—I discovered that my own themes and conflicts and issues were those of humanity in general. What was personal, to a surprising degree, *was* universal. Further, my students' themes, to varying degrees, mirrored my own, bringing the image of my own adolescence into clearer focus.

It became increasingly clear to me that I would need to teach not as I was taught—since school had limited me to skills and promptly forgotten information—but as I learned.

If through understanding myself I could come closer to understanding the human race, couldn't my students?

Didn't *they* have something to say?

To find beauty, strength, and wisdom—through reading, writing, discussion, and conversation—in one's family, social, or political life, one must pursue and follow the pain. One must surrender to true emotion. Intellect obfuscates the vision and fogs the view. Anxiety and hysteria are distractions, intellectual manifestations of fear, which as an emotion must itself be fully realized, i.e. felt, before it can dissipate and give way to the true pain in one's heart. Beware of convention, which sends out a multitude of disguises and decoys to lure our posse into a wild goose chase. The truth is hard to find, much less catch. Beware of piety and sanctimony, martyrdom and self-pity, blame and righteous indignation, clichés and platitudes, psychobabble, furrowed, pensive brows (they reflect an intensity of thought that is anathema to true emotion), rationalizations (they seduce rationalism as deftly and unnoticed as a patient slipping under anesthesia), socially, politically, or psychologically correct axioms, Oughts and Shoulds, generalizations, and any verbal offering that smacks of altruism or a Concern for Others (never have I seen a kid in turmoil over another's problem unless she was personally affected by it—in other words, unless it was somehow contagious).

Also, remember, Truth is ultimately logical; it has to make sense. If the child doesn't, he's untrue to himself; he's somehow covering up or lying. He's sheltering himself in a way that will harm his life and his work. The more his heart opens, the more his mind will; the more profoundly he discovers and expresses whatever truths he possesses or acquires, the smarter he'll be.

Indeed, isn't that the sum total of a creative intelligence?

Intelligence, I hope I've shown, is indeed determined less by conventional academic means such as I.Q. or achievement test scores or even the spit-up of reorganized, regurgitated logic (safely and conveniently required by most schools) as it is by personality, depth, wit, humor, and perceptiveness. What does one *see* and how beautifully or persuasively does one express it? Whether we are talking about writing, speaking, acting, or reacting—whether, in fact, we are talking about counseling sessions—the old artistic and academic saw has never been more true than it is in my classroom: the outlaw is the generalization, the good guy the detail; the truth, i.e. genuine emotion, must be discovered and dramatized—very simply, *shown* rather than told about.

Boredom is the most telltale sign that a person, far from the truth, is telling you only what he *thinks* you want to hear, what is socially, artistically, and intellectually acceptable.

Most people, most of the time, aren't really listening because most of us, most of the time, aren't really saying anything.

Only when we truly become ourselves are we truly—and inevitably, I have learned from my students—interesting.

The truth of one's soul—genuine emotion, in other words, true passion and inspiration—catapults talent and intelligence over a thousand classrooms, curriculums, and standardized test scores.

A surprising number of my students, as you know, suffer from attention deficit disorder or learning disabilities, as do most of us were we to be truly *seen*, recognized, or discovered. Yet they score impressively on standardized tests; many attend elite colleges and universities.

They have something to say because they know who they are.

Because their personal issues, conflicts, and themes are inevitably universal and consequently and coincidentally classic, we read and reread the great books, as you also know, ears to the tracks in anticipation of the roar of the Great Truths approaching. Yet my fundamental question upon a student entering my classroom, I can't help but repeat, is Who is he?

Indeed, *who* is he?

How might I bring him out socially, morally, artistically, and intellectually?

Through writing and literature? Social studies, i.e., the class government and court system? Counseling?

To know a child is to understand her heart and soul. Listening carefully, you may use many of the same pedagogical skills to bring her out emotionally, morally, socially, and artistically as you do to bring her out intellectually: cajole, whine, get on your knees and beg, confront, challenge, shame (if you have to), probe, probe, and probe, dig deeper and deeper and deeper until the truth—the revelation—begins to stretch, yawn, awaken, and tiptoe about her face like a smile. Follow her, until her feelings match her thoughts, until all questions are answered and she makes sense. You will know, because you will see in her face and her body language relief and satisfaction. She will be, at that point, happy.

If you don't know, ask her: How do you feel? Oh, not great, well, let's go a bit further, okay? If she can't, but feels at least better than she did before, which means she *understands* more than she did before, wait until she *can* go further. Go to the next student. Make sure, however, that you understand what she understands. "Is this what you're saying? Is this what you're feeling?" *Your* understanding liberates her to go further.

Throughout this process, knowingly or unknowingly, you will be learning from her. The more honest her teaching, the more authentic is yours. Tell her. Let her, to the degree that she can, with your help, take charge. Even when she leads you astray—again intentionally or otherwise—you will soon learn to distinguish between the false tracks and the authentic ones, becoming ever sharper at this.

Despite racial, cultural, socioeconomic and, most importantly, individual differences, the more I've learned about kids, the more I've learned how fundamentally alike they are. An open heart is an open mind, regardless of who they are or where they come from. All have heart, all have soul, all certainly, once they break the surface emotionally and shake the hair out of their eyes, can see—see far beyond the limits of conventional wisdom—and express what they see.

The great themes and issues of the humanities and social sciences (English and Social Studies, per middle school age) are already jostling for attention in the heart of the child, whether he's a student in the rural school in which I taught before coming to Paideia, the ghetto school of which I was principal, or my classroom at Paideia. Remember: What child has not fantasized the demise of a sibling, particularly the less likely it is to occur? Popularity to a child is social status, perhaps even the equivalent of fame to an adult; the Gap tee shirt may be the status symbol at the suburban or prep school, the fashionable sneaker at the inner-city school. The pangs of first love can be felt as early as kindergarten. Sex, romance, violence, death, extortion, racism, illness, identity, rebellion, friendship, and betrayal—the history of the world, I have tried to show, is in the heart of the child, regardless of race, class, or socioeconomic status.

Further, such themes, already to varying degrees a part of every child, are the untapped sources of inspiration for their stories, poems, essays, debates, and discussion, their natural plugins to literature, civics, government, and history.

Does the schedule and curriculum allow for such a personally inspired program in most schools, public or private?

Yes, to varying degrees, and that's how it should be. *If Holden Caulfield Were in My Classroom* will broaden and deepen your vision of kids. It will open your eyes to your own students; still, it takes time to see them as individuals. You can only go as far as you can see, and since it takes time to see your own students, the program can develop gradually. Take risks. Acknowledge what you don't know to your students. Because it's about them—and the knowledge you seek is somewhere inside them—they will naturally become surprisingly involved and helpful; they will assume even more responsibility for their learning.

Still, no need to suddenly ditch your total curriculum. Already, in fact, creative writing is not only a major in many colleges and universities, but also it is a staple of many elementary and secondary school curriculums. To some degree, you're probably already teaching it, or feel you should be doing so. Personalizing it saves time in that it improves the content and the language of the students' writing a thousandfold. The stories my students wrote that are included in this book, totally unedited and untouched by me, should prove that to you. It does take more time to help each student discover his theme, his story idea, since it must truly matter to him, since it must be so important that he must, deep down, *need* to write it, but since content inspires form, as you've seen, the story will largely style and shape itself, and you will spend significantly less time teaching him *how* to write it.

To help her students discover their story ideas, one public school teacher, who didn't have as much time as I to spend on this process, periodically wheeled into the classroom a cart of library books, had each student select and read a story, and then had them write down their *personal* reasons for selecting their particular stories. Each student's personal reason became his own story idea.

Often I do the same thing, only more directly and immediately: when the discussion in literature class becomes personal, story ideas can develop. "Write them down," I suggest, "and save them for when you need them."

In fact, when *any* discussion becomes personal—a discipline problem or a counseling session or the particular fear that sparks a law in the class government and court system—I have them note it as a possible story idea for later.

Never have them write their stories during class. Though yours may spend less, depending on how much time you want them to devote to it, mine usually spend about forty-five minutes each weeknight and four or five hours over the weekend working on their stories. Remember, it's about them, so as anxiety-producing as it can be, often resulting in their stomping about the house complaining about you, it's also interesting and engaging.

Save class time only for what can never be done elsewhere.

That's what makes class special, essential, and inviting.

Most expository writing should be taught during social studies, again with the writing itself done at home. If the language arts and social studies teacher is not the same person, regular communication becomes necessary.

Some of the grammar and punctuation you will teach through their writing, so class time you spend on it may be somewhat reduced, though not significantly. You might suppose that because they develop a reason for learning it that it makes it easier to teach. Because I have so many students with language or spelling disabilities, I emphasize punctuation and spelling as custodial acts rather than writing, i.e., an act of expression. Since they see it this way, it remains a bitch to teach.

Nevertheless, because it is a part of their writing and essential for clear communication, they do a fairly effective job of learning it. I spend about two and a half periods weekly on it. Again, exercises they can do at home.

Literature: Certainly some stories or novels are preferable to others. Whatever your literature curriculum, however, whether state-, county-, school-, or teacher-inspired, the themes of the stories or novels will naturally coincide with those of your students. Thus, it's not necessary to alter it. More attuned to themselves and the people and places around them, the students will be more attuned to literature, particularly as you help them see the connection.

Social studies? A bit trickier. At some point you'll have to decide how much time you need and want to devote to the class government and court system. Some classes use an abbreviated system; some, as does mine, go whole-hog. However, as with creative writing and literature, one can move slowly. No need to suddenly ditch your present social studies curriculum.

But if your major purpose is to transmit information (which they'll promptly forget anyway) purely for the sake of conveying information, or if you insist on their doing expository writing as reorganized and regurgitated spit-up, forget the class government and court system. There won't be time for it. In fact, forget learning.

If the generally accepted definition of learning is "a change in behavior," then it's got to be therapeutic, active, or both. In the class government and court system, it's both. What are laws, for example, but the reverse side of fears? Information used to debate laws—or rights or procedures, for that matter—is important because it affects their day-to-day lives in the classroom. Communicating it is important, so developing and cultivating the skills and persuasive powers of writing and speaking become essential to the students as citizens and participants in a classroom democracy.

They *create* history, government, and a civil community rather than merely reading about it. Abstract ideas, it's worth remembering, require greater complexity of thought and feeling and are more easily and thoroughly understood when concretely and *personally* experienced rather than remotely examined. When students create a "balance of power" or a "separation of powers" or a system of "checks and balances," such a formidably abstract concept is more profoundly understood by them. "Invasion of privacy" assumes greater meaning for the student when classmates break into his locker, steal the love notes from his girlfriend, and post them on the bulletin board. The proper balance and tension between "rights" and "laws" becomes a serious issue for students when they have to decide whether or not a proposed law against put-downs, probably the most lethal social crime in the middle school, is a violation of "freedom of speech," probably the most sacred right in my classroom.

Still, don't suddenly ditch your present curriculum. In fact, if you're teaching American history and government or civics, usually staples of the middle school social studies curriculum, you can use the U.S. Constitution, as we initially did in my class-room, as a guide to developing your class constitution.

It is natural to move into the class government and court system gradually, particularly since laws, rights, and proce-dures are not all made at once, right out of the starting blocks, but rather as the need arises.

If laws are external manifestations of our fears, time must initially be allotted to discover of whom and of what in the classroom students are most afraid. Honesty is essential, else the foundation of the system—the laws, rights, and the proce-dures of the court and government that protect the students—will be fragile, unsound, and of little value to them, at most a game, reducing their arguments, discussions, debates, essays, speeches, and trials to the trivial and juvenile. Again, more than the conventional notions of what is required for intelligence, it is courage you are seeking. You are looking, again, for what they are most afraid to tell you. Remind them that if they speak truly, they will speak, in some form or another, for a surprising number of their classmates. They will have followers. They will become leaders.

Conviction must be behind the laws they propose; for that we need to hear the source of their fears. Ask them: Of whom are you most afraid? Why? Who bullies you, picks on you, snubs you, excludes you, ridicules you, extorts lunch or homework from you, makes you afraid to be yourself? Why do they do it? Help them. Point out what you see. If they're hesitant, get them to write down their fears, anonymously at first, if that's the only way to begin. Then read them aloud, one by one, ask who has the courage to claim them, and begin with a general discussion. Grade them on how specific they are. Donate names to their di-lemmas—theft, extortion, assault and battery, social manipula-tion, exclusion, degradation, sexism, destruction of property, etc.—and they will discover the laws that can rescue them from their daily misery. Tragedy inspires action and law as much as it does literature. The laws, rights, and governmental or courtroom procedures they propose—or their opposition to such proposals—and the personal reasons behind their convictions, along with their qualifications and critiques of their opponents, will dominate the campaign speeches—all given on the same day—of the candidates running for your first congress.

Consequently, time must be allotted before campaign speeches for several discussions of the issues and the fears that spawn them. Meet with congressional candidates to critique their speeches. Work with them on their deliveries. I let the entire class help them; it involves and teaches them also. Beware of loaded or nitpicky criticism that comes from either an opponent or a jealous classmate. Simply asking for the motive, or suggesting what you think it might be, is usually enough to curtail it.

Allot a period or two for the official speeches and voting. Afterwards, a chairperson must be elected to run the congress.

Then time must be allotted for the members of congress to meet and write up, based partially on the speeches and discussions, the laws, rights, and procedures, subject to amendment, of the class constitution. (Use my class constitution—see my website—as a guide, as well as the U.S. Constitution.)

Because it will provide for a judicial system, elections will need to be held also for judges, the class prosecuting attorney, court officers, bailiffs, and what in our classroom we call the cleanup checker, i.e., the giver of punishments. Time must be allotted for you to help them with their speeches (again, I prefer involving the whole class here) and for students to deliver them.

Remember, in your training of lawyers and judges after the elections you are not expected to be a legal expert, but a teacher. The basic rules of composition—relevance, clarity, logic—apply whether you are talking about a lawyer's opening statement and questions to witnesses, a judge's ruling, or a congressional debate.

The amount of time you spend on the class government and court system, once it's established, depends on how abbreviated or expansive you want it to be. Left to its own devices, it will allow you to periodically challenge your students to be more courageous, more honest and more industrious, on the one hand, and you'll spend a great deal of time, on the other, catching up to it, which is the way I prefer it. It means it's going on its own steam. You might need to allot certain periods for it. You might also want to prepare the kids for it in a brief mini-course. If you want to use it to develop almost every conceivable academic skill, as I do, from memorization and quick recall to critical thinking, action research, and expository writing, then your preparatory course can take as long as an entire semester, as mine does. Aside from the preparatory course, the system isn't terribly time-consuming. I meet with kids to help decide whether there is sufficient evidence to warrant a case going to trial; I meet with lawyers before trials to review and critique their cases; and I usually attend court and meetings of congress.

Allot about one or two periods weekly for students with guilty pleas to be run through the docket and sentenced to punishment. Allow one period per week—even if recess—for congress to meet, and one period monthly for congress to meet with the class, since constitutionally the class will probably reserve the power to pass or defeat bills.

It is simpler to create and sustain a class government and court system if the English and social studies teacher is the same person; if not, because of the thematic relationships between literature, creative writing, and the class government and court system, it will save time if there is ongoing communication between the teachers. Also, if the social studies teacher needs help teaching expository writing, the English teacher can offer expertise.

At the ghetto school in Mississippi of which I was principal prior to teaching at Paideia, the departmentalization of courses was so heavily institutionalized that to have a realistic government and court system we divided the school into "houses" (itself not a new concept at the time). Each house was a wing of the school consisting of four teachers (math, English, history, and science) and about a hundred and twenty kids. (Specialists were adjuncts to all houses.). In each house representatives from each homeroom, who comprised the house congress, met weekly to propose and debate bills, and met monthly with their entire house (120 kids) to propose bills for approval or veto. At the time, a two-thirds majority prevailed in both the house congress and the entire house.

Unless yours is a small school, strongly departmentalized, a schoolwide government is probably superfluous and unnecessarily time-consuming. In Port Royal, South Carolina, however, where I was teaching principal (again before coming to Paideia) of a school of about a hundred and fifty kids, a schoolwide government worked quite well, with the student council serving as the class congress, presenting monthly bills to the student body in school meetings for approval or veto. Again, allot time for court, probably one or two periods weekly, particularly if you want to involve all the students, either as participants, critics, or spectators.

Remember too after each session of court or congress to allot time for a general evaluation session involving everyone. Kids will be interested; it's about them and their lives. That creative writing, literature, and court are so much about them and the people with whom they are in everyday contact is the biggest time-saver of all. The inspiration for a law, for example, might well be the inspiration, once plumbed to its origins, for a story; it might be a plug-in or a response to literature. Also, one kid's issue, brought out in the classroom, inspires countless others; once ignited, the whole classroom catches fire.

It takes time to help a child discover what he has to say. That saves time, however, because what a child has to say, more than anything else, informs how he is to say it.

To the pedagogical techniques you use to bring him out emotionally, which by and large are no different than the ones you use to bring him out intellectually, I would add relaxation. Middle school kids are often hyper, and like most of us, defensive and hyper-rational. They can know what they feel without feeling it, which does them no good. Talking about the problem can in and of itself become a way of avoiding it. You'll know this if you (or your students) start feeling bored. Mine were so hyper and rude and excitable and defensive all at once one day that I found myself saying, "Shut up, just sit there for God's sake, be quiet." Then, lo and behold, I discovered I *liked* the quiet. Still, they were staring at me, curious, anticipating. Instinctively, I said, "Close your eyes. In fact, keep them closed. Relax. Don't open them until the feeling comes."

I didn't know what was going to happen, but anything beat all that confounded verbiage.

After a minute or so, one kid opened her eyes and said, "I got it." Then another, and another...

It turned out to be a real time-saver. I've been using it as a technique ever since. When they close their eyes, go limp, and relax, the feeling—the truth, that is—more easily surfaces.

Still, one must probe, and that does take time. The big pedagogical question, of course, is Why. Just as Jamila Cade's racial confusion would later prompt her law against racial put-downs, Neelima Puri's ethnic confusion would inspire her law against ethnic put-downs. (In fact, Jamila would later realize that Neelima's confusion re-awakened her own and that Neelima's law inspired hers.) Note the similarity and consistency of the class' and my responses. You want a law against ethnic put-downs, Neelima? Why? Because I'm from India, and Indians are always being slighted, put down, discriminated against. In this classroom, Neelima? Sure, why not? she shrugs. Who's doing it? What'd they say or do? I don't know, she says. No one, now that I think of it. So why do you want a put-down law? Don't think. Relax, close your eyes, and let the true feeling come up. That'll tell you why. Take your time.

I don't know, she says, but I know I want the law. You're not being stubborn? I ask. No, she says quietly, and she's convincing. She's truly puzzled. When you relaxed, I ask her, what feeling came up? Was there a hint of one? Fear, she says. I was afraid. Try it again, I suggest. Close your eyes. One, two, three, relax... (I count slowly, it makes it easier for them to relax; the class relaxes too, curious). After less than a minute she opens her eyes. I'm afraid, she says, of people knowing who I am. And who are you? I ask. She hesitates. Indian, she says, and shrugs. The class smiles.

So who's putting you down? I ask gently, with some humor. *I* am, she answers, blushing happily. I'm putting myself down.

Still, she's not entirely satisfied. Only when they're fully satisfied has the truth fully emerged. What's left? I ask. I *still* want the law, she says.

Can anyone help? I ask the class. Anna Rossini raises her hand. Why are you afraid for us to know you're Indian? she asks. Yeah, I ask, what does that mean? Try to be specific. I'm afraid, says Neelima, you'll all laugh at me. That you'll be embarrassed? I ask. Over what? ask several kids at once. (They've heard me do it, so they listen and probe naturally.) She looks at me, for relief, for escape, but she really doesn't want it. They never do. You'll see. What are you hiding? I ask. What are you afraid they'll see?

I ask the class: Who's been to Neelima's house?

No one raises their hands, yet clearly she is well-liked and has friends.

Why not, Neelima?

I'm ashamed, she says. We eat *Indian* food, not McDonald's. Do you like McDonald's? I ask. Yes, she says, laughing. Do you like Indian food? Yes, she says, I do. But you're afraid your friends won't? Right, she says.

Hell, says Lester Hardwicke, we eat Indian food all the time. That's all my mom serves.

The class smiles. Shut up, Lester, says Anna.

Right, says Lester.

And you know, says Neelima, we pray...differently...

And that might embarrass you?

Yes.

And the saris your mom wears?

God, she says, that is *so* embarrassing.

Everybody starts talking at once about how their moms embarrass them—particularly by singing along with the radio during carpool—and how they would "just die" if their friends saw such-and-such...

You want the law, I offer (as I later would Jamila), to make it safe for you to come out in this classroom?

Yeah, she says, and now she is satisfied; she smiles, breathing a sigh of relief, since now she knows. She's learned.

Well, I say, looking around the room, looks like you're not the only one.

They never are.

Her theme, of course, is identity. She has a story to write, if she traces it back to its origin; she has the inspiration and law for a speech or proposal to congress. She has a natural connection to literature. Of equal importance, she has an opportunity for a more intimate relationship not only with her classmates and friends, but also her parents. No longer is she so alone.

Can a program so personal and unconventional be politically acceptable in a public school?

Yes, as long as you progress only as you learn from the kids. Let things develop. Parents will be excited because their kids are and because their talk at home, as well as their writing, will be so much more exciting and sophisticated; many of the parents, in fact, will profess envy of their child's education. Also remember, it brings family (and friends) together; when Neelima accepts herself, she is more accepting of her family.

Know, however, that the more rational or repressed the student—or his parents—the greater his resistance to the program, particularly to the story he might be writing, since always we expect it to be personal. Paradoxically, the more powerful the story, the more frightening it can be and the greater the resistance. Parents who have a family secret such as abuse or neglect certainly may not wish to have their child inform his classmates and teacher about it. They may not be aware or may be indifferent to the fact that it may boil and fester until not only their child, but also his entire classroom community is plagued by it.

Yet the key to my students' success, their ability to write far better than other kids their age, their wisdom, maturity, and capacity for loving, *is* their secret(s). None of my students has ever failed either to elevate his writing or to become happier by revealing it. Families, far from becoming more estranged, become closer. And when parents see their kids' writing, they are almost always more than satisfied; to tell you the truth, they seem grateful.

The lesson I learned in Mississippi still holds true: the worse the school, the more disastrous the educational environment, and the more frustration, resignation, and ennui people feel about it, the more susceptible it is to change. The public has given up, they're ready for anything, as long as the kids are happy, stay in school, and learn. Believe me, kids challenged, stimulated, and inspired to read, write, and talk about what truly matters to them will not only come to school but also take it home with them. That is the surprise they offer the community. Remember too that Paideia itself, though private, was born from parental and student dissatisfaction with the local offerings, both public and private.

When the heart is touched, the mind opens, and openness is contagious.

At the ghetto school of which I was principal in Mississippi, I discovered, purely by accident, the folly of underestimating the strength and tenderness of kids. Causing a near-riot, a group of thirteen black girls terrorized a cluster of five white girls at recess. They accused the white girls of having lured the sexual attentions of the black boys away from them The white girls' responses consisted of sullen denials and retaliatory accusations. We were all seated in an empty classroom, the black girls on one side, the white girls on the other. Listening to them trace the cause back to who-did-what-to-whom-way-back-when, I felt like an adult often feels in this situation, like a frustrated detective helplessly sifting through unfathomable evidence.

Their indignation and shouting hid the truth. Without their generosity, authority could never truly touch their hearts.

"Solve it yourself," I said, and left the room. A white girl sat off by herself, crying.

I closed the door behind me, walked down the hall a few paces, then quickly returned, like a good Jewish mother, to observe through the keyhole. It didn't take long for the kids to find a civil, orderly way to address each other. A circle of desks was formed, and apparently for a person to speak she had to stand in the middle. When she finished, another would take her place. Apparent also was that anyone who interrupted was shushed by the group.

I wondered: Had I been in the way?

With the exception of the lone white girl on the periphery of the circle, quietly crying, they all looked expectantly at whomever was speaking. A few black girls spoke, then a white girl; at one point the middle yawned empty, they seemed to be negotiating not whose turn it was but who would be the most appropriate to speak. Finally, after the last speaker, people turned in their chairs, speaking directly to each other, and one of the black girls left the circle, walking toward the door.

She caught me half way down the hall. "We've solved it," she announced, as we entered the room.

Everyone nodded but the white girl off to herself, her head in her hands.

And they had. No problem among these girls ever reoccurred. *They* had established civility and respect among themselves. Friendship, in the state of Mississippi in 1972, was possible.

As I was leaving, the same kid who had come to fetch me in the hall, the kid in fact who had been not only the leader of the peace movement but the instigator of the war, walked over to the lone white girl, knelt, put an arm on her shoulder, and began whispering to her. The white girl nodded, slowly nodded…

QUESTIONS AND ANSWERS

When you're working with your students, is there a line, a boundary that you don't cross?

No, there isn't. If there were, the implied lesson I might be teaching them would be, Stay on safe ground, Don't risk yourself, Keep the most frightening parts of yourself boarded up. You're really *not* safe in here. It's like saying to them, we want you to search for Truth, but once you approach danger, head back the way you came—when in fact the longer you stay in the danger zone, the safer it becomes. It's like saying to the pitcher, your best stuff, leave it at home, or to the student in my classroom, your most powerful, inspiring stuff, keep it to yourself, there's no place for that in school, which is in fact what most schools *do* say. Yet kids couldn't keep it to themselves even if they wanted to. If it doesn't come out openly and honestly, it'll show itself subversively and destructively: Betsy Robinson with her promiscuous behavior, Norman Stewart's destruction of his classmates' lockers, Maury Michael's passive-aggressive behavior towards her father, Marvin Pazol's gaybashing, Laura Daye's put-downs—based on the kids you've seen just in my classroom, we could go on and on.

Now, if you reversed the question and asked, Do I respect *their* boundaries, their lines, i.e., their fears, the answer would be Yes, unequivocally. And for three reasons. First, humility requires that I acknowledge that what I have learned about them over the years I have learned from *them*. I only know what they know, which as you have seen, without time and work is very little. I only know what they tell or show me, either directly or indirectly, but until *they* know, there's no way I can. That can't be forced. Oh, I can push, prod, poke, whine, get on my knees and beg, listen, try to understand, point out contradictions, ask questions, let them know if they're not making sense, if they're not quite believable, but I can't know, or hope to know, before they do. So I can only go as far as they're willing to take me. And once you think you know, beware, because often later you find you don't.

Maury Michael's story, if you remember, wasn't really about her tennis match. Norman Stewart still hasn't written his story. Why? All I know is what you know. Everything points to the fact that he's scared, but of what, exactly? Of feeling abandoned by his parents, of feeling inadequate, responsible for his abandonment? Sure, this he's already told us. So if he knows, and I know, why can't he write it? Well, knowing and feeling, i.e., re-experiencing through remembering and writing, are two different things. Feeling is painful. It hurts your heart. So maybe he's just not ready to face it, so he can't. Maybe. Or maybe there's something else down there in that memory, something perhaps still lost to him, that I can't possibly know until he does (and until he trusts himself to reveal it), that frightens him away from his story. He wants to write it. He's told me, if you recall, and experience leads me to believe him. To disbelieve him would suggest that he is comfortable with loneliness and distrust, with fear. No one is. And besides, if he were, he wouldn't have ransacked his classmates' lockers and stole their money. He wouldn't, as he said, be so "angry." What else *can* I do, but respect his hesitation? If he doesn't know, I don't.

Besides, if I push too hard, they usually tell me—they know I want them to—in one way or another, after which we discuss it. What they don't want is for me to give up on them. They know that the only knowledge I have is theirs. And if I were to be *too* pushy, they'd show me who was boss. They'd clam up, or somehow save themselves by leading me astray. So, my second reason for respecting their reluctance and hesitation is simple: strategically, pushing too hard ends up with me in a frustrating bout with myself—and the kid, for a while at least, an amused fan with a front row seat.

Finally, my third reason: going too fast can be dangerous. Remember Raquel Millsey's story about the death of her father? She dealt with her grief, as I pointed out after her story. And though she realized, as she told Checker Blumenthal, that words could not cause cancer, it was not as if suddenly informed, her feelings of guilt and responsibility suddenly vacated the premises of her subconscious. Consequently, in her social life, she tended to avoid responsibility for some of her behavior. She would blame, using the second person "you" instead of the first person "I," escaping from the personal to the analytical. Culpability, of any kind, was too much for her to handle, since what she was really feeling, she told me without telling me, was culpability for her father's death. It just stands to reason that to suddenly stand up to that overwhelming blizzard of guilt would be not only impossible but unhealthy. She's also telling me, by not dealing with it, to let the weather clear and warm up a bit.

Are you practicing therapy without a license?

What therapist could bring kids out the way they're brought out in my classroom? Have you ever seen the writing kids produce for therapists? God spare me such punishment. Yet for the story to be good, it has to be somehow therapeutic, as you have seen, has to show a revelation on the part of the protagonist, a slight alteration in his mood or behavior, perhaps a dramatic change. The suffering he went through to face it must in the end leave him somehow more mature, perhaps lighter, happier. His relationships, to a degree, should be positively affected. This is a natural law, however, established long before Freud saw his first patient. Even he, I think, acknowledges that. It is the law of art, of creativity.

I don't diagnose my students. I wouldn't know how. There have been times when I have referred them to therapists, to get extra help, advice, or perhaps to have them tested for medication. My view of teaching is that it's an art more than a science. Feelings may be necessary to the process of therapy, but they're essential too to creativity, to true intellect, and to one's social and moral development. I think it's a bit ludicrous, perhaps nuts, to argue that for a person to express his deepest, innermost feelings he's got to go to a doctor and pay for it. You go the doctor if you can't do it, when you need help doing it. At least that's when I've gone. Feelings, or the expression of them, should not be institutionalized. I mean, do you take your partner to the doctor to tell her you love her?

Only if you have to. My program—art, creativity—if nothing else might serve to place feelings where they ought to be, in the natural order of things, in learning, for example, in the home, among friends, in the classroom.

It seems as if so many of your kids have been abused? Have they?

No. Of the ones in my classroom in 1990, a typical year, only four were—four at least that we knew of. That's less than one-quarter of them, which is slightly less than the national average in any classroom, cutting across racial or socioeconomic lines. All of my students, thank God, do have problems—areas if explored and understood do make them more liberated, but that's because they happen to be human beings capable of love, and therefore the corresponding negative emotions, which can disturb them. Laura Daye felt guilty because she was unable to "feel," to "cry," at her grandmother's funeral. Remember? Yet once she realized *why*, that it would hurt too much, that she loved her so much she couldn't face it, well, she felt better because the issue, she realized, was not guilt, but love. She only felt guilty because she *cared* so much. Many, many kids suffer this same guilt finding themselves unable to cry at a grandparent's funeral. It's normal and natural. The only thing I find sad about it is that most kids either have to live with it or repress it. Still, that's not a problem of abuse or neglect. It's a problem, like most of them, of loving and not knowing it.

Sexism on the playground, procrastination, issues of identity, of sibling rivalry, of social or family relationships, shyness, perfectionism—these are your normal issues, which once explored, simply make you smarter, inspired, happier. Let's face it, it's also nicer for the people around you.

Your students express their emotions often in the presence of the whole class. You show that they and their classmates profit from it, learn from it, and generally seem to be uplifted by it, even to the point of admiring the classmate who does it. Isn't it also humiliating?

Not for the reason that you suggest, which is that it's public, that is to say, in front of their classmates, since *they're* opening up also, often at the same time. It's their goal: intimacy. That's what makes them happy. In fact they want it so badly, those who have the most trouble with it are sometimes jealous of those who are more successful at it. Why? Because, as Tessa Monroe said to Laura Daye after Laura finally revealed the story of finding herself unable to cry at her grandmother's funeral, "You're so *human*." Tessa didn't know it before, even though they were supposedly best friends, because Laura hadn't shown her. Not only is Laura happier with herself, a weight off her shoulders, she's closer to Tessa. And believe me, she wants that closeness. All kids do. Now when Laura, out of jealousy, spread rumors about Tessa and her boy friend, suggesting she was "slutty," did Laura, once exposed, feel humiliated? Probably, a bit, but less because of what her classmates thought about her, once she fully admitted to herself what she was doing, than what she thought about herself. (Hopefully, at least briefly, she *was* ashamed by what she'd done.).

When kids are judging themselves, like Laura at her grandmother's funeral, they assume the whole world is judging them just as harshly, when in fact most people don't care all that much. They've got their own problems to worry about. Besides, if sanctimony reared its ugly head, well, you'd have trouble finding me a kid who *hasn't* ever engaged in the kind of malicious gossip Laura did. Finally, more importantly perhaps, once she finds out why she did it, and is forced to concede to herself and her classmates her jealousy, then Tessa is free to admit *her* jealousy of *Laura* and to own up to the fact that she's also put *Laura* down. Voila! Underneath jealousy, what do we find, smiling up at us? Admiration! How about that? Now the friendship, much more positive and intimate, can deepen. *That* is a very nice feeling. Because the whole time, underneath all the subversive activity, as I've pointed out, that's what they're looking for.

That's why Marvin Pazol, once he admitted he was afraid he might be gay, felt better. It was out, he was no longer alone, and *real* friends awaited him. R. J. Peabody was hurt when Ian Gardiner refused to applaud her story. But once she found out why, that she was always putting him down in math class, she acknowledged, she apologized, and she was happy. And when she explained to Ian that the only reason she'd done it was to cover up her own feelings of stupidity in math, was she humiliated? No, she was offering her motive, and yes, she was ashamed of it, but she also was connecting, if you will, which then liberated Ian to show how much he liked her story. Finally, both felt better. Ian realized that R. J. had really been putting down herself in math, and R. J. realized he liked her story. Kids *understand*. When Carrie Enright told us she'd been sexually abused, all the kids wanted to go beat up the guy. They were *with* her, on her side. Openness didn't humiliate her, a pervert did.

Once in a court hearing Checker, confronted with a million inconsistencies, had to admit to Tessa that he'd accused her falsely of stealing his candy bar. Why? Well, because he'd *liked* her, and well, she didn't seem to like him. Sure, he was a bit embarrassed, but not nearly as embarrassed as he was by what he'd done to her. Her reaction? Total shock. You sure have a hell of a way of showing it, she told him. Every time I walk by you hold your nose, and you're always sneering and making nasty comments to me. Really? You like me? Yes, said Checker, glumly. Wow, said Tessa, I'm really flattered. It's okay if you don't like me, Checker said. Oh, said Tessa, But I do! I think! Not only does Checker learn that flattery will get you everywhere, but he learns the right way to get attention. As long as the kids tell the truth about themselves, not about others, but about *themselves*, they'll not only be surprised, as Checker was at Tessa's response, but they'll learn, become more intimate with each other, act out less, i.e., Laura, Tessa, Marvin, R. J. *(all* of them) have more fun, and feel better.

Remember too, for example, as Laura admits to her foray into malicious gossip, every kid in that class feels closer to her, they respect her honesty, because they have done just as badly, if not worse. Often one kid's revelation invites a whole roomful of them. *Everybody* gets closer.

Does their openness about their relationship with their parents ever cause a rift between them and their parents, or between their parents and you?

The purpose of that openness is to bring them closer together, which both parties want. The kids, as you could tell— Betsy, Maury, Danny—certainly want that, even if at first they might deny it. In fact what often thwarts the relationship is that because they're kids, naturally they want more than their share of their parents' love and attention and don't understand when they don't get it. Sometimes they *aren't* getting their share, as with Maury, with her dad working late, but her openness, if you remember, did bring them closer. Naturally, parents are happy with the class when that happens, as it often does. And why shouldn't they be? We want for their kids the same things: creativity, intelligence, courage, strength, and loving relationships.

Remember too that the kid is responsible for telling his

parents if he's upset with them or needs their help in some way. If he can do it privately, at home with them, fine. Often, however, he can't (or he would've) so that often happens in a parent-teacher conference in which the kid is included. More often than not, parents are impressed with their kids' courage, their sensitivity, and their openness. Certainly, they often say, they could not have done that with *their* parents. And of course, often too, we get the parents' side of the story, which the kid can no longer lie about, since they're sitting right there. Parents and I work very closely together. I couldn't do what I do without them, and I'm very grateful to them and honored that they would entrust their kids to me. As long as I'm talking with them, we're for the most part delighted with each other. They're helpful, and if the kid's been finger-pointing to absolve himself of wrongdoing, like being lackadaisical about his work, that comes out in a phone call or conference. Obviously if a parent has been abusive, as over the decades a few have been, and I've turned them in to the authorities, naturally they'd like to see me dead, but that's to be expected.

Also, the one requirement I have—the only one, as a matter of fact—for a child to be in my class is that his parents place no taboos, no censors on him. (It places him in a potentially traitorous position, and I certainly don't want him feeling as if he's betrayed his parents.) Fortunately or unfortunately, depending on your point of view, openness is the price one pays for Truth and Beauty. Obviously, that requirement keeps away the ambivalent, which means less potential pain and suffering on my part.

Remember too—and I can't stress this enough—ultimately these kids are talking about *themselves*. We're working with them, not their parents. And these kids are not in a position to judge, a posture that's absolutely anathema if you're looking for Truth. Judging others is just a way of avoiding it about yourself. You can certainly be angry at someone, but the problem's still yours.

How do you know they're not just telling you what they think you want to hear?

Often they are, at least initially, but it's hard for them to know what I want to hear if I don't. Remember too that unless what they're saying is true, true to their feelings, it begins to unravel and not make sense after a while. And that inevitably becomes boring, which no one likes. Once Joe Popular wrote on the bathroom wall that Irving Nerd "sucked." At the time there was no law against that kind of thing. Make one, I suggested to the kids, so it won't happen again. Afraid they'd be Joe Popular's next designated victim, they played it safe and proposed a law against "defacing classroom property." Who cared? They did it to please me. So naturally it withered on the vine. It's hard to sustain an interest in something you could care less about. After a while they get the picture that it's got to truly come from them, that I don't have a whole lot of the questions, much less the answers for them.

Who's really in charge, with respect to the class government and court system, you or the kids?

They're in charge of the class government and court system—with my help and guidance, of course—which is a large part of our classroom, but I'm in charge of the classroom. Theirs is a democracy granted by the teacher, a benevolent dictator. I really rarely interfere or overturn anything they might do for the simple reason that it would be pedagogically counterproductive. The more mistakes they make, under the system, the more they learn. Nevertheless, the class constitution itself acknowledges that it is subject to "teacher-made" laws. And it is.

How well do your students fare academically in high school or college?

As you might surmise from what you've seen, they certainly do read and write well. Naturally, its not surprising that they have a "presence," many of them, that they show independence, that they know perhaps better than many kids what they want and how to get it. They participate well in class discussions, most of them. They do quite well in high school, on the whole, and a large percentage get into the colleges they want, many of them among the more elite ones. Their high grades and. S. A. T. scores most of them would have anyway, no matter whose class they came from, as long as the core skills and information were taught. I can't take credit for the fact that many come from well-educated families. The fact that along with having the core skills, they're creative and handle themselves well, that I understand gives many of them a plus. They do quite well. But what pleases me so much is that the classroom is so memorable to them.

Can other teachers and parents do this, or is this a one-personality program?

They do, and they are. I've supervised numerous teachers over the years, and they in turn have contributed by adding not only to my growth, but to each other's. Several have conducted workshops for parents who wanted to more profoundly understand their kids or who saw what their kids were getting and wanted the same thing for themselves. "The child is father [or mother] to the man [or woman]." When parents remember, unclouded by nostalgia, who they were as children, it not only brings them out, making them more sensitive, aware, and creative (as the same process does their kids), it enables them to better understand their kids, which brings out their kids even more. Basically, in our supervisory sessions or workshops we put ourselves through what the kids go through. It's very intimate, and of course, confidential. The same kind of talking and writing the kids do, we do. I've been meeting every Wednesday afternoon after school with groups of teachers for years. Each meeting usually lasts several hours because my rule is, You can't leave unless you feel better, at least better than when you came in, which is the same rule I apply to kids in my classroom.

Everybody contributes, and we all learn from each other. A teacher comes in, for example, who's finding it difficult to stand up to his assistant. He discovers first that he couldn't stand up to his mother, because she frightened him by yelling at him. For example, he explained, she'd yell that he was making her late for school—she was a teacher herself—because it took him so long to tie his shoes. Why *did* he take so long? one of us asked him. Well, to get her back for yelling at him, to drive her out of her mind, and then assume his role as the family martyr, which was exactly what he was doing with his assistant, as well as, he said, laughing at himself, his wife. This discovery—that he was passive-aggressive—let him know that he could be mean, that indeed he was powerful, to say nothing of the fact that without knowing it, he'd been pissing everybody off. No wonder, as he said, he was having trouble with his assistant

Another teacher, an art teacher, the child of alcoholics, expressed anxiety over putting too much of herself in her students' art work, "adding something here or there" to make it "perfect," concerning herself too much with appearance, neatness, and order, perhaps robbing her kids, she worried, of something valuable. She also complained about the constant "messiness" of the art room itself. Her subsequent poem about tidying up after her parents' drinking bouts was perfect, we all thought, not at all "messy," ironically enough, and unhesitatingly took her to the source of her problem: What was a child supposed to do with the terror, chaos, and confusion of her parents' alcoholism? Make it orderly, she concluded, clean it up, make it perfect. How? She couldn't stop her parents' drinking. Make it *look* perfect, god-damn it, she writes.

This whole idea that creativity comes from within, that it's a personal experience obviously did not originate with me, but with my wife, Martha, at the time also a teacher. (Where she got it in such a way as to internalize it so naturally, I don't know. When I asked, her answer was, "If the butterfly were to pause in mid-flight to analyze how he flew, he'd plummet.") As a consultant working with a think tank in a small Southern state I had an altercation with my boss. Martha said Write a poem about it. I said, I've never written a poem in my life. She said, Just sit down with pen and paper, as upset and worked up as you are, believe me, it'll come out on its own. Well, I did. And of course, some of it was terrible. But in the poem, as in real life, after I rant and rave, my boss props his feet on his desk, leans back in his chair, smiles, exhales a Pall Mall, then "issues a thin line of smoke like a silent directive."

In other words, you can rant and rave all you like, he's saying with his "directive," but I'm the boss.

"… issues a thin line of smoke like a silent directive." Wow, I thought, where in the hell did that line come from? That's not bad. From me, just like she said. From inside. I couldn't stop writing after that. And I certainly paid a lot more attention to the way *she* was teaching. I didn't know it then, but most writers and artists, instead of teaching as they *learned*, unfortunately teach as they were formally *taught*. If they did otherwise, they'd be great teachers.

So obviously just as most kids can do all this, since they're human, so can most teachers. So can most anybody, anybody sincerely interested in seeking and expressing the truth of their feelings.

Can your program work with older adolescents and adults?

Oh yes; absolutely. As I've said, several teachers including myself have run workshops for adults, both parents and teachers. I've run countless workshops for high school kids, usually creative writing, and for years taught a creative writing class in the high school. The writing among older kids is even better than among middle school kids because their personalities are more developed, but only if I teach them the same way I teach the middle school kids. In other words, the workshops and classes are, as you might expect, intensely personal.

Also, for decades now, I've taught adults in the evenings. Sometimes they come for writing, sometimes just to get freer and happier. Same results. But those, my editor tells me, are for another book.

What about younger kids?

Honestly, I don't know. Certainly if they have a particular problem, they are surprisingly open and honest about it, and in specific cases I have seen this approach work quite comfortably for them. I just don't have enough teaching experience with them to know, as a program, how it might be. And I certainly would want them to maintain their innocence, their real innocence, for as long as possible.

I will tell you an interesting story, however.

Our class published annually, at one time, a collection of the kids' stories called *Hidden Places*. To advertise it, I'd haul a copy around to the elementary, high school, and other middle school classrooms and read them a story. Well, I didn't want to leave out the little kids, the first and second graders but (perhaps in my naiveté) I was afraid the stories might be too mature for them to handle. I mean, even the funny ones are about *problems*.

What's the hurry, right? So clever man that I am, I'd always tell them a story, one I might tell my own kids (now my grand-kids) at bedtime, say an animal story, one not too scary.

So I'm in this first and second grade classroom telling my animal story, and when I'm finished this second grade kid named Michael Haskell raises his hand and says, "My mom died."

I was flabbergasted. I said, and the kids agreed, nodding their beautiful heads, "That's sad."

And he nodded, "Yes."

And I held up *Hidden Places,* opening it to a story written by Darwin Moore, and I said, "This story is about Darwin's mother dying. His mom died too. He's also sad. Would you like to read it?"

He nodded, vigorously.

"For you, Michael, a free copy." I looked at the class. "Don't you agree?"

"Yes," they chorused.

"Come to my classroom on Monday morning, Michael, and I'll have one waiting for you. Okay?"

I didn't think about it at the time, though I should've, but it takes a lot of courage for a seven-year-old boy to even be in the same building with a bunch of rambunctious thirteen-year-olds running around all over the place before classes start.

He was there, however, waiting for me at the door to my classroom, seemingly oblivious to the goings-on around him.

Leaving, he held *Hidden Places* to himself as if it were sacred.

Later, his writing mentor, Thrower Starr, was a teacher I had mentored.

Last year, at age twenty-six, Michael won the prestigious Whiting Award for his poetry. I love that kid.

Hell, I think I love them all.

How can you not, particularly once you truly get to know them?

About the Author

In his over forty years as an educator, Bernie Schein has "gotten personal" with countless students, bucking the conventional wisdom that education must be impersonal, formal, and objective. In countless talks and workshops, he has shared his views on everything from the shortcomings of the SAT and No Child Left Behind to the need for students to be emotionally open and aware before true learning can take place.

Schein was the principal of three different schools in Mississippi and South Carolina before he taught full time at the Paideia School in Atlanta, which he helped to start. The subjects he taught included creative and expository writing, literature, drama, and social studies, where his approach was distinguished by its group dynamics and his unique class government and court system. He has been an educational consultant throughout his career and continues to teach creative writing to both adolescents and adults. He was chosen District Teacher of the Year in the Atlanta, Georgia area in 1978.

Schein holds a Master of Education degree from Harvard University, with an emphasis in educational psychology. His stories and essays have been published in *Atlanta Magazine*, *Atlanta Weekly*, *Creative Loafing*, and the *Mississippi Educational Advance*. His book *Open Classrooms in the Middle School* was a featured selection of the Educators' Book Club. Bernie Schein lives in Beaufort, SC, near Charleston, and can be reached at bernie1@hargray.com. His website is www.bernieschein.com

Sentient Publications, LLC publishes books on cultural creativity, experimental education, transformative spirituality, holistic health, new science, ecology, and other topics, approached from an integral viewpoint. Our authors are intensely interested in exploring the nature of life from fresh perspectives, addressing life's great questions, and fostering the full expression of the human potential. Sentient Publications' books arise from the spirit of inquiry and the richness of the inherent dialogue between writer and reader.

Our Culture Tools series is designed to give social catalyzers and cultural entrepreneurs the essential information, technology, and inspiration to forge a sustainable, creative, and compassionate world.

We are very interested in hearing from our readers. To direct suggestions or comments to us, or to be added to our mailing list, please contact:

SENTIENT PUBLICATIONS, LLC
1113 Spruce Street
Boulder, CO 80302
303-443-2188
contact@sentientpublications.com
www.sentientpublications.com